Evaluation of Employee Assistance Programs

Evaluation of Employee Assistance Programs

Michael J. Holosko
Marvin D. Feit
Editors

The Haworth Press
New York • London

Evaluation of Employee Assistance Programs has also been published as *Employee Assistance Quarterly*, Volume 3, Numbers 3/4, 1988.

The Haworth Press, Inc., 12 West 32 Street, New York, NY 10001
EUROSPAN/Haworth, 3 Henrietta Street, London WC2E 8LU England

Library of Congress Cataloging-in-Publication Data

Evaluation of employee assistance programs.

Published also as v. 3, nos. 3/4 of the Employee assistance quarterly.
Includes bibliographical references.
1. Employee assistance programs—Evaluation. I. Holosko, Michael J. II. Feit, Marvin D.
HF5549.5.E42E93 1988 658.3'82 88-759
ISBN 0-86656-741-0

Evaluation of Employee Assistance Programs

CONTENTS

ABOUT THE EDITORS

Michael J. Holosko, PhD, is Associate Professor at University of Windsor School of Social Work at Windsor, Ontario. He has been a consultant to the human services field for the past ten years, and is consulted internationally in the areas of administrative skills training, program evaluation, and stress management. Dr. Holosko currently serves on the Board of Directors of the American Association of Industrial Social Workers. He has served on Boards of Directors for a variety of human services organizations including the Health and Welfare Canada Research Advisory Committee for the past five years.

Marvin D. Feit, PhD, is Associate Professor at Norfolk State University School of Social Work at Norfolk, Virginia. He has given presentations at the local, state and national level on employee systems programs and was the director of a national one week course entitled, "Consultants' Role in Employee Systems Programs." Dr. Feit has published articles on evaluation of employee systems programs and substance abuse. He is author of *The Management and Administration of Drug and Alcohol Programs*, and is co-author with Dr. Michael J. Holosko of *Workbook for Internal Management*.

PREFACE

EAPs: Assessing How They Work

EAPs have experienced some 40 years of longevity and growth in the United States and Canada. During this time, they have evolved and have been subject to a variety of changes and influences. The field itself is still experiencing some growing pains, and evaluation efforts parallel this growth process. To date, evaluations of EAPs have been largely fragmented, in-house publications, based in industry. The methods and findings used have not been adequately disseminated to those working in this field. As a result, there was a need for a manuscript which brings together the latest developments in the field of evaluating EAPs. The key question germane to any evaluation effort and one at the heart of this manuscript is – do these programs work or not work? The articles included in this text all address this question, and highlight a number of issues related to it.

The purpose of this text is to document issues and concerns, and to bring together in one volume articles centering on developments in evaluating EAPs, as well as illustrating a number of actual case examples. As a result, the text is organized into three main categories. Section one addresses the concept of evaluation in its broadest sense, i.e. determining the "state of the art" of the EAP field. Specifically, articles in this section are directed toward identifying the growth, development, trends and issues, and capture the essence of where we have been, where we are at present, and where we are going. Thus, they serve as a point of departure for the remaining articles in the text as they set the stage for understanding how EAPs have emerged and how they are being evaluated.

Stern's lead article highlights significant changes in our economy affecting the American workplace and the role of EAPs in those changes. His article considers how such changes may influence the development of EAPs and their future, and he provides a societal basis for understanding how EAPs and their evaluations will evolve. McClellan and Miller provide empirical data to substantiate many of the claims made by Stern. They show how EAPs are in transition and how they have responded to changes in the workplace and in the economy. McClellan and Miller make the point that all EAPs have several universal functions which evaluators need to recognize if their evaluations are to be successful. The final article in this section, by Straussner, illustrates that despite the national growth of EAPs, upon examination of survey data in the New York Metropolitan area, it was found that in reality, EAPs serve only a very small proportion of industries, corporations and human service organizations. She further develops a comparison of in-house and contractual EAPs, and highlights issues related to them.

Section two, the context of EAP evaluations, deals with the planning, some models, the rationales, issues to consider, obstacles and organizational realities. The articles in this section clearly illustrate that proceeding to conduct an EAP evaluation without a consideration of such contextual issues is shortsighted.

Holosko identifies some common sense yet essential prerequisites for EAP evaluators to consider prior to the conduct of their evaluations. These prerequisites are discussed within the context of a cooperative planning process between the administrator, EAP coordinator and the EAP evaluator. Taylor et al. enunciate the same point but address it from the perspective of the role social work may play in planning EAP evaluations. This article concludes with a series of process questions which should be addressed prior to the conduct of any EAP evaluation. Battle stresses the same theme and examines a variety of issues to be considered in planning EAP evaluations. He describes a model that EAP evaluators should use in evaluating their programs. Balgopal and Patchner chip away at the same issue from yet a different perspective. They define specific obstacles, issues and strategies that EAP evaluators need to address prior to conducting their evaluations.

Cole and Teram focus on organizational contexts and the important role they play in EAP evaluations. Cole describes a detailed account of an organizational development model which was used through the EAP in order to evaluate how the organization impacted on employees. Teram makes the case for formative rather than summative evaluation of EAPs by studying the role perceptions of organizational cultures in Israel.

Yamatani offers an evaluation model based on an EAP benefit and cost structure analysis and illustrates how it can be utilized for establishing program accountability and planning purposes. He effectively accomplishes the difficult task of relating cost to units of service. Cayer and Perry provide a practical framework to guide comprehensive evaluations of EAPs, based on five programmatic aspects: effort, program performance, adequacy of performance, efficiency and process evaluation. They see the framework as forming the basis of a strategy for evaluating the success or failure of EAPs. Kim also sees the same need and presents four generalizable types of evaluations to use in an overall evaluative scheme: intervention planning, program monitoring, impact assessment and economic efficiency. In his typology, he illustrates how several evaluation methods, such as needs assessment, cost-benefit analysis, program development, utilization analysis, and so forth, can be used in the evaluative research design.

The third section presents a series of case examples of EAP evaluations. In this section, each of the authors downplays the study's findings and highlights the strategies, methods used, designs, and outcomes of the research. In essence they focus on what worked and how it worked. Thus, we selected articles for this section that were "practitioner friendly," as results of any evaluation tend to be highly idiosyncratic to the respective host organization. Thus, we chose to feature articles here related to what methods were used and what problems were encountered so that other EAP evaluators or practitioners could learn from these examples.

Maiden presents data on a 30 month project conducted by the

U.S.D.H.H.S. employee counselling service program. He highlights the cost-effectiveness of the evaluation, the design, and the methodological issues encountered. Wright describes three models of EAP evaluations used by the Family Service Association which were tailored to the specific needs of different organizations. He highlights the uniqueness of EAPs, but also the importance of using straightforward methods to evaluate such programs. He also reminds us how easy it is to become lost in complexity. Stanley et al. discuss case management from their own organization's experience as they continue to implement and evaluate the approach, while Roberts-Degennaro proposes how to develop and evaluate case management.

Chandler et al. describe how an EAP was established and evaluated in a small plant operated by a large distillery in another location. The article details a chronology of events associated with the EAP and suggests a practical model related to a participatory philosophy and simple outcome evaluation. Dicks, after conducting a telephone survey of EAP development in rural North Central Louisiana, focuses on the salient factors contributing to the limited development of rural EAPs. Her findings are consistent with expected difficulties in developing EAPs anywhere, but highlight the uniqueness of rural characteristics and how they influence EAP growth, development and evaluation. Finally, Browne applies a system of estimating cost in EAPs and demonstrates the importance of understanding how cost is determined and the issues surrounding the use of cost estimates.

This text strives for a blend of academic and practical insights into the field of EAP evaluation. The range and diversity of articles reflects EAPs in transition, their growth patterns, evaluation needs, and evaluation methods. EAPs and their evaluations have been shown to be constantly changing and evolving, as much from within the field as in response to the environment. Overall, these articles stand as testimony to the point that successful evaluations depend on not just methodological expertise but a consideration of much broader salient and societal issues.

Michael J. Holosko, PhD
Marvin D. Feit, PhD

SECTION I: "STATE-OF-THE-ART" OF THE EAP FIELD

Economic Change and Social Welfare: Implications for Employees' Assistance

Mark J. Stern

Employee assistance has been a growth industry during the past decade. Virtually unknown in 1975, EAPs and other emotional health programs have become one of the many ways that industry is becoming involved in the everyday lives of American workers.

Those actively involved in the employee assistance movement—social workers, alcoholism counselors, and other mental health professionals—have generally viewed these events positively. They have paid attention to the scope of the problems of workers and the nature and structure of helping. At the same time, the movement has been buoyed by an optimistic belief that American business has adopted a new humanistic management philosophy. This new attitude includes an increasing sophistication about the nature of the work motivation, a recognition that mental health problems hurt productivity and profitability, and a recognition of corporate responsibility for a range of human problems which may not have their origins in the workplace.

The optimism and growth of employee assistance contrasts sharply with other trends in social welfare. While EAPs have expanded during the 1980s, public and voluntary social welfare institutions have undergone repeated cuts and retrenchment. The public social insurance programs—old age, survivors, and disability insurance (OASDI) and unemployment insurance in particular—have experienced some cuts, while public assistance programs directed at mothers and the "able-bodied" poor have suffered more severe re-

Mark J. Stern, PhD, is affiliated with the University of Pennsylvania.

ductions. The voluntary sector, as well, has faced an uncertain period in which maintaining services, rather than expanding services has become the primary preoccupation. While many of the bleak predictions of the early 1980s have turned out to be false, others have been more accurate.

The contrast between EAPs good news and public welfare's bad news has led many critics to question the motives and results of industry-based social services. They have been portrayed as at least the unwitting tool of big business and at worst an active participant in a conspiracy to impose more thorough social control on workers. EAP professionals have understandably resisted these charges, calling attention to the many benefits that the programs have brought to workers and management alike and invoking a "new era" in which the two sides could work together for their mutual advantage.

This debate has distracted attention from a much more vital task: an understanding of how employee assistance does fit into current trends in the workplace. The political and ethical issues are certainly worthwhile, but do not provide the detailed understanding of the changes of the work force that is necessary for planning and evaluation. Neither caricature – the humanistic corporation or the cynical social controller – provides a solid basis for program or policy analysis.

In this paper I examine the major changes which are now affecting the American workplace and the role of EAPs in those changes. A split image emerges reminiscent of Dickens's opening to *A Tale of Two Cities*: "It was the best of times, it was the worst of times." Because of changes in the structure and organization of the labor force, the American corporate community is indeed becoming more involved in enriching and improving the work lives of many Americans. At the same time, however, for many of the same reasons, corporations are abandoning, displacing, and impoverishing other workers.

This big split in the economy explains the contrast between the sunny optimism of EAP professionals and the grimness that grips the public welfare community. It also suggests that while employee assistance is central to the new American workplace, a wider view of employee assistance's role and future is in order.

In this paper we examine four trends: (1) the impact of technological change in the composition of the labor force; (2) changes in management philosophy; (3) the changing position of labor unions in the economy; and (4) the impact of displacement on unemployment, poverty, and inequality. This discussion sets the context for a better understanding of the environment in which employee assistance programs have recently flourished.

TECHNOLOGY AND THE CHANGING COMPOSITION OF THE LABOR FORCE

Since their discovery, computers and other advanced technologies have been seen as the harbinger of a revolutionization of the workplace, yet it is only in the past decade that the contours of this revolution have become clearer. High technology affects what workers do, the skills and training they need, and the duration and nature of their work lives.

The clearest impact of economic change has been the rise of the service sector. By 1985, nearly three-fourths of all jobs in the economy were service-producing. Moreover, of the 23 million new jobs created in the American economy between 1970 and 1984, fully 22 million were in service industries; at the same time, only 1.3 million new jobs were created in goods-production. While the growth of manufacturing employment—which is more cyclical than service-employment—is likely to increase, the dominance of service employment has become a permanent feature of the economy.[1]

For many years, the growth of the service economy evoked the image of millions of computer programmers going off to the office. Recently, as the reality of service dominance has emerged, it has become clear that this is not true. Rather, the service sector is split quite sharply between well-paying and poorly-paying jobs. For example, by one estimate, of 56 million service-sector jobs in 1985 9 million were in high-paying occupational categories (managers and professional workers) and 20 million in low paying occupations (service workers, clerical workers), leaving less than half of the jobs in "middle-income" job categories (technical, production, and sales workers). By contrast, nearly three-quarters of manufacturing jobs are in the middle-income categories. Thus, the shift to the service economy implies a shift from a middle-income society to one dominated by class differences.[2]

The slow growth of manufacturing employment, however, does not suggest that this sector is stagnating. Quite the opposite. While employment in manufacturing hardly increased, the value of consumption goods increased by almost 50% in real terms between 1970 and 1985.[3] The declining importance of manufacturing employment was testimony to the rapid productivity increases in this sector.

The key to the rapid transformation of manufacturing over the past decade has been the impact of technological change. Since the 1950s, Americans have been announcing the coming of automation, but today its impact is finally being felt. The application of computers and robotics is changing the nature of manufacture from design of goods to their delivery. This switch is changing the nature of employment throughout the economy.

The byword for this change is flexibility. The last industrial revolution was based on the assembly line and huge integrated production facilities which turned out the mass-market goods which transformed American life: cars, appliances, and other consumer goods. Supply and demand forces have combined recently to alter this picture. The undifferentiated mass-market goods which used to fuel the economy have saturated the American economy.[4] As a result, the market for manufacturing goods is now more specialized, directed at specific (often foreign) markets. As consumers became more selective, the production run for manufacturing goods was reduced from six or seven years to one or two. As a result, the change in demand required American industry to be more flexible, to be able to switch from product to product cheaply and without huge expense.

The computer revolution met these requirements. The centerpiece of computerization is the industrial robot which actually replaces the production worker, but this is only the most visible of the many ways in which technological innovation alters the modern factory. Computer-assisted design and manufacture (CAD/CAM) have reduced the time it takes to get a good from conception to production and have reduced the needs for mounds of paperwork formerly done by middle-managers. At the same time, the application for computers to inventory management has led to the development of just-in-time (JIT) manufacture, through which material bottlenecks and waste have been reduced. The new technologies—combined in computer-integrated manufacturing (CIM)—have allowed manufacturing to become as flexible as the new consumer market demands.

These changes signal the obsolescence of the huge integrated production facility. In its place, the new realities require "flexible specialization": a model based on the flexible, multi-use equipment, skilled workers, and the decentralization of production facilities, linked together through a variety of arrangements.[5] The most complete example of this switch from large, mass-production to decentralized, flexible specialization is the American steel industry. The expansion of the integrated steelworks based on open-hearth technology symbolized the industrialization of American society during the early 20th century, just as its collapse symbolized "deindustrialization." Yet, at the same time that basic steel was stumbling, speciality steel based on electrically-powered, minimills expanded. Between 1970 and 1985, electric furnaces more than doubled their share of domestic steel production. Because of higher productivity, lower wages, product specialization, and geographical specialization, minimills were able to beat the older integrated facilities and to stay ahead of foreign competition.[6]

The rise of flexible specialization has immense implications for the American labor force. The biggest impact is to decrease the number of workers needed. The most affected group in the semi-skilled production workers of the old industrial giants. In their place, flexible specialization requires a smaller, more skilled, and more flexible workforce. At the same time, the permanent revolution sparked by high technology means that—just as product lives are reduced, so does the career life of the production workers. In the future, workers will not enter a factory at 18 and leave when they retire. Workers will experience several career shifts—and the resulting life crises—during their working years.

White collar jobs, too, are placed in jeopardy by the new manufacturing technologies. Flexibility calls for a responsiveness that is inconsistent with layers of middle managers that swelled the white collar workforce. Instead, computerization allows the flattening of management pyramids which in time leads to a reduction in lower skilled white-collar jobs as well. The greater job stability of white collar workers, too, is being eroded, increasing their vulnerability to unemployment, layoffs, and job dislocation.

The current industrial revolution, then, is Janus-faced. On the one hand, it can appear as a disastrous combination of deindustrialization, dislocation, unemployment, and increasing poverty. On the other hand, it produces possibilities for job enrichment, increased skill and diversity, and more humanistic management styles. We need not decide which of these is the real face of the economy, they are both underway.

FLEXIBLE SPECIALIZATION AND THE QUALITY OF WORK LIFE

The new economy presents a host of exciting possibilities. It has implications for the training and skill requirements of economy, for quality of the work lives of employees, and for the philosophy of management toward its workers. It is within this context that EAPs fit most comfortably.

Flexible specialization leads to the replacement of masses of semi-skilled production workers with a smaller number of more trained employees. Yet, what are the skill and training requirements of the new factory system?

One trend is the reemergence of a more craft-like occupational model. In place of the deadening and alienating detailed division of labor that dominated the old factory system, flexibility requires workers who are able to perform more tasks and who have more control over their use of time and resources. In many of the more advanced sectors of the economy, this has led to the abandonment of the narrow job classifications that long dominated industrial organization. For example, the Saturn division—that General Motors is hoping is the automobile of the future—will eliminate many of the job classification and restrictive work rules which were the basis of labor relations in traditional automobile factories. In its place, the Saturn factory will be based on small work teams led by an elected "counselor" and linked to other groups by a work unit advisor.[7] In other countries, the trend toward broader skills and responsibilities has progressed even further.[8]

This shift in skill has obvious implications for the training of workers. In the past, industrial skill referred to competency in a limited number of concrete tasks. As jobs become broader, training must be reoriented from mastering specific tasks to developing *judgment* to make informed decisions about what to do and when to do it. This requires workers to be more thoroughly educated and more motivated to do their jobs well. The system of external supervision which dominated the assembly line can no longer substitute for workers' internal motivation.

These new requirements are illustrated most graphically by Larry Hirschhorn in his study of nuclear power plant workers. He discovered that workers at Three Mile Island were trained not with a focus on judgment and motivation, but on concrete skills and external supervision. As a result, they were unprepared to make the complex judgments that were necessary when faced with a possible meltdown. The recent examples of nuclear plant workers falling asleep on the job suggest that plant management is yet to address the motivational problems it faces.[9]

Worker motivation is the genie that American industrial psychology has tried to capture for the entire century. Taylorism believed that external control and incentives could substitute for the internal motivation, while the human relations school of Elton Mayo and his followers looked to group solidarity and sociability as the essential features of the well-run factory. The most recent addition to this history is the quality-of-work-life (QWL) movement which has flowered in the last ten years.

Quality-of-work-life is a broad term used to cover a variety of strategies for increasing worker involvement in task-related decisions; it breaks with the basis of labor management relations since the New Deal, which stressed the right of management to determine the structure of work. In its most limited form, QWL focuses only on workplace issues: quality circles (discussion groups which examine the organization of the work unit), broader worker-supervisor communications, and the use of worker attitude surveys. In its broader forms, QWL can be linked to broader issues like work restructuring, the sharing of business knowledge, employment security, or union involvement in management or training programs.[10]

While QWL is hailed as the solution to the productivity crisis, its realities are a good deal more complex. Each party – management, workers, and (if present) unions – enters a QWL program for different reasons. Companies hope to increase productivity, workers hope to improve their jobs, gain more secure employment, or gain income, and unions hope to use the process to achieve collective achievements for the work force and thereby secure their position. In a recent examination of QWL and labor relations, Kochan, Katz, and McKersie concluded that those programs that were most successful were those which linked shop floor issues with broader concerns; yet, ironically, these programs are most likely in companies with strong unions. Given current trends in unionization, the authors conclude, there are severe limits on how generalized these programs can be.[11]

Participation and flexibility are popular among white collar as well as blue collar workers. The ability to flatten hierarchies has led to a decisive shift from hierarchical organizational structures. Matrix management systems, temporary work groups, and the simulation of independent business initiative (intropreneurship) are possible means to improve the efficiency and competitiveness of white collar workers. As with QWL, these innovations' goals is to increase the involvement of the worker in the purposes of the enterprise.

The fate of QWL and organizational innovation is still very much in question. While there are a number of outstanding examples of their success, the evidence to date is mixed. While the pressures toward cooperation will continue, countervailing pressures to cut costs, maintain discipline over the work force, and maintain strategic flexibility will hamper its growth, particularly among nonunion firms. As high-tech industry matures, it will face greater competition which will increase the pressure to cut costs and adopt less liberal employment policies. In addition, as the supply of high-tech workers increases, the need of companies to retain this scarce resource will decline.[12]

Employees assistance programs fit comfortably into the current economic environment. As broader social forces encourage management to take a wider view of workers and their motivation and to attempt to retain skilled workers, the provision of a range of social services – ranging from alcoholism counseling, stress management, child care, broader assessment and referral services – will increase. EAPs fit into recent trends in management policy.

Yet, as we have noted, this is only one side of the future of work in America. Before we can draw definitive conclusions about the future position of EAPs, we must examine some more troubling trends in the economy.

THE DECLINE OF LABOR-MANAGEMENT COOPERATION

There is little doubt any longer that America has entered a new economic epoch, one dominated by the service sector and high-tech manufacture. Yet, as with previous economic revolutions, the current transformation is producing many losers. While it is too early to fill in a scorecard, it is clear that literally millions of Americans have become the casualties of post-industrialization.

Some of those who are now suffering are already in the advancing sector. For example, while technological innovation has led to record numbers of business formations, it has led at the same time to an avalanche of business failures and bankruptcies.[13]

Still, the major losers in the current industrial revolution are the old industrial work force. The semi-skilled workers in basic industry and a host of supporting sectors have been forced to undergo the painful dislocation, unemployment, and psychological harm that have accompanied post-industrialization. A combination of technological, economic, and political forces have worked to make this transition more painful that it might have been.

The American industrial working class has had a unique history. Throughout the 20th century, the "American standard of living" has been the envy of the world. Indeed, it was the success of the working class during the postwar period that sparked the belief that the working class had become "middle class." While these claims were wildly exaggerated, they did reflect in a distorted way the rapid rise in the income of workers during and after World War II.[14]

The reasons for this success were complex. At its base, the improved standard of living derived from the vast technological and productivity edge that the United States had over the rest of the world.[15] Yet, the prosperity of the working class was not simply the automatic benefit of technological and economic power. It was a result as well of the American labor relations system which had been imposed on American business and the rise of the American welfare state which provided workers with unprecedented security and opportunity.

The economic crisis of the 1970s and economic transformation of the 1980s has undercut this prosperity. Labor peace has been superseded by increasing conflict, with labor unions the usual loser. Millions of workers have found themselves displaced and unemployed. As a result economic inequality and poverty have both increased rapidly. The "middle class" blue collar worker has borne the brunt of these changes.

The postwar labor management system was based on a number of propositions: (1) unions were a permanent feature of the industrial landscape; (2) labor and management could work in partnership to raise productivity and wages; and (3) the government would serve as a neutral referee, holding each side to living up to agreements and avoiding unfair labor practices. During the 1970s, this system fell into disrepair. The declines in productivity growth, inflation, and foreign competition led both labor and management to question the older social contract. At the same time, management formulated ways of keeping unions out of new enterprises and challenging them in existing businesses. Finally, government policy—in the form of tight money policies, the deregulation of transportation and communications, and a more laissez-faire stance by the National Labor Relations Board—encouraged management to free itself of union constraints.[16]

As a result, the strength of unions in the American economy has declined precipitously. Unions today represent a little over half of the proportion of the work force that they did in the late 1950s. In some sectors, including mining, construction, transportation, and communications, the decline has been even steeper.[17]

THE CASUALTIES OF POST-INDUSTRIALIZATION

The decline of unions is only one symptom of the pain that economic transformation is imposing on American workers. Workers in older smokestack industries are finding themselves thrown out of secure jobs, while the high-tech sector promises new jobs, but ones which require more skill and possess less security than the old. The deregulated labor market poses risks for both the old and new working class.

The combination of business closings, deregulation, and the decline of unions has resulted in a massive increase in labor displacement. In January 1986, for example, the Census Bureau found that over five million workers had lost their jobs since 1981 after having been employed for over three years. Of this number, only about a quarter had found jobs that paid as well as the ones they lost. Nine hundred thousand of the five million displaced workers were still unemployed (18%), another 800,000 had left the labor force (16%), an another 1.1 million were now working at lower paying jobs (22%). While these figures compared favorably to a similar study in 1984, they suggest that massive job displacement has become a significant element of the current economy.[18]

In addition, poverty and unemployment have increased significantly over previous decades. During the recession of 1981-82, unemployment rose to 11%, the highest rate since the Great Depression. While the civilian unemployment rate fell to 6.3% in the spring of 1987, it remained significantly higher than it had been at comparable points in past recoveries. Similarly, poverty, which had fallen to 11% during the early 1970s, rose above 15% in 1983 and has remained in the 14% range. While the rising poverty of black female-householders has attracted much attention, the poverty rate of white male-householders has increased even more rapidly.[19]

The rise of unemployment is even more troubling because it appears that the twin goals of the economy – low unemployment and rapid economic growth – are no longer consistent with one another.

Increasingly, economists have claimed that the "natural" (noninflationary) unemployment rate has risen to the 6 to 7% range; they believe that economic health will be built on the economic redundancy of eight million Americans. Even more troubling, it now appears that to maximize economic growth in advanced industrial economies, higher dislocation and unemployment will have to be tolerated; economic growth no longer leads to increased employment. The old belief that "a rising tide lifts all boats" no longer holds.[20]

Even if massive unemployment can be reduced, the post-industrial economy appears no longer capable of producing "good" jobs. The size of the labor force has expanded rapidly, adding over nine million jobs between 1979 and 1985. Yet, according to a study by the Joint Economic Committee of Congress, the vast majority of these have been low-paying jobs. Bluestone and Harrison estimate that whereas in previous expansions, only about one in five new jobs was low-wage (under $7,400 constant 1986 dollars), in the current recovery, 44% of the new jobs have fallen into this range. The new economy is producing more jobs, but a larger share of them are either low-wage or part-time. The middle-income jobs which used to dominate the economy are no longer there.[21]

As a result of these conditions, there has been a significant increase in inequality during the 1980s. In 1984, the top fifth of the population held 42.9% of aggregate income, while the share of the lowest fifth, was 4.7%. In 1979, the top fifth held eight times as much income as the bottom fifth; by 1984, it held over nine times as much. The index of income concentration – a summary measure of income inequality – rose from .365 in 1979 to .386 in 1984, the highest figure recorded since data were first collected in 1947.[22]

American society is going through a dangerous polarization. Since the 1960s, the economy has turned out more poverty, more unemployment, more low wage jobs, and more inequality. While the "middle-class" has not disappeared, it has been significantly eroded. In place of an economy which generates a bulk of middle-income white and blue collar jobs, the 1980s American economy is turning out high and low wage jobs. These trends have continued even as the economy has recovered from the recession. They appear to have become a permanent structural feature of the economy.[23]

IMPLICATIONS FOR PUBLIC AND OCCUPATIONAL WELFARE

Today's workplace is characterized by increasing polarization. The middle of the 20th century produced trends toward greater equalization of incomes and skills, labor peace, and increasing prosperity. As we move toward the 21st century, these trends are no longer present. While the economy is producing many hopeful innovations, it is at the same time producing more poverty, displaced workers, and unemployment.

The complex context of the 1980s workplace is the dangerous terrain in which the employee assistance movement has flourished. As we have seen, EAPs are solidly lodged in the quality-of-work life strategy which has recently been fashionable in American business. In those industries and occupations where management is interested in increasing motivation and loyalty and assuring a stable, healthy work force, EAPs will continue to experience the growth that they have had in the past decade. Yet, the current organizational environment provides risks and turbulence which we must take into account.

First, the success of QWL strategies has generally occurred in unionized settings. It is only these settings in which QWL shop-floor innovations are linked to higher level business decisions that it is likely to succeed. Yet, given current trends in union representation, less than 15% of the labor force may be organized by the turn of the century. This suggests that while EAPs may currently be facing a growth market, soon the room for expansion in these prime locations may decline.

Of course, EAPs are not only present in unionized settings. They have spread rapidly into partially unionized and union-free environments as well. Here, the dangers for the future success of EAPs are greater. In order for work innovations to be successful, there must remain a high degree of trust between employers and employees and the linkage of innovations to broader business issues. Yet, in nonunion settings, there are tremendous pressures to adopt different strategies, ones that do not foster long-term trust.

These strategic decisions will directly affect human resource strategies. As Kochan, Katz, and McKersie note:

> Many of the totally unorganized firms that started up and grew rapidly in the 1960s and 1970s are now facing the challenge of adapting their human resource management practices to maturing, more price-competitive markets. Like their unionized counterparts, these firms will experience increased pressure to lower labor cost, streamline staffing levels, adopt labor-saving technologies, and redeploy workers and assets. Human-resource management professionals will be asked to adjust policies away from those that were designed to serve a business strategy that valued low turnover and high commitment to ones that better serve emerging strategies that depend on low labor costs. As these pressures increase, so does the potential for the emergence of conflict between employee expectations for employment continuity and career progression and management's efforts to contain costs.[24]

Only companies with the resources, competitive clout, and culture to resist these trends are likely to retain their "humanization" thrust. For example, IBM has gained a reputation as an innovator in labor relations with its commitment to life-time employment and the training of its work force. Yet, in recent years, IBM has come in for criticism on financial markets for its unwillingness to abandon this tradition in the face of increased competition. At the same time, many of the companies that have been noted for their enlightened personnel practices have abandoned these strategies as their market situation changed.

As companies move from "humanizing" to cost containment, the ground is likely to shift beneath the feet of EAP specialists. While the shift may open up new opportunities for EAP professionals in exit counseling, relocation aid, and vocational guidance, the decline in trust that will be engendered in this strategic shift is likely to be inimical to the success of EAPs.

Even in those companies which retain QWL strategies, the macroeconomic context may pose severe challenges to employee assistance. As poverty and inequality continue to engulf a larger part of the population, the humanized companies will find themselves as pristene preserves in a society descending into increased conflict and social breakdown. Only through the successful use of large social blinders will EAPs be able to continue their work in this context.

In short, EAPs cannot insulate themselves from the negative side of the current economic transformation. In the short-term they may be able to treat unemployment, declining worker representation, and poverty as "other people's problems." In the long run, they are likely to do so at their own peril.

The spectre of a society dominated by overt class conflict and social disorder is not inevitable. To avoid it, however, we will need to reverse the trends toward deregulation of the labor market that have been popular over the past decade. We will need to articulate a labor policy that allows workers to organize without the intimidation and maneuvers that the current NLRB has allowed. We will need public programs to protect a larger share of the unemployed and provide a wider set of retraining and employment opportunities. We will need to assure that the disabled, low-skilled, and children are not forced to endure the level of deprivation to which they are currently relegated. In short, the public sector in cooperation with business, labor, and the voluntary sector will have to commit themselves to a broad program of workplace activism. While it may seem like a pipe dream today, the nightmarish alternatives may further its realization.

EAP professionals must become advocates and supporters of these strategies, not only out of altruism, but because their own success will hinge on it. Occupational social welfare can become a permanent part of the social landscape, but only in cooperation and partnership with an expanding commitment to public and voluntary social welfare. The current situation of private growth and public decline is insupportable in the long run.[25]

Unfortunately, there is scant evidence that current EAP practitioners appreciate their current choices. More often than not, EAP professionals appear to adopt the management goals – profitability, cost containment, and efficiency – as their own. Rather than extending their practice to examine the organization and social origins of workers' problems, they are more likely to use their expertise to individualize and medicalize dysfunction.[26] Practitioners have increasingly hitched their star to that of management.

History provides examples of the error of this strategy. During the 1920s, welfare capitalism became a major movement among American businessmen. Expanding benefits, providing services, and hiring "special secretaries" became increasingly popular. Rather than maintain their independence or advocate for public expenditure, the social secretaries concentrated on the private sector and their narrow organization environment. When the Great Depression brought a new era of private cost-cutting and public activism, welfare capitalism and its practitioners were swept from the scene.

Today's EAP practitioners need not repeat the mistakes of their predecessors. The trends to humanize the workplace are not illusions; they grow out of real changes in the economy. Yet, unless EAPs are linked to an expansion of social responsibility and public expenditure, they are unlikely to continue the success they have enjoyed during the past few years.

NOTES

1. U.S. Congress, Office of Technology Assessment, *Technology and Structural Unemployment: Reemploying Displaced Adults* (Washington, DC: Government Printing Office, 1986), p. 154.
2. Ibid, p. 157.
3. U.S. Commerce, Department of, *Statistical Abstract of the United States 1987* (Washington, DC: Government Printing Office, 1987) p. 417. See also, U.S., *Economic Report of the President*, January 1987 (Washington, DC: Government Printing Office, 1987), 26-29, 45-50.
4. By 1980, there was one car for every two Americans; 99% of households had televisions, refrigerators, and radios; and 90% had washers, toasters, and vacuum cleaners. Michael J. Piore & Charles F. Sabel, *The Second Industrial Divide: Possibilities for Prosperity* (New York: Basic Books, 1984), 184.
5. Piore & Sabel, *Second Industrial Divide*, 17, passim.
6. D. F. Barnett & Robert W. Crandall, *Up From the Ashes: The Rise of the Steel Minimill* (Washington, DC: Brookings Institution, 1986), 6-16.
7. "How Power Will Be Balanced On Saturn's Shop Floor," *Business Week* (August 5 1985), 65-66.
8. Piore & Sabel, *Second Industrial Divide*, 221-259.
9. Larry Hischhorn, *Beyond Mechanization: Work and Technology in a Postindustrial Age* (Washington, DC: MIT Press, 1984), 74-86.
10. Thomas A. Kochan, Harry C. Katz & Robert B. McKersie, *The Transformation of American Industrial Relations* (New York: Basic Books, 1986), 148-149.
11. Ibid.

12. Roseabeth Moss Kanter, *The Changemasters: Innovation for Productivity in the American Corporation* (New York: Simon and Schuster, 1983), 246-248.

13. Between 1978 and 1985, the annual rate of business incorporation increased from 478,000 to 669,000, an increase of 40%. During this same period, the number of business failures rose from 6,600 to 57,100, an increase of 765%. The *rate* of business failure (per 10,000 listed enterprises) rose from 23.9 to 114.0, an increase of 378%. *Economic Report of the President, 1987*, Table B-92, 351.

14. Godfrey Hodgson, *America In Our Time* (New York: Random House, 1976).

15. For example, in 1960, American Gross Domestic Product per Worker was 70% higher than that of any of nation. "Survey: High Technology," *The Economist* (August 23, 1986), 1.

16. See, for example, Sam Rosenberg, "Reagan Social Policy and Labour Force Restructuring," *Cambridge Journal of Economics* 7 (1983): 179-196.

17. The decline in the rate among nonagricultural workers has been from 35% in the mid-1950s to approximately 18% in 1984. For specific industries declines, see Kochan, Katz & McKersie, *Transformation*, 48-50.

18. U.S. Department of Labor, *News*, October 14, 1986.

19. Axinn & Stern, "Race, Inequality, and the Welfare State." Unpublished manuscript, November 1986.

20. Lester Thurow, *Zero-Sum Solutions: An Economic and Political Agenda for the 1980s* (New York: Simon and Schuster, 1985).

21. Bluestone & Harrison, "The Grim Truth About the Job Miracle," New York Times, February 1, 1987. In response, Janet Norwood, "The Job Machine Has Not Broken Down," NYT February 22, 1987, argues that the upsurge in low-wage work is simply a cyclical phenomenon.

22. U.S. Bureau of the Census, *Money Income in the United States* Current Population Reports, series P-60, number 151 (Washington, DC: Government Printing Office), Table 12, 37.

23. Lester Thurow, "A Surge in Inequality," *Scientific American* 256:5 (May 1987): 30-37.

24. Kochan, Katz & McKersie, *Transformation*, 246.

25. Sheila Kammerman & Alfred J. Kahn, "Private Sector Social Policy Responsibilities," *The Journal of the Institute for Socioeconomic Studies* (Fall 1986), pp. 44-60.

26. William J. Sonnenstahl, *Inside an Emotional Health Program* (Ithaca, NY: ILR Press, 1986), 166-167.

EAPs in Transition: Purpose and Scope of Services

Keith McClellan
Richard E. Miller

SUMMARY. This paper is a survey report of EAP purpose and practices. One hundred and eighty-two ($n = 182$) randomly selected EAP practitioners responded to a questionnaire designed to measure purposes, services, staff specialties and characteristics, service users, and related background information. The findings provide an empirical evaluation of the "state of the art" of the growth, development and trends in the employee assistance field. Also, while the findings indicate that EAPs are in transition several basic functions common to all are identified.

INTRODUCTION

A survey of the literature has indicated that the purpose of employee assistance programs (EAPs) has been changing (Spicer, 1987; Steele, 1982). Twelve years ago EAPs were usually advertised to employers as programs for "improving productivity." Today EAPs are often sold as an "employer benefit," although these programs may be recommended for resolving management problems, reducing health and safety risks, promoting wellness, containing health care costs, and even limiting employer liability. Obviously, important shifts have been taking place in the purpose of

---

Keith McClellan, PhD, is Director, Health Interventions, Council on Health Costs and Richard E. Miller, EdD, is Manager, Xerox Health Management Program. Direct inquiries to Keith McClellan, at Council on Health Costs, Suite 1020, 730 East Trade Street, Charlotte, NC 28202-3021.

EAPs. These shifts have profound implications for the way EAPs are organized, staffed, and designed to function.

This paper is a survey report of EAP purpose and practice. The investigators randomly selected EAP practitioners and requested responses to a questionnaire designed to measure purposes, services, staff specialties and characteristics, service users, and related background information. The findings are discussed in relation to past, present, and future trends in the employee assistance movement.

SAMPLING AND DATA COLLECTION

During the fourth quarter of 1986, a sample of professionals and practitioners in the EAP field was constructed by randomly selecting subjects from the current membership directories of the Association for Labor/Management Administrators and Consultants on Alcoholism (ALMACA) and the Employee Assistance Society of North America (EASNA). Member records, alphabetically listed in the directories according to region of residence, were numerically labelled. Using a table of random numbers (Slakter, 1972), the investigators proceeded to select 150 subjects from each directory. If duplicate records were selected (subjects being members of both associations) only one version (either ALMACA or EASNA) of that record was chosen. Subject selection proceeded until 150 records were drawn from each directory for total sample size of 300 records.

The 300 subjects were mailed the questionnaire, EAP Purpose and Practice, resulting in the return of 187 questionnaires. Five of the questionnaires were incomplete and accompanied by a message indicating the subject was not directly involved in EAP. Thus, 182 subjects completed and returned questionnaires representing a response rate of .61.

The questionnaire, EAP Purpose and Practice, was constructed by the investigators and purposed for the collection of descriptive information on the EAP in which the respondent was employed. Three of the 11 questionnaire items were designed for the collection of respondent's background information regarding source of employment, staffing, and years of practice (see Table 1).

A little less than half of the respondents (44.9%) were employees

Table 1: Background information

Your EAP specialists are	Per cent
employees of employer to whom EAP services are provided	44.9
employees of external company/agency providing contracted EAP services	29.1
independent practitioners	14.6
other	11.4
Formal training of EAP assessment specialist(s)	
relevant undergraduate degree	18.3
relevant graduate degree	32.9
certified alcoholism/drug counselor	21.3
on-the-job training/professional workshopping	22.3
other	5.6
Size of your EAP staff	Mean
full time	3.1
part time	1.1
contract	2.8
Years you have practiced EAP	6.8

of the employer to whom EAP services were being provided. About 29% of those answering the survey indicated being employees of external company/agency providing contracted EAP services. Independent practitioners comprised 14.6% of the group whereas 11.4% responded to "Other" (e.g., multi-client organization being "internal-external-independent").

Formal training of the EAP assessment specialists in the response group varied. Nearly one-third of the EAP assessment specialists (32.9%) were reported to have an advanced degree in the social sciences. Approximately 18% in the group reported specialists having a relevant undergraduate degree. About 21% of the respondents had a staff person certified in alcohol/drug counseling. Twenty-two percent of the assessment specialists received training on-the-job and/or through professional workshops. About 5% of the respondents indicated formal training of assessment specialists to be in the "Other" category (e.g., "certificate programs").

Subjects responding to this survey had a mean staff size of 6.7 persons of whom approximately three were full-time, one was part-time, and three were contracted. The mean number of years the respondents practiced EAP was 6.8.

EAP PURPOSE(S)

When asked to report "purpose(s) of your EAP," 6% of the respondents listed one purpose, whereas the majority (85.5%) listed two to seven purposes. Eight percent of the respondents listed eight or more purposes. The mean number of reported purposes was 4.9.

Improve employee production was the most commonly cited purpose by the responding EAPs (87.8%). Bearing in mind that respondents could indicate more than one purpose, improve employee production represented 18.0% of the total responses (see Table 2). The second most frequent purpose was reduce health risks (74.1%) comprising 15.2% of the responses. An equivalent portion of the respondents cited reduce safety risks (68.7%) and resolve management problems (67.9%) as purposes representing 14.1% and 14.0% of the responses respectively. Contain health care costs was cited by 69.5% of the respondents representing 14.3% of the responses. Approximately 61% of the respondents indicated their purpose to be

Table 2: EAP purpose(s)

	% of Respondents	% of Responses
Improve employee production	87.8	18.1
Reduce health risks	74.1	15.2
Reduce safety risks	68.7	14.1
Resolve management problems	67.9	14.0
Promote wellness	61.8	12.7
Contain health care costs	69.5	14.3
Limit employer liability	31.3	6.4
Other	25.2	5.2

promote wellness, comprising 12.7% of the responses. Limit employer liability was registered by 31.2% of the respondents representing 6.4 percent of the responses. "Other" (e.g., "save jobs and families") was an indicated purpose by 25.2% of the respondents comprising 5.2% of the responses. Only 5% of those returning the questionnaire, however, submitted improve employee production as sole response.

Responses to the questionnaire item "purpose(s) of your EAP" were categorized by the investigators as "benefit to the employee" or "benefit to the employer." EAP purposes considered as "benefit to the employee" were reduce health risks, and promote wellness. EAP purposes considered as "benefit to the employer" were improve employee production, resolve management problems, contain health care costs, and limit employer liability. The percent of reported purposes representing "benefit to the employer" was higher (52.7%) than percent of responses reflecting "benefit to the employee" (27.6%). The responses, reduce safety risks, and "Other," were considered an employer/employee benefit category and comprised 19.7% of the total responses. It is interesting to note that 15.3% of the respondents submitted program purpose(s) categorized exclusively as "benefit to the employer" whereas 6.1% indicated purpose(s) categorized exclusively as "benefit to the employee."

SERVICES

Subjects were asked to reply to "Your EAP services" (see Table 3). The mean number of identified services for respondents of this survey was 11.7. The more commonly offered services indicated by the respondents were assessment (91.6%), referral (96.2%), and supervisory training (90.1%) representing 8.2%, 7.8%, and 7.7% of total responses respectively. Large portions of the response group reported aftercare/follow-up (82.4%), employee education (80.9%), and management consultation (78.6%), comprising 7.0%, 6.9%, and 6.7% of the total responses respectively.

In comparison, smaller portions of the response group reported services related to diagnosis (54.2%), short-term outpatient counseling (58.0%), "key employee" training (41.9%), motivational counseling (45.8%), research/evaluation (36.6%), policy develop-

Table 3: Services

	% of Respondents	% of Responses
Assessment	91.6	7.8
Diagnosis	54.2	4.6
Referral	96.2	8.2
Short-term outpatient counseling	58.0	5.0
Aftercare/followup	82.4	7.0
Management consultation	78.6	6.7
Supervisory training	90.1	7.7
Employee education	80.9	6.9
"Key employee" training	41.9	3.6
Referral agent training	18.3	1.6
Motivational counseling	45.8	3.9
Drug screening	14.5	1.2
Research/evaluation	36.6	3.1
Policy development	61.1	5.2
Internal case review	39.7	3.4
Utilization reviews	40.5	3.5
Pre-admission	21.4	1.8
Concurrent case reviews	22.9	2.1
Case management	53.4	4.6
Benefits consultation	38.2	3.3
Health promotion	48.1	4.1
Marketing of services	38.2	3.3
Health risk appraisals	9.2	.8
Other	9.9	.8

ment (61.1%), internal case review (39.7%), utilization reviews (40.5%), concurrent case reviews (22.9%), case management (53.4%), benefits consultation (38.2%), health promotion (48.1%), and marketing of services (38.2%). The least commonly offered EAP services indicated by the respondents were referral agent training (18.3%), drug screening (14.5%), pre-admission certification (21.4%), health risk appraisal (9.2%), as well as replies to the "Other" (e.g., "pre-retirement counseling") category (9.9%). Bearing in mind that respondents could indicate more than one service, each reported service proportional to total responses has been presented in Table 3.

The investigators observed that 78.6% of the EAPs answering this questionnaire provided one of the problem resolution services. Short-term counseling, motivational counseling, and case management—in addition to referral—were placed in this service category by the investigators. A little more than 20% provided all the problem resolution services. There was a low percent of responding EAPs (5%) that provided problem resolution services but no referral.

A high percent of respondents (92.4%) offered some type of person-to-person outreach. The investigators considered the services comprising this category to be management consultation, supervisory training, employee education, "key employee" training, referral agent training, motivational counseling, drug screening, and health promotion. Only 3.1% offered the full range of person-to-person outreach functions.

Likewise, there was a significant linkage between health education/promotion/benefits and most EAPs in this response group. More than 76% of the respondents provided at least one education/promotion/benefit related service such as drug screening, utilization reviews, pre-admission certification, concurrent case reviews, case management, health promotion, or health risk appraisals.

Aftercare, follow-up, and case management were also observed in a service cluster according to those EAPs responding to this survey. Just over 71% of the respondents offered at least two services in this cluster. About 9% of the respondents provided no aftercare, follow-up, or case management services.

Finally, the investigators examined what was considered "the traditional EAP package": assessment, referral, aftercare/follow-up, management consultation, supervisory training, employee education, motivational counseling, and policy development. Only 16.8% of the respondents provided *all* of these services. Interestingly enough, about 3% of the respondents did not provide any one of these services.

CASEFINDING

Identification of individuals (employees and/or eligible dependents) who have personal problems is one of the central concepts of an EAP. People who have personal problems must be identified before intervention, referral, or remediation can take place. The distribution of reported casefinding techniques in proportion to respondents and total responses has been shown in Table 4.

All of the EAPs returning the questionnaire used more than one casefinding technique. The typical respondent utilized a mean of five techniques. Nearly all of the respondents (96.2%) permitted self-referral. A comparable portion of the respondents (94.7%) utilized constructive confrontation by supervisors – an interesting observation since a slightly smaller portion of respondents (90.1%) provided supervisory training for this casefinding technique or any other related task (see Table 3). Family referrals were also commonly used, with 86.2% of the respondents reporting this source of casefinding. Two other common casefinding techniques according to the respondents were peer referrals (78.5%) and labor union EAP committee referrals (60%).

Table 4: Casefinding

	% of Respondents	% of Responses
Constructive confrontation by supervisor	94.7	18.2
Assumed closing by supervisor/ "key employee"	20.6	4.0
Self referral	96.2	18.5
Peer referral	78.6	15.1
Family referral	86.2	16.6
Court referral	22.9	4.4
Union EAP committee referral	59.5	11.5
12th Step calls	16.8	3.2
Other organizations in company	29.0	5.6
Other	15.3	2.9

Internal referrals from other organizations in the company (i.e., medical and/or personnel departments) were cited by 29% of the respondents. The early stage problem casefinding technique known as "the assumed closing" by supervisors or other "key employees" was used by 20.6% of the respondents. Court referrals, resulting from drunken driving convictions, for example, were accepted by about 23% of the responding EAPs.

Only 16.5% of the respondents appeared aware of or admitted linkage to 12th Step calls or networks of Alcoholics Anonymous and other self-help groups. This observation appears to be somewhat at variance with the majority of respondents (59.5%) that reportedly utilized union EAP committee referrals. Referrals of this kind are frequently linked to the 12th Step work of union members who are active on the EAP committee. About 15% of the respondents indicated "Other" (e.g., "working with other local EAPs") as a casefinding technique.

The investigators observed that of the respondents using constructive confrontation (94.7%), only 52% of this subgroup provided referral, aftercare and employee education services. About 70% of this subgroup provided two of these three services.

STAFF SPECIALIZATION

The investigators examined staff specialization of the EAPs responding to this survey (see Table 5). Approximately 45% of the respondents reported having an administrator and about 20% indicated having assessment/referral specialists on staff. Alcoholism/drug counseling (30.5%) and education/training specialists (29.0%) were commonly reported specialties. Lesser portions of this response group reported staff specialties in marketing (20.6), clinical direction (19.1), and record keeping (17.6). About 18% of the respondents indicated "Other" (e.g., "legal specialist").

These findings indicated a variety of specialties on staff. The typical EAP in this response group had a mean of 2.4 specialists. Since respondents could indicate more than one staff specialty, the distribution of specialties in proportion to total responses has been shown in Table 5.

Table 5: Staff specialization

	% of Respondents	% of Responses
Marketing	20.6	8.6
Assessment/referral	41.2	17.2
Clinical director	19.1	8.0
Education/training	29.0	12.1
Alcoholism/drug counseling	30.5	12.7
Family counselor	18.3	7.6
Record keeping	17.6	7.3
Administrator	45.1	18.8
Other	18.3	7.6

EMPLOYERS SERVICED

Subjects in this survey were asked to respond to "Employers serviced by your EAP" (see Table 6). A majority of the respondents (54.9%) reported manufacturing. About 47% of the respondents indicated business whereas a little more than 42% indicated labor unions. Noticeable portions of this response group reported government (30.5%), hospitals/health centers (25.9%), and public sector providers (17.6%) are "employers serviced."

A comparable percent of respondents identified the "employers serviced" as schools (15.3%). private sector providers (14.5%), wholesale/retail operations (13.7%), and colleges/universities (12.9%). A low percent of respondents indicated employee associations (5.3). About 10% of the respondents reported "Other" (e.g., "professional sports team").

These observations implied a variety of employers were being serviced by the EAPs responding to this survey. The mean number of "employers serviced" was 2.9. The distribution of "employers serviced" in proportion to total responses has been shown in Table 6.

Table 6: Employers serviced

	% of Respondents	% of Responses
Manufacturing	54.9	18.8
Business	47.3	16.2
Labor union employees	42.7	14.7
Schools	15.3	5.2
Colleges/universities	12.9	4.5
Government	30.5	10.5
Wholesale/retail	13.7	4.7
Employee associations	5.3	1.8
Private sector providers	14.5	5.0
Public sector providers	17.6	6.0
Hospitals/health centers	25.9	8.9
Other	10.7	3.7

IMPORTANT SKILL

Sampled EAPs were asked to respond to "The skill you believe is *most* important to employee assistance work" (see Table 7). Assessment/referral was by far the most commonly identified skill representing the largest portion of the response group (58.8%). Much smaller portions of response group indicated labor-management relations (6.9), employee relations (6.9), alcoholism counseling (6.1), and differential diagnosis (6.1) as most important skill. An even lower percent of respondents reported administrative skills (2.3), marketing (1.5), and benefit management (0.8). No respondent identified legal/safety skills as most important. Interestingly enough, about 5% of this response group reported "Other" as the most important skill. Examples of this category were: "people skills translatable into organizational functions," "motivational counseling," and "building trusting relations between management and employees."

IMPORTANT CHARACTERISTIC

EAPs completing this survey responded to "All other things being equal, the employee characteristic you favor most in an employee assistance Program Director" (see Table 8). Relevant professional experience was most noticeably the most common identified important characteristic representing 63.4% of the respondents. Knowledge of work group was identified by 19.1% of the respondents. Lower percents of respondents indicated personal

Table 7: Important skill

	% of Respondents
Labor-Management relations	6.9
Employee relations	6.9
Alcoholism counseling	6.1
Differential diagnosis	6.1
Marketing	1.5
Assessment/referral	58.8
Case management	6.1
Administrative skills	2.3
Benefit management	.8
Legal/Safety skills	0.0
Other	4.5

Table 8: Important characteristic

	% of Respondents
Personal recovery experience	7.6
Relevant professional experience	63.4
Relevant college degree	2.3
Knowledge of work group	19.1
Other	7.6

recovery experience (7.6) and relevant college degree (2.3) as most important characteristic. Approximately 7% of respondents indicated "Other" (e.g., "ability to communicate and, solve problems") as most important characteristic.

DISCUSSION

The findings from this study seem to indicate that EAPs are in transition. The responding EAPs are multipurpose services considering that approximately 93% reported more than one purpose. These programs seek to be both employer and employee benefits, and are perhaps experiencing role conflicts from time-to-time. Approximately 87% of the respondents identified their purpose to improve employee production. Nearly 62% of the respondents also believed their purpose was to promote wellness. Two-thirds of the responding EAPs presented purposes indicative of containing health care costs.

Clearly, a majority of practitioners (69%) in this response group viewed their EAPs as multipurpose programs having benefits for both the employer and the employee. Upon closer examination, however, "benefit to employer" category of purpose was represented by more of the responding EAPs than "benefit to employee." Yet, as previously cited, the typical EAP in the field is more likely to be marketed as an employee benefit (Spicer, 1987).

In the early 1970s, Trice and Roman (1972) popularized the concept of using social controls in work organizations to contain and solve employee problems. Specifically targeting the alcohol abuser, occupational alcoholism programs were promoted as methods of utilizing traditional supervisory responsibilities to provide the social controls for enacting behavior changes in alcoholics. These programs were based on the assumption that deteriorating job performance frequently results from the behavioral and physical impairment associated with alcoholism and can be effectively dealt with through means typically available in the workplace. By training supervisors in how to document and confront employees whose job performance had deteriorated, the employer, it was asserted, could exert stronger social controls and thereby improve employee production, while encouraging remediation from alcoholism.

By the 1980s, Roman (1985) decried the medicalization of the workplace. He asserted that EAPs were changing the nature of supervisory control in an adverse way. "Employee Assistance Programs," he claimed, "embody a series of concepts about the management of job performance that diverge from traditional management approaches." What was not acknowledged in this claim was that traditional management approaches were being replaced by new management styles independently from any EAP influence. EAPs were changing to conform to new working conditions and styles of management (McClellan & McClellan, 1987). The nature of effective social controls on workers was changing. The role of supervisor was changing and hence, the role of the EAP was forced to change. These changes are still underway in the EAP field and are reflected in this survey findings.

Traditional, unionized manufacturing employers continue to be the most common users of EAP services, as such, the traditional occupational alcoholism model of employee assistance maintains an adequate fit for these employers. However, schools, colleges/universities, hospitals/health centers, governmental units and many businesses do not have a work environment that is compatible with the constructive confrontation model of employee assistance. Hence, a "new wave" of EAPs has been introduced; programs more focused on health intervention.

Health intervention EAPs emphasize a different set of purposes. These programs are more likely to be presented as an employee benefit than are traditional occupational alcoholism programs. Health intervention EAPs emphasize reduction of health risks, reduction of safety risks, wellness, limitations on employer liability, and containment of health care costs. Results of this survey indicate these new purposes are becoming established in the EAP field.

As the purpose of an EAP changes, so must its services. Once again, survey findings indicated that the lexicon of EAP services has been expanding and shifting. More than half the EAPs respondents to this survey provided diagnosis, not simply assessment. More than half the EAPs in the response group provided counseling as well as referral. More than half the respondents provided formal case management services. These findings imply that a growing number of EAPs are moving beyond policy development toward active policy implementation in the form of utilization reviews, concurrent case reviews, benefits consultation, drug screening, and even health risks appraisals. This "new wave" of EAPs is blending health intervention activities with alcoholism, drug abuse, and mental (ADM) casefinding and assessment.

Another clear evidence of transition in the EAP field is the emergence of such "new wave" casefinding services as "key employee" training, referral agent training, assumed closing, and greater employee education activity. Substantial numbers of EAPs in this survey reported offering these new types of services. The investigators in this study observed that even traditional EAPs, more oriented toward alcoholism services, appear to be offering a broader range of services than those originally defined by Trice and Roman (1972). In the current work of Roman and Blum (1986), these researchers observed two types of EAPs: one primarily offering assistance to management whereas the other primarily offering assistance to employees. Accordingly, Roman and Blum have recommended to organizational consumers the careful coordination of parallel activities (health promotion, drug screening, and prepaid mental health services) with EAPs and not integrated into EAPs.

This survey suggests that neither the "core technology" of EAPs (Roman & Blum, 1985) nor ALMACA's credentialing instruments (Law, 1985; 1986) adequately reflect the emerging scope of EAP activities. A noticeable portion of EAPs responding to this survey offered services that are not accounted for in either the "core technology" or ALMACA's credential. The ALMACA credential is potentially problematic because it seeks to place a single credential on a multifaceted, multifunctional field of work. Referral agents, assessment and case management specialists, administrators, consultants, trainers, and employee counselors each have different functions.

There also are different methods of achieving similar EAP functions. An EAP has several basic functions: (1) program authority, (2) identification of employee problem, (3) determination of nature of employee problem, (4) motivation for employee to secure and accept help, (5) linkage of employee/eligible dependent with problem remediation, (6) monitoring assistance, and (7) determination outcomes of assistance.

Program authority can be established with a job description or contract. It also can be established by formal/informal policy, benefit design or the formation of an EAP committee. There are at least nine systems for identifying employee problems that have or, if unaddressed, will have an adverse effect on the employer. These systems are: (1) employee education designed to promote self-referral, (2) supervisory training designed to result in formal supervisory referrals, (3) "key employee" training designed to create informal management or peer referral by means of assumed closing, (4) referral agent training designed to result in peer referral, (5) family education designed to foster family referral, (6) drug screening designed for referral of drug users, (7) health risk appraisals designed to identify and refer employees whose life-style places them at risk of health problems, (8) health screening designed for medical referrals, and (9) 12th Step calls designed for self-referral.

In turn, each EAP function can be achieved in several ways. Diagnosis, which is governed by licensed psychological and medical practice, can be interchanged with assessment, which is currently ungoverned by law or regulation. Both are methods of determining the nature of a personal problem. Motivational counseling, which can use positive/personal motivational tools, can be interchanged with constructive confrontation—a pragmatic, problem solving technique likely to lead to formal discipline (Sonnenstuhl & Trice, 1986); or with benefits design, which is structural, to achieve similar objectives.

Different techniques appear appealing to different work groups, problem areas, and stages of problem development, better than others. Constructive confrontation may work better with middle-late stage male alcoholics than with females with certain types of mental health disorders.

Proper linkage of EAP with primary care can take place through a referral network to community resources or by offering outpatient counseling. An EAP can have routine follow-up or authority-driven case management. Pre-admission review and concurrent case review, techniques regularly used by insurance carriers, are becoming more commonplace EAP functions.

Methods of determining outcome can rely on the information secured during routine follow-up. Aftercare groups, which are more proactive than follow-up in nature, are being offered by increasing numbers of EAPs. Research and evaluation studies are being encouraged by professionals in the field. Attention to the management of job reentry has emerged as a critical issue.

The focus of the EAPs reflected in results from this survey obviously transcends chemical dependency to other behaviorally linked health problems. Services such as outpatient counseling and motivational counseling activities extend EAPs into areas of regulated and licensed health care services. Formal utilization reviews, case management, and concurrent case reviews imply formal training. Yet the investigators of this study observed that 17% of the responding EAPs who reportedly offered these services did not have the skilled staff necessary to legally provide them. Marketing is another service requiring specialized training or knowledge. Survey results did not reflect adequate staff qualifications to provide this service.

As EAPs develop more sophisticated methods of outreach and utilize a broader scope of services, they will have a greater need for formal education. Currently, the field is almost evenly split between occupational transplants and recovering, self-educated EAP practitioners on the one hand, and social workers, psychologists and other degreed professionals on the other hand. As health intervention EAP approaches are adopted, the balance of power in the field is likely to swing to the formally educated practitioners. In the future, experience in EAP work by itself is unlikely to be as important as the kinds of experience and skills the EAP practitioner has to offer.

REFERENCES

Law, J. (1985). Competency validation. *The ALMACAN*, 15:4-7.

Law, J. (1986). Certification commission holds first meeting. *The ALAMACAN*, 16:4-6.

McClellan, K. & M. McClellan (1987). The dark side of megatrends. *Employee Assistance Quarterly*, 2:1-21.

Roman, P.M. (1985). From employee alcoholism to employee assistance. *Journal of Studies on Alcohol*, 42:244-272.

Roman, P. & T. Blum (1985). The core technology of employee assistance programs. *The ALAMACAN*, 15:8-19.

Roman P. & T. Blum (1986). Educating organizational consumers about employee assistance programs. U.S. Public Health Service, National Institute on Alcohol Abuse and Alcoholism (No. AA-05703).

Slakter, M.J. (1972). *Statistical inference for educational researchers*. Reading, MA: Addison-Wesley Company.

Sonnenstuhl, W.J. & H.M. Trice (1986). *Strategies for employee assistance programs: The crucial balance*. Ithaca, NY: ILR Press.

Spicer, J. (1987). *The EAP solution – Current trends and future issues*. Center City, MN: Hazelden Educational Materials.

Steele, P.D. (1982). Characteristics of employee assistance programs throughout the United States. U.S. Public Health Service, National Institute on Drug Abuse (No. 271-76-4413).

Trice, H.M. & P. Roman (1972). *Spirits and demons at work: Alcohol and other drugs on the job*. Ithaca, NY: Cornell University Press.

A Comparative Analysis of In-House and Contractual Employee Assistance Programs

S. Lala Ashenberg Straussner

SUMMARY. This paper aims to expand the present state of knowledge regarding employee assistance programs (EAPs) through the presentation of the findings of a study which explored the existence and the nature of such programs in the New York Metropolitan Area. The identification of all EAPs in this area allowed for the development of a typology encompassing the identified programs, and for a comparative analysis of in-house and contractual EAPs in the finance/insurance, manufacturing, and service industries.

INTRODUCTION

Empirical research studies of employee assistance programs have traditionally focused either on in-house alcoholism-oriented programs (see Mannello, 1979; Beyer & Trice, 1978; Steel, 1984, etc.), or on cost-benefit and programs outcomes (Foote et al, 1978; Myers, 1984) of broadbrush programs – either in-house or contractual. While numerous articles listing the benefits of in-house or contractual programs can be found in the literature (Phillips & Older, 1981; Hellan & Campbell, 1981; Kolben, 1982; Minter, 1983; Fleisher & Kaplan, 1984; Stein, 1984; etc.), they are not based on empirical research findings, but purely on the "conventional wis-

S. Lala Ashenberg Straussner, DSW, is Assistant Professor, New York University, School of Social Work and an EAP Consultant. Address correspondence to 124 West 79 Street, New York, NY 10024. This paper is based on a dissertation study entitled *Helping Troubled Employees: An Analysis of Selected Employee Assistance Programs Under Management Auspices*. Columbia University, 1986.

dom," or in the author's own practice experience. The single empirical study on this subject (Sudduth, 1984) is limited to six EAPs—only one of which was internal or in-house.

The purpose of this paper is to expand the programs (EAPs) by presenting the findings of a study which examined the scope and nature of all identified EAPs in the New York Metropolitan Area and compared a representative sample of fifteen (15) in-house and eight (8) contractual programs within three industries.

While a preliminary study of EAPs conducted by the author found that the organizations which offer EAP services to their employees in the New York region tend to be larger than in other parts of the country, in this author's opinion, this sample of EAPs based in the Metro New York area can be considered to be reflective of EAP programs throughout the United States.

METHODOLOGY

This was an exploratory descriptive study whose purpose was (1) to provide an overview of the scope and the models of all identified EAPs in the New York Metropolitan Area, (2) to provide a detailed analysis of a representative sample of in-house and contractual programs.

The first part of the study was the identification of the universe of employee assistance programs operational as of June 1982, in the Metropolitan New York Area (New York City, Long Island, and Westchester County). These programs were identified on the following basis:

1. All programs self-identified as EAPs in specialized literature (EAP Digest, ALMACAN, etc.), and in professional journals (i.e., personnel, social work, sociology, and psychology related literature).
2. All program-members of the Metropolitan New York Chapter of the Association of Labor-Management Administrators and Consultants on Alcoholism (ALMACA).
3. All programs identified as EAPs by the staffs of the NYSDAAA/Occupational Branch, and of the Industrial Department of the New York Council on Alcoholism.
4. Through the utilization of key informants who were asked to

> examine the list of programs which was developed through the above means and to add any additional programs of which they were aware.[1]

Any program whose existence or date of inception seemed questionable was contacted by the author for verification. While employee assistance programs were found to be located in both private (both for-profit and voluntary) and public sectors, the special forces operating in the public arena (legal mandates, political factors, civil service regulations, etc.), and the unique nature of union and other membership-sponsored programs mitigated against lumping all of these EAPs together. Therefore, the second part of this study was limited to examining only those EAPs which were located in the private-sector and which were under management auspices.

The second part of the study consisted of the selection and analysis of a sample of 23 management-sponsored employee assistance programs in the private sector. Fifteen of the programs were based in-house and eight had contracted out for the EAP services. These programs were selected on the basis of a non-probability quota sampling technique stratified according to program model (in-house and contractual[2]); type of industry of the organization providing the program (finance/insurance, manufacturing, and service); and size of the company (small, medium, and large). They represented 45% of all EAPs under management auspices in the three industries under study, i.e. finance/insurance, manufacturing, and service (see Table 1).

The research instrument utilized consisted of both structured and open-ended questions examining over 200 different variables under 15 categories (see Straussner, 1986). Data were obtained from 67 respondents including program administrators and representatives of top management of the companies and of contracting firms.

Data were collected during the years 1983 and 1984 and are based on 1982/1983 figures. The information was analyzed utilizing the Statistical Package for Social Sciences. Frequency tables and cross tabulations were done on all the variables by the three independent variables which were controlled in the sampling process: program model, company size, and nature of industry. Chi-square tests of association, Kruskal-Wallis one way analysis of var-

Table 1

The Universe And The EAPs Studied In Three Industries
Stratified By Program Model, And Size

Type of Industry	In-House Programs				Contracted-Out				Total
	Size			N	Size			N	
	S	M	L		S	M	L		
Finance/Insurance	3* (2)**	5 (3)	4 (2)	12 (7)	5 (2)	1 (0)	1 (1)	7 (3)	19 (10)
Manufacturing	3 (1)	3 (1)	8 (3)	14 (5)	4 (2)	0 (0)	3 (2)	7 (4)	21 (9)
Service	7 (2)	1 (1)	0 (0)	8 (3)	3 (1)	0 (0)	0 (0)	3 (1)	11 (4)
Total	13 (4)	10 (5)	11 (5)	34 (15)	12 (5)	1 (0)	4 (3)	17 (8)	51 (23)

1. Classification based on U.S. Department of Labor Bureau of Labor Statistics classification code of private industries
2. Sizes of companies are defined as follows:
   Small--Less than 10,00 employees
   Medium--Between 10,000 and 30,000 employees
   Larte--Over 30,000 employees

* Top number indicates total EAP universe in this category.
** Bottom number indicates number of programs studied.

iance by ranks, and t-test for two dependent samples in matched group design were utilized.

FINDINGS

Part One – Overview of EAPs in the Metropolitan New York Area

It was found that in the Metropolitan New York Area consisting of over 5.5 million employees and over 182,000 companies (NYS DOL, 1982), only 125 employee assistance programs were fully operational as of June 1982.[3] All the identified EAPs were classified according to a typology based on program auspice (management or union); sponsorship (individual or consortium); program model (in-house or contractual); and sector (public or private). Table 2 provides a breakdown of the identified programs utilizing this typology.

Over three-quarters (78%) of all the EAPs were found to be existing under management auspices. These programs were most likely to cover those employed in manufacturing industries (33% of all the EAPs under management auspices), followed by those working in finance/insurance (30%), service industries (20%), and transportation/public utilities (14%). Those employed in trade industries as well as those in construction industries were the least likely to have access to an EAP under management auspices (2% each), and were most likely to be covered by a union based program.[4]

An examination of the size of private sector organizations with EAPs reveals that 94% can be classified as "large" organizations, i.e., companies having more than 1,000 workers. The number of employees in firms sponsoring EAPs ranged from 120 to 847,768 workers with a mean of 41,561 and a median of 10,173 employees per organization.

An analysis of all the New York area EAPs based on their program model reveals that 82% of the 125 programs were based in-house and only 18% were contracted-out. It is important to note that only one union/peer group and one public sector EAP were contracted-out.

An analysis of program models chosen by management reveals that there were twice as many in-house as contractual program (43 vs. 21). While the majority of all contractual programs (66%) were found among the companies with fewer than 10,000 employees, there was *no correlation* between in-house programs and size of the work force, although this finding could have been an artifact of the sample.

Part Two – Comparison of In-House and Contracted-Out EAPs

Table 3 provides a summary of some of the major variables studied by program models. Statistically significant differences were found to be related to: year of program inception; original program goals; computerization of records; consultation/training provided to

Table 2

Metropolitan New York Based EAPs Operational as of June, 1982
Stratified by Auspice, Sponsorship, Program Model, and Sector

Auspice:	Management					Union/Peer Group					
Sponsorship:	Individual		Consortium			Individual		Consortium			N
Model:	In-House	Contractual	In-House	Cont	N	In-House	Cont	In-House	Cont	N	
Sector											
Private	42	20	1	1	64	19*	1*	4*	0*	24	88
For Profit	35	20	0	0	55						
Voluntary	7	0	1	1	9						
Public	32	0	0	1	33	4*	0	0	0	4	37
Federal	5	0	0	1	6						
State	8	0	0	0	8						
City	12	0	0	0	12						
County	7	0	0	0	7						
Total Number	74	20	1	2	97	23	1	4	0	28	125

*More discrete classification is not applicable for union-based programs.

Table 3

Major Variables Studied by Program Model
(in Percentages)

VARIABLE	In-House	Contracted-Out	P
Nature of Industry:			NS
Finance/Insurance	47	38	
Manufacturing	33	50	
Service	20	13	
Size:			NS
Small	33	63	
Medium	33	0	
Large	33	37	
Year of Inception			.02
1947-1969	20	0	
1970-1974	7	13	
1975-1979	67	25	
1980-1982	7	63	
EAP Title	53	75	NS
Unionization of Company	60	38	NS
All Establishments Covered	80	50	NS
Provision of Medical Services	93	87	NS
Union Involvement in Program Development:			NS
None	44	100	
Some	33	0	
Full	22	0	
Original Program Goal:			.02
Alcohol Focused	60	13	
Broadbrush	27	88	
Other	13	0	
Administrative Location:			NS
Personnel/Human Relations	33	74	
Medical	34	13	
Employee/Industrial-Labor Relations	13	13	
Other	20	0	
Separate On-Site Office	80	50	NS
Separate/Confidential Records	100	100	NS
Computerized Records	7	57	.05
Services Provided:			
Information & Referral	100	100	NS
Motivational Counseling	93	100	NS
Diagnoses/Evaluation	80	88	NS
Formal Follow-Up	93	88	NS
Consultation/Training with Supervisor	93	88	NS
Short-Term Therapy (≤ 6 Session)	73	75	NS
Family/S.O Counseling	53	88	NS
Self-Help	73	38	NS
Consultation/Training with Unions (asked of unionized companies only)	56	0	.05

TABLE 3, continued

VARIABLE	In-House	Contracted-Out	P
Didactic/Educational Lectures	47	25	NS
Group Therapy	47	0	NS
Long-Term Therapy (>6 sessions)	33	13	NS
24-hour Hot Line	7	63	.02
Emergency Coverage	43	100	.03
Other Services	33	25	NS
Services Changed Over Time	67	25	NS
Program Available to Families	73	100	NS
Problems With Confidentiality	47	25	NS
Support of Top Management:			NS
Very supportive	60	88	
Somewhat	33	12	
Not at all	7	0	
Feedback to Referring Supervisors	85	57	NS
Union View Re Program:			.02
Positive	56	33	
Negative	0	0	
Mixed	44	0	
Unknown	0	67	
Referral Sources:			
Self	44	75	.01
Employer/Supervisor	31	14	.01
Medical	15	9	.02
Other (union, peer, etc.)	10	2	.03
Nature of Presenting Problems:			
Work Related	10	7	NS
Alcoholism	31	12	.03
Marital/Family	18	17	NS
Mental Health	16	32	.01
Financial	7	7	NS
Drug Abuse	5	5	NS
Medical	6	3	NS
Social	3	8	NS
Legal	3	9	.02
Other	2	2	NS
Annual Utilization Rate	3.8	5.7	NS
Are Employees Referred-Out	100	100	NS
Preference of Resources:			
Community Agencies	43	29	NS
Private Practitioners	57	71	NS
Clients Given Choice of Referrals	36	86	.01
Basis of Selection of Resource:			
Location	60	86	NS
Skills of Provider	47	57	NS
Insurance Coverage	20	86	.01

unions; the provision of 24 hour hot-line and emergency coverage during nonstandard shifts; union views regarding the program; referral sources; percentage of employees with alcohol, mental health, and legal problems; the provision of choices to employees regarding referral resources; and selection of referral resources based on insurance coverage.

Additionally, contracted-out programs were found to report to higher level officials than in-house programs ($p < .001$), and the mean cost per eligible employee was more than three times as high in contracting programs than in in-house EAPs ($25.6 vs. $7.5 per employee per year, $p < .001$).

An examination of the nature of the work force of the companies and of the users of these companies' EAPs by gender, occupational status, and ethnicity revealed interesting findings although the data were too limited for valid statistical analysis. As reflected in Table 4, in-house programs saw proportionately the same percentage of males and females as existed in their work force; however, contractual programs saw an overrepresentation of women and were underutilized by the men in their companies.

The limited data regarding occupational status and ethnic/racial characteristics of employees and program users indicate that while in-house program users (n = 8 EAPs) tend to reflect the occupational levels of the work force, contracted-out programs (n = 5 EAPs) tend to be overrepresented by higher level workers.

While the ethnic/racial characteristics of employees were similar for companies with either in-house or contractual programs, analy-

Table 4

Gender, Occupational Status and Ethnicity of Employees in the Organization and Program Users by Program Model

Variable	In-House		Contracted-Out		
	In Organiz.	EAP Users	In Organiz.	EAP Users	P
Gender: (N=18)					
Male	50	50	57	47	NS
Female	50	50	43	53	NS
Occupational Status (N=13)					
Official/Professional	29	27	32	43	--
Non-Managerial	71	73	68	57	--
Ethnicity/Race (N=7)					
White	77	55	74	82	--
Minority	23	45	26	18	--

sis of program users indicates that whites were more likely to use contracted-out programs (82% vs. 55%), while conversely, minority employees, who were most likely also lower level employees, tended to use (or be referred to) in-house programs (45% vs. 18%).

DISCUSSION AND IMPLICATION OF FINDINGS

While the number of employee assistance programs has grown rapidly since 1975, this study found that the proportion of employees covered by EAPs remain minuscule, and thus the overwhelming majority of workers do not have access to such work-based programs but remain dependent on any available community-based services.

The private sector companies providing EAP services tend to resemble those which were, historically, in the vanguard of providing welfare capitalism—large, somewhat paternalist companies wishing to maintain the goodwill and prevent the unionization of their workers, and with the ability to pay for these programs (see Brandes, 1976). In essence, the companies sponsoring these programs are already in the forefront in the provision of fringe benefits. Thus, EAPs tend to be made available to workers who are already likely to have access to numerous other employer and/or union sponsored benefits. This issue of equity must be taken into account when considering future public policies benefiting EAPs.

The comparative analysis of in-house and contractual programs indicates that contracted EAPs tend to be newer, are more likely to have originated as a broadbrush program, report to a higher level within the organization, and cost more per employee (although how one arrives at in-house costs will affect this finding [ed.]). They are also more likely to provide 24-hour or emergency coverage, and to have a computerized data retrieval system. They are more likely to see self-referred employees with mental health or legal problems, and to offer employees several community referral resources based on their insurance coverage. (For additional discussion of contractual EAPs see Straussner, 1985.)

In contrast, in-house programs, while more numerous, tend to be older, are more likely to have originated as alcohol-based programs, report to lower within the organization and cost less per covered employee. They are also more likely to provide consultation and training to unions, and are viewed somewhat more positively by the unions in their company. In-house programs receive a higher percentage of supervisory and medical referrals, and are more likely to see employees with alcohol problems than are contractors.

Such comparative analysis shows that each program model tends to serve different groups of workers. As described previously, in-house programs are more likely to reach employees with alcohol problems, males, and minority workers; while contracted-out programs tend to be used more by women, and higher level, white employees with mental health problems. The users of contractual employee assistance programs thus tend to replicate the pattern found among users of community-based mental health and family agencies. This pattern may indicate that men, as well as minority employees of both sexes, are more likely to be seen by EAPs because of supervisory referrals which are more commonly seen in in-house programs, while women are more likely to self-refer themselves to contractual EAPs. The finding that higher level employees of both sexes were more likely to use contractual programs may be reflective of a greater concern regarding confidentiality among higher level workers. The implications of such differential use by employees are profound and need to be researched further.

In order to maximize the advantages inherent in each EAP model, the ideal employee assistance program may need to be composed of two separate components. One, exemplified by the in-house model, would focus on the identification of employee's behavioral problems based on job performance with the identification of alcohol and drug problems as its central focus. This model would thus encompass the EAP "core technology" identified by Roman and Blum (1985). A separate component, exemplified by the contractual EAP model, would aim at reaching a different segment of the work force through the provision of information and referral services and short-term counseling to self-referred employees with a variety of personal problems. Since such a proposed model can be expensive, companies with limited resources may wish to provide one or both of the above EAP components with part-time staff and through the utilization of consortia arrangements.

The difference in the nature of employees utilizing the two program models implies that research findings based on studies of single program models, such as those conducted by Erfurt and Foote (1977) and Jones (1983) have to be restricted to the model studied and should not be generalized to all EAPs. Based on the findings of this study, Table 5 provides benchmark figures which can be used for comparison by other programs and researchers.

CONCLUSION

This paper summarizes the findings of a research study which examined the various EAPs found in the New York Metropolitan Area.

The limited geographic location of programs studied, the relative small sample and the lack of any input by program users may limit the generalizability of these findings. Nevertheless this study provides important preliminary data regarding the scope and nature of today's EAPs and identifies the differences between in-house and contractual employee assistance programs.

Table 5

Benchmark Figures by Program Model

Variable	In-House Programs	Contractual Programs	ALL EAPs
% Workforce Utilizing EAP	3.8	5.7	4.4
% Self Referred	44	75	54
% Supervisory Referred	31	14	25
% Clients With Alcohol Problem	31	12	25
% Clients With Drug Problem	5	5	5
% Clients Referred Out	66	70	67
% Male Clients	50	47	49
% Female Clients	50	53	51
Number Clients Seen Per Month (Per company)	45	16	36
Cost Per Employee (1982/83)	$7.5	$25.6	$14.7

NOTES

1. For a description of utilization of such key informant technique see Roman, "Survey Methodology in Occupational Alcoholism Research," 1982.
2. Only one of all the identified EAPs could be viewed as a joint labor-management program.
3. The author also identified another 48 programs which were established between July 1982 and December 1984.
4. A more detailed analysis of the organizations sponsoring EAP and of the characteristics of these programs is available elsewhere (Straussner, 1987).

REFERENCES

Beyer, Janice M. & Harrison M. Trice. *Implementing Change: Alcoholism Policies in Work Organizations*. New York: The Free Press, 1978.

Brandes, Stuart D. *American Welfare Capitalism*. Chicago: The University of Chicago Press, 1976.

Erfurt, John C. & Andrea Foote. *Occupational Employee Assistance Programs for Substance Abuse and Mental Health Problems*. Ann Arbor, MI: University of Michigan – Wayne State University, 1977.

Fleisher, Dorothy & Barbara Kaplan. "Components and Trade-offs of Four, ECP Models," in McBroom, Elizabeth (Ed.), *Social Work Papers*, Vol. 18, Summer, 1984, Los Angeles: The School of Social Work, University of Southern California, 1984.

Foote, Andrea, John C. Erfurt, Patricia A. Strauch & Toni L. Guzzardo. *Cost-Effectiveness of Occupational Employee Assistance Programs: Test of an Evaluation Method*. Ann Arbor, MI: Worker Health Program, Institute of Labor and Industrial Relations, University of Michigan – Wayne State University, 1978.

Hellan, Richard T. & William J. Campbell. "Contracting for EAP Services," *Personnel Administrator*, 26(9), September, 1981.

Jones, Donald. *Performance Benchmarks for the Comprehensive Employee Assistance Programs*. Center City, MN: Hazelden Fdn, 1983.

Kolben, Nancy S. *Human Services Programs – Employer and Union Sponsored: Current Trends in New York City*. New York, NY: Community Council of Greater New York, January, 1982.

Manello, Timothy A. *Problem Drinking Among Railroad Workers: Extent, Impact and Solutions*. Washington, DC: University Research Corporation, 1979.

Minter, Jack. "A Contracted or In-House EAP?" *EAP Digest*, 3(4), May/June, 1983.

Myers, Donald W. "Measuring EAP Cost Effectiveness: Results and Recommendations," *EAP Digest*, March/April, 1984.

Phillips, Donald & Harry J. Older. "Models of Service Delivery," *EAP Digest*, Vol. 1(4), 1981.

Roman, Paul H. "Pitfalls of 'Program' Concepts in the Development and Maintenance of Employee Assistance Programs," *Urban and Social Change Review*, 9(1), 1983.

Roman, Paul H. "The Environment for EAP Research: Comments on Structure of Organizational Support," in Grimes, H. (Ed.), *EAP Research*. Troy, MI: Performance Resource Press, Inc. 1984.

Roman, Paul H. & Terry C. Blum. "The Core Technology of Employee Assistance Programs," *The ALMACAN*, Vol. 15(3), March, 1985.

Roman, Paul H. & Harrison M. Trice. "Alcohol Abuse and Work Organizations," in B. Kissin & H. Begleiter (Eds.), *The Biology of Alcoholism*, Vol. 4., New York: Plenum Press, 1976.

Steel, Paul. "Assessing Employee Assistance Programs: Intra and Extra-Organizational Influences," in Grimes, H. (Ed.), *EAP Research*, Troy, MI: Performance Resource Press, Inc., 1984.

Stein, Robert L. "The Pentagon Employee Referral Service," *EAP Digest*, Vol. 4(5) July/August, 1984.

Straussner, Lala A. "The Nature and Growth of Contractual EAPs," *The ALMACAN*, Vol. 15(9), September, 1985.

Straussner, Shulamith L. A. *Helping Troubled Employees: An Analysis of Selected Employee Assistance Programs Under Management Auspices*. Ann Arbor, MI: University Microfilm Int'l, 1987.

Sudduth, Ann B. "Assessing Employee Use of Internal and External Employee Assistance Programs for Alcohol and Control Groups," in Grimes, C. (Ed.), *EAP Research*, Troy, MI: Performance Resource Press, Inc. 1984.

SECTION II: THE CONTEXT OF EAP EVALUATIONS

Prerequisites for EAP Evaluations: A Case for More Thoughtful Evaluation Planning

Michael J. Holosko

SUMMARY. This chapter's main contention is that EAP evaluators, coordinators and administrators need to spend more time in thoughtfully planning EAP evaluations as such activities directly influence the quality of any subsequent evaluation. The chapter outlines four prerequisites to be considered in this regard. These are: (1) a sincere commitment to evaluate the program; (2) answering the why, when, and how of the evaluation; (3) the goals and objectives of the EAP require specification; and (4) information should be in retrievable form. These prerequisites are discussed within the context of a cooperative planning process between the administration, the EAP coordinator and EAP evaluator(s), and are described as to how they may directly influence the EAP evaluation.

INTRODUCTION

Employee Assistance Programs (EAPs), in their various forms, have been operational for approximately 40 years and have increased rapidly in number and popularity in North America. These programs aimed at identifying problem employees through deteriorating work performance have had success rates purported to be as high as 85%, and as secondary benefits improved working relationships, increased worker morale, and improved labour/management cooperation (Brant, 1979). Nevertheless, when one closely examines the occupational, addictions, or EAP journals, the lack of attention directed toward why these programs work or don't work is

---

Michael J. Holosko, PhD, is Associate Professor, School of Social Work, University of Windsor, 401 Sunset Avenue, Windsor, Ontario, Canada N9B 3P4.

quite conspicuous. More specifically, there is distinct literature void related to scientifically based evaluations of EAPs.

The reasons for this may include any one or combinations of the following: (1) there is a lack of resources (e.g., money and personnel) devoted to evaluating EAPs; (2) there are a lack of scientific instruments developed for use in this field; (3) organizations are reluctant to evaluate their EAPs for one reason or another; and/or (4) there has been a lack of attention directed toward planning EAP evaluations.

In regard to the latter point, the premise of this chapter is that EAP coordinators, and/or evaluators need to spend more thoughtful time in planning EAP evaluations in order to conduct them in more meaningful ways. For example, Myers (1984) noted that in the haste and enthusiasm that often accompanies the development and implementation of an EAP, evaluation planning is either ignored or assigned a low priority on everyone's "things-to-do" list. Further, when pressured for evaluation data or information, many EAP directors/coordinators compile meaningless statistical tables or graphs, make frantic and belated attempts at scraping together any haphazard program information, or rationalize for the program's existence or importance in nonevaluative ways. It is little wonder that the resulting "evaluations" are poorly designed and produce meager and even erroneous results (Shain & Groeneveld, 1980).

The purpose of this chapter is to identify specific prerequisites in planning EAP evaluations. The major assumptions are: (1) that EAP coordinators (evaluators) have been negligent in thoughtfully planning EAP evaluations; (2) that subsequent evaluations of EAP will be more meaningfully developed, conducted, and disseminated if more time and energy is devoted toward such planning activities; and (3) that the host organization, EAP personnel, and EAP evaluators may learn to work together cooperatively in planning EAP evaluations.

PREREQUISITES FOR EVALUATING EAPs

Certain prerequisites must be in place prior to conducting any EAP evaluation. These are construed as essential ingredients for successful evaluations, and all must be systematically addressed to some degree at the beginning of the evaluation process. In another sense, if any one of these is not addressed, subsequent evaluative efforts could be seriously undermined. These prerequisites include:

1. a sincere commitment on behalf of the organization and program to both conduct and support the evaluation;
2. answering the *why*, *when*, and *how* of the evaluation;
3. the goals and objectives of the EAP, or components of it which are being evaluated, need specification in measurable terms; and,
4. information needed to conduct the evaluation should be in retrievable form.

Although these may seem obvious they require elaboration, as numerous organizations and EAPs continue to conduct evaluations without considering them, and invariably such efforts usually prove unsuccessful. Each of these will be briefly discussed and where appropriate, the roles and relationships between the host organization, EAP personnel, and EAP evaluators will be highlighted.

Organizational and Program Commitment

Any EAP program which embarks on an evaluation without having the support of the administration, managers, or key decision-makers in the respective organization and program is seriously remiss. It doesn't matter whether the impetus for the evaluation comes from the external organizational environment (e.g., the community, other organizations, funding sources, etc.) or the internal environment (e.g.. line staff, the union, EAP personnel, supervisors, administrators, the board of directors, etc.). In either case, a sincere administrative commitment is critical to the evaluation's development and conduct.

Administrative support from both the host organization's administration, and coordinators of the EAP program, is the key to influencing and obtaining other levels of support in the organization or program, and as a result, needs to be obtained first. Consistent with the "domino theory," other levels of support (e.g., rank and file workers) quickly follow the administrative lead, although their motivation for desiring the evaluation may be very different from the organization or EAP program coordinators. Thus, gaining support for EAP program evaluations is an area in which much reciprocal learning and cooperation between managers of the host organizations, union officials, EAP administrators, and EAP evaluators (whether in or out-of-house evaluators) needs to come about. For example, administrators or key decision-makers can learn to provide input to program evaluations and support them in more effective ways, and program evaluators can learn how to tailor their evaluative efforts to meet the needs of the respective organization or program which they are evaluating. This first level of support solidifies the purpose of the evaluation and shapes its subsequent assumptions, design, conduct, and ultimate dissemination.

The Why, When, and How of the EAP Evaluation Must Be Answered Prior to Its Conduct

These three questions seem harmless enough, yet if they are not satisfactorily answered prior to conducting the EAP evaluation, a veritable "Pandora's Box" of problems may unfold. These questions are best answered in sequence such that *why* must be answered before *when* and *how*. It matters less whether the latter two (*when* and *how*) are out of sequence because they are usually addressed simultaneously, as the answer(s) to one usually influence the answer(s) to the other, and vice versa. However, it is imperative that the question *why* be answered first.

EAP programs should not be too concerned if their answers to the question – why conduct an evaluation?. . . . seem as frivolous or obvious as some of the standard responses. These include: (1) it was mandated (e.g., by a funding source); (2) it was recommended (e.g., by EAP personnel, the host organization, the union, etc.); (3) the EAP may be having some difficulties, and would like to determine why; (4) other EAPs have conducted evaluations which have influenced this organization and EAP to conduct an evaluation; (5) it may be "politically astute" for the organization or EAP conduct an evaluation at this time (e.g., for program justification, etc.); or, (6) it seemed like a good idea at the time. Regardless of the reason, which could be any one of these (or combinations of them), the point is that at the onset of the EAP evaluation, the host organization and EAP coordinator must agree in an open and honest way to answer *why* they are conducting the evaluation which in turn, directly influences *when* and *how*.

When the evaluation should be conducted is an important issue which EAP coordinators/evaluators need to be sensitive to. The general preference is the earlier the better, as EAPs may build the potential for subsequent evaluations into their overall planning and operational frameworks. Examples of this may include: addressing issues of confidentiality; establishing baseline data for comparisons at some point in the future; recording information which can be updated or elaborated on in the future; formatting records, files or forms for subsequent retrievability; and, commencing the process of socializing the organization or program toward the evaluative process and its implications. Without question, *when* the evaluation occurs determines both the nature and outcome of the actual evaluation.

Ironically, the least favourable yet most frequent situation which occurs are post hoc evaluations conducted after the EAP has been operational for some time. These types of evaluations must face a host of inevitable problems such as: tracking the history of the program; tracking clients or staff who participated in the program; contending with staff turnover; and, contending with missing, lost, misplaced or forgotten information which inevitably occurred over time. Such difficulties may be avoided by commencing the evaluation process at the onset of the program.

Finally, *how* to do the evaluation is best resolved by those who are conducting it. More specifically, *how* clearly implies issues which may be beyond the scope of those not directly involved with the evaluation (e.g., resource utilization, research methodology, costs involved, etc.), and one should leave such matters for those who are best trained to do them, namely, program evaluators. Thus, administrators, managers, and EAP coordinators should defer judgment to such expertise, and work with the evaluator (or the evaluation team) in ensuring that the evaluation does not consume the operational aspects of their programs which may in turn, influence service delivery. This model suggests a cooperative approach which allows for EAP evaluators to do what they do best, yet at the same time ensures that they are accountable to the host organization and EAP for planning and conducting the evaluation.

Goals and Objectives Require Specification

EAP evaluators have a justifiable "hang-up" about goals and objectives because they cannot evaluate programs without them. Goals and objectives when operationalized in evaluation terms become efficiency and effectiveness criteria which are the lifeblood of any evaluation. In fact, evaluation research is distinguished from basic or applied social science research in that it always assesses program processes, efficiency, and/or effectiveness (Knott, 1986).

In order for EAP program evaluations to evolve in this area, EAP goals and objectives require: (1) specification; (2) consensus agreement about what they are; and, (3) operationalization in measurable terms. This process (of determining goals and objectives) is both deductive and reductionistic in nature. In simpler terms, one proceeds from general EAP goals to specific goals and objectives, and during this process, breaks the EAP down into component parts, each having different (or similar) goals and objectives.

The logical place to commence this process is the operations manual or planning document of the EAP as most specify such criteria in their mandates, proposals, operational aspects, guidelines, or requirements. Thus, these criteria constitute the first level goal or mission statements which guide the EAP or components of it. Although it may seem surprising to some (in this day and age of scarce resources and accountability), I would be remiss not revealing that in some instances, many host organizations (Probably the majority of them) are negligent in holding EAPs accountable for service delivery. Further, some EAPs operate on the basis of informal, loose, or ill-defined criteria. In organizations or EAPs such as these, evaluators through the process of determining goals and objectives, may inadvertently assist the EAP in clarifying its relationship to the host organization and workers it purports to serve.

In regard to having consensus agreement about goals and objectives, the operative word here is consensus. Certainly in some instances, workers, supervisors, managers, EAP coordinators, and/or EAP evaluators may have differing perceptions about the goals and objectives that guide such programs. Thus, this process may further help articulate and clarify what the goals and objectives are to all of these respective parties. As well, asking a variety of organizational personnel to define their goals and objectives may also prove a meaningful human relations exercise in getting those involved directly or indirectly in the evaluation to begin communicating toward consensus goals and objectives. Through ongoing and open dialogue between the evaluator(s), organizational members and EAP personnel, consensus agreement about this issue usually emerges.

Finally, the specification of goals and objectives in measurable terms is once again a task best left to those conducting the evaluation. This involves the operationalization of concepts into measurable and attainable terms which are usually: (1) time-framed (i.e., they occurred, or will occur over specified period of time); and (2) quantifiable (usually based on units of service delivered and the outcome of those services). In the past decade, the literature in the field of program evaluation has focused attention on better ways of measuring goals and objectives at both a micropractice level (Hersen & Barlow, 1976; Bloom & Fischer, 1982; Hudson, 1982), as well as macrolevels (Tripodi, 1983; Isaac & Michael, 1977; Holosko & Feit, 1981; Austin & Associates, 1985).

Information Retrievability

Organizations and EAPs, have a peculiar relationship about collecting information for purposes of planning, evaluating, and decision-making. This relationship is peculiar for a number of reasons. First, most organizations are "information short" when it comes to having meaningful and retrievable information available for program evaluations, yet they perceive of themselves as having an information overload. Second, most EAPs have a disproportionate amount of background information about their employees (too much), and very little about what services or activities these employees received (too little). Third, most EAPs collect information for the wrong reasons. For example, three standard reasons are either: (1) because they have to (it is a requirement); (2) because they have always collected information as such; or (3) so they may better internally manage themselves. The latter reason is the only one that remotely resembles a rationale which applies to program evaluation research.

Information (referred to as data by evaluators) must be in accessible and retrievable form if any evaluative effort is to occur. Astute evaluators will usually appraise the "state of the art" of the data, prior to conducting an evaluation due to its critical importance in this process. Again, the significance of having the evaluation commence early on in the program planning development stage, ensures that data will at least be formatted in retrievable form at some point for future use. The final point to be made about information retrievability is that most evaluations, through the actual process of their conduct, will inevitably assist the EAP to organize and systematize its information for subsequent evaluations, program planning, or service delivery. For example, formatting or monitoring files or cases, establishing data sources, and developing protocols for subsequent data collection are all part of any comprehensive evaluative effort, and should be construed as a positive spin-off effect or benefit of the EAP evaluation. As a result, the process of the evaluation effort will yield a benefit for any subsequent effort.

CONCLUSION

The preceding chapter outlined specific evaluation prerequisites which should be used to assist program evaluators, coordinators, administrators, and managers plan better quality EAP evaluators. These prerequisites are suggested as guidelines to be used in the planning process, and they should be considered prior to the conduct of any EAP evaluation. The main contention of this chapter is that more time and energy should be devoted toward more thoughtful planning of EAP evaluations. Too frequently, good intentioned evaluators or coordinators embark on EAP evaluations without such rigorous planning and usually such endeavours prove unsuccessful.

REFERENCES

Austin, Michael J. & Associates (1982). *Evaluating your agency's programs*. Beverly Hills, CA: Sage Publications, Inc.

Bloom, M. & Fischer, J. (1982). *Evaluating practice: Guidelines for the accountable profession*. Englewood Cliffs, NJ: Prentice-Hall Inc.

Brant, W. G. (1979, January/February). The labour scene. *Labour/Management Alcoholism Journal*, p. 137.

Harsen, M. & Barlow, D. H. (1976). *Single-case experimental designs: Strategies for studying behaviour change*. New York: Pergamon Press.

Holosko, M. J. & Feit, M. D. (1981). *Workbook for internal management*. Knoxville, TN: University of Tennessee Press.

Hudson, W. W. (1982). *The clinical measurement package: A field manual*. Homewood, IL: The Dorsey Press Inc.

Isaac, S. & Michael, W. (1977). *Handbook in research and evaluation*. San Diego, CA: Edits Publishers Inc.

Knott, Tara D. (1986, Summer). The distinctive uses of evaluation and research: A guide for the occupational health care movement. *Employee Assistance Quarterly*, *4*, 43-51.

Myers, D. W. (1984, March/April). Measuring E.A.P.: Cost effectiveness—results and recommendations. *E.A.P. Digest*, pp. 22-27.

Shain, M. & Groeneveld J. (1980). *Employee Assistance Programs: Philosophy, Theory, & Practice*. Lexington, KY: D.C. Health.

Tripodi, T. (1983). *Evaluative research for social workers*. Englewood Cliffs, NJ: Prentice-Hall Inc.

Paving the Way for EAP Evaluations: Implications for Social Work

P. A. Taylor
M. J. Holosko
B. Wayne Smith
M. D. Feit

SUMMARY. The theme of this chapter centers on the development of key process questions that precede and direct the development of EAP evaluations. The main assumptions of this chapter are: (1) that nonthreatening process-type questions may be used in helping EAP evaluators plan their evaluations; and (2) that the profession of social work can meaningfully assist in developing and answering such questions. These process questions emerge from considering issues related to: (1) policies and procedures; (2) services; and (3) the administration of EAP programs. The role of the social worker in this process is described, and the unique knowledge and skill of the social work profession in this particular role is explored and identified.

BACKGROUND

The growth of industrial social work in the past decade has been impressive, to say the least. The tremendous loss of employee productivity that may be saved by the introduction of Employee Assistance Programs (EAPs) has been well documented in the literature

---

P. A. Taylor, MSW, is Associate Professor, School of Social Work, University of Windsor, Windsor, Ontario, Canada. M. J. Holosko, PhD, is Associate Professor, School of Social Work, University of Windsor, Windsor, Ontario, Canada. B. Wayne Smith, BA, BSW, is Social Policy Analyst, Executive Council, Government of Newfoundland & Labrador, St. John's, Newfoundland, Canada. M. D. Feit, MPH, PhD, is Associate Professor, School of Social Work, Norfolk State University, Norfolk, VA 23504.

(Byers, 1978; Howe, 1978). Although social workers are still relative newcomers to this field, the basic skills and techniques of social work readily adapt to workplace environments. Many authors (e.g., Googins, 1975; Roman, 1982; Trice & Hunt, 1981) have suggested that both systems and role theory are operational within the EAP processes. Indeed, the social work concept of "person-in-situation" seems an appropriate way of showing how problems in the workplace have causal links to the outside world and may influence home life, and/or significant other persons or systems. In this regard, employment settings provide potent and legitimate sanctions for controlling behaviours that violate specific role obligations (Weissman, 1975). Further, social controls and social pressures identified within an individual's value systems, cultural mores, beliefs, etc., provide clear and direct links between work, the worker, his/her family, and his/her company.

Generally defined, EAPs are employment based services whose purpose is to assist individuals experiencing personal problems, by assessing the nature of their difficulties, and by making referrals to appropriate helping resources (Alcohol and Drug Addiction Foundation, 1978). They operate within the context of the work environment and are consequently influenced by their positions within the organizational structure. Problem identification is generally made when the behaviour of the employee affects the quality of the work performance. EAPs are based on the premise that the workplace provides an ideal setting for this identification through deteriorating work, absenteeism, accidents, morale, etc.

Despite the rapid growth of EAPs, there is a paucity of literature related to the evaluation of these programs. The profession of social work, as well as industry have recognized that the tendency to accept EAPs based on general, and/or causal feedback rather than scientific investigation is frequently related to concerns about the validity of the EAP, its financial costs, confidentiality and effectiveness. These concerns are real and can only be addressed through well planned and executed evaluation. Indeed, viewed in the context of these concerns, evaluation becomes a critical component for the continuation and growth of any EAP and as Hayward, Schlenger and Hollon (1976) concluded, EAPs provide an ideal structure for evaluation. These authors suggested that the workplace can be a situation where one may develop a sampling procedure and control of variables unlike many social environments. In a sense, an EAP is a captive experimental "laboratory" setting for evaluation.

The purpose of this chapter is to articulate critical questions that should be answered before entering the arena of evaluation. The importance of identifying potential program problems through questions about (i.e., gaps, inaccuracies or inadequacies) is paramount. In fact, the thrust of this chapter suggests that the process of planning, exploration, and discovery related to the functioning of any EAP is an essential prerequisite for the direction of the evaluation. These process questions, as well as the role of the social worker in working within the organization to help identify the problems and seek accurate answers to them, will be outlined. Prior to discussing these issues an outline of basic EAP components, which form the basis for such questions will be described.

COMPONENTS NECESSARY FOR EAP EVALUATIONS

In order to evaluate EAPs, it is essential that the components of the program be identified and reviewed in terms of their real presence for evaluation purposes. Sorenson (1978), for example, described "paper programs" where a written policy statement is placed on file and no appointments are ever made to commence the evaluation process. Googin (1975) identified four fundamental dimensions critical to any EAP as well as basic to the evaluative process. These are:

1. Policy – policies should reflect a supportive understanding by management, recognizing their role in employee problem solving;
2. Training – training is essential from the highest level of management to the front-line supervisors;
3. Services – services relates to the availability of resources with which to match the workers needs;
4. Follow-up – follow-up provides the opportunity to monitor the

employee progress during the treatment phase and his adjustment back into the workplace.

Although these dimensions can be viewed as cornerstones to any EAP program, and many authors will similarly list EAP evaluation ingredients; they are global in nature and idiosyncratic to any particular organization of EAP. As such, these dimensions are starting places to commence EAP evaluation planning, but require specification in more precise terms.

To evaluate an EAP, it is necessary to identify data that will enable the employer to determine how a program is doing in relation to future decisions about continuation, modification and improvement of the program. Consequently, planning for evaluation is essential. To accomplish this, the development of key process questions to use as a basis of exploration with EAP coordinators and evaluators is critical in "paving the way" for more rigorous evaluative efforts. Such questions will identify the priority EAP coordinators and researchers need to place on key variables. For example, if a company can assess particular problem areas prior to collecting data through such questions, the subsequent research can substantiate more dramatically whether the EAP is effective or not.

PROCESS EVALUATION QUESTIONS

It is important that the evaluation planning process incorporate social research techniques, including variables such as program use and case outcome, wherever possible. In addition, such planning should include key process questions to use as a basis of exploration with EAP evaluators and coordinators which could lay the groundwork for rigorous evaluations. As previously suggested, such questions may help identify issues and priorities that the evaluators may need to place on dimensions or variables in the program which need focus or attention. Three main areas are obvious ones for planning the process-type questions listed below.

(1) Policies and Procedures

- Is there a comprehensive written company policy of the EAP that reflects contemporary views of employee problems and an earnestness of intent to help?
- What resources (i.e., monies, professional staffing, space, etc.) have been allocated to promote company policies relating to helping employees?
- Are the policies of the EAP nondiscriminatory?
- Are certain employees exempt from certain policies?
- Is there a safeguard for confidentiality for EAP participants?
- Are the policies abstract ("paper policies") or real (reflecting practice)?
- Are the policies readily accessible (i.e., a manual) to all employees?
- Are policies reviewed systematically?
- What are the goals and objectives of the EAP?
- How are these policies stated, e.g., long/short-term goals, behavioural objectives etc.

(2) Services

- Is there a clearly written procedure for identification of employee problems and referrals?
- Are EAP programs perceived as mandated from top management with potential for reprisals (i.e., demotion, job loss)?
- To what extent are the services suggested available?
- What is the relationship between service providers, the EAP, and host organization?
- Are a list of services available to all employees?
- Are service providers located proximally to the organization?
- To what extent do the potential users of the EAP (supervisors and employees) have input into the EAP?
- Does the EAP signal out any particular group in the employee population for service (e.g., front line, blue collar etc.)?
- How are EAP services provided?
- How is service information collected or organized?
- Are there any other issues related to services which might in-

hibit use (e.g., costs, employees' perception of services, informal stigmatization, etc.)?

(3) Administration of EAP Programs

- Is there a formal orientation for upper management about EAP programs and company implications?
- Are all supervisors trained in the philosophy and functions of company EAPs?
- How extensively are all employees made aware of the philosophy and company functions of EAP programs (i.e., dissemination of written, verbal, and media material)?
- What mechanisms are used to insure worker/client confidentiality?
- Is there a formalized mechanism for EAP coordinators to receive an employee outcome assessment through supervisors' follow-up?
- What is the EAP utilization rate since the program was implemented?
- Does the utilization rate compare with general statistical evidence about worker/client type (i.e., alcoholic workers in industry)?
- Are there any significant changes in such areas as attendance, sick leave, and productivity?
- Has baseline data been compiled prior to the initiation of the EAP?
- Does the administration support the EAP in meaningful ways?
- Are adequate statistics about the EAP being gathered presently?

This list of process questions is certainly not exhaustive. However, it does define a guideline for beginning the dialogue process between the host organization, EAP coordinators and evaluators. While process questions alone cannot predict the capacity of an EAP evaluation, they may go a long way in avoiding obstacles which may accrue in subsequent EAP evaluations.

IMPLICATIONS FOR SOCIAL WORK

As Rothman (1982) states in his chapter on the development of industrial social work, the community of work and the social work community have not worked easily together. Indeed, as advocates for clients experiencing problems in the workplace, social workers frequently have been antagonistic towards the workplace. However, the logic of the availability of economically viable and psychologically satisfying jobs has both a preventive and therapeutic consequence for clients (Akabas, Kurzman & Kolben, 1982). Consequently, the involvement of social work in humanizing the workplace has been increasing steadily. EAPs, their planning, functioning, and evaluations are all concerns of social work.

Social workers seem to be the appropriate professionals to work in the process planning phase of EAP evaluations and develop and utilize such questions. The history of social work is rooted in the areas of identifying needs and problem solving (Johnson, 1985). Indeed, basic skills endemic to the profession highlight increasing communications through asking relevant questions, listening, understanding, and responding.

Additionally, social work attributes and skills, such as approachability, ability to encourage trust, identification and expression of verbal/nonverbal feelings, ability to define conflicts constructively, confrontation, safeguarding confidentiality, negotiation, and stress management could all be critical in working through a successful process planning phase of an EAP evaluation.

The position and role of the social worker in business and industry is another important feature which can contribute to this planning process. For example, social workers are not aligned with employer or employee, and as such, they have the potential to be viewed by both parties as being impartial and consequently in a position to ask critical and probing questions. At the same time, social workers can bring an understanding of cooperativeness and facilitation within both employer-employee and union-management boundaries. Thus, they are in a unique position to "network" with people at various levels and within various groups (i.e., employers, administrators, supervisors, workers, EAP coordinators, evaluators, etc.) in the organization in order to more fully and accurately understand critical EAP issues. In fact, part of this process of planning the evaluation could involve reaching out to explore and gather opinions, attitudes, and experiences about the EAP. This type of outreach activity is particularly relevant to the problem solving process identified extensively within the social work literature.

Large organizations are complex systems. How well workers perform is linked not only to the workplace but also to other aspects of their life. Sustaining a productive and competitive work force is a primary concern for the employer. EAPs can be seen as one strategy for working toward this goal. Carefully planned evaluations of these programs add immeasurably to their reliability as a viable service to the organization as well as a humane resource. Social work's philosophy, values, and skills can assist in accomplishing both of these goals.

REFERENCES

Akabas, S., Kurzman P. & Kolben, N. (1982). *Work, workers and work organization: A view from social work*. Englewood Cliffs, NJ: Prentice-Hall, Inc.

Alcohol and Drug Addiction Foundation (1978). *EAP, a discussion guide*. ADAF of Newfoundland and Labrador.

Brant, W. G. (1979, January/February). "The Labour scene." *Labour/Management Alcoholism Journal*, p. 137.

Byers, William. (1978). Kelsey-Hayes company center for counseling and guidance. In Sheila Akabas, Paul Kurzman & Nancy Kolben (Eds.), *Labor and industrial settings: Sites for social work practice*. New York: Council on Social Work Education.

Googins, B. (1975, November). "Employee assistance programs." *Social Work*, *20*, pp. 464-467.

Hayward, B. J., Schlenger, W. E. & Hollon, J. B. (1976, June). *Occupational programming: A review of literature*. Raleigh, NC: The Human Ecology Institute.

Howe, Michael (1978). Northern states power company social resource center and training. In Sheila Akabas, Paul Kurzman & Nancy Kolben (Eds.), *Labor and industrial settings: Sites for social work practice*. New York: Council on Social Work Education.

Johnson, Louise C. (1985). *Social work practice: A generalist approach* (2nd edition). Toronto: Allyn and Bacon Inc.

Roman, P. (1981). "From employee alcoholism programs to employee assistance." *Journal of Studies on Alcohol*, *42*(3), 244-270.

Rothman, Jack (1982). Taking account of the workplace in community organization practice. In Sheila Akabas, Paul Kurzman & Nancy Kolben (Eds.), *Work, workers and work organizations: A view from social work*. Englewood Cliffs, NJ: Prentice-Hall Inc.

Sorenson, D. (1978). *The art of preserving human resources*. Nebraska: National Publications.

Trice, H. & Hunt, G. (1981, Winter). "Coercion, confrontation, and self-referral." *Journal of Drug Issues*, *11*(4), 40.

Weissman, A. (1975, September). "A social service strategy in industry." *Social Work*, *20*, 401-403.

Issues to Consider in Planning Employee Assistance Program Evaluations

Stanley F. Battle

SUMMARY. This article examines a variety of issues to be considered in planning Employee Assistance Program (EAP) evaluations. It focuses on issues of definition, the importance of primary prevention, intervention as a strategy, types of evaluative issues to consider, and basic assumptions in EAP evaluation research. These issues lead to the presentation of a detailed and prescriptive model that EAP evaluators should consider prior to evaluating EAPs.

A systematic comprehensive approach is needed to evaluate the effectiveness of programs in human services, health, public health, and industry. But because of varied philosophies and theories, it is difficult to design one appropriate model.

One of the best examples to highlight this dilemma is the emergence of Employee Assistance Programs (EAPs). The evaluation of these programs are important for several reasons. First, they provide a framework for the delivery of human services within the workplace. Second, the majority of these services are provided by occupational social workers. Third, by their very design, EAPs are providing a needed service in industry and in the general workplace.

Stanley F. Battle, MSW, MPH, PhD, is Associate Professor of Welfare Policy and Health at the University of Connecticut School of Social Work. Dr. Battle is the coordinator of the Black Experience Sequence. He serves as a consultant to several local, state, and federal programs. His research is on mental health issues affecting minorities with a special interest in Black adolescent males and social epidemiology. Address correspondence to 1 Haviland Rd., Bloomfield, CT 06002.

Employee Assistance Programs combine a unique blend of prevention (primary, secondary, and tertiary levels) from a generic human services approach. Various ideological orientations are used to design services; consequently it is difficult to recommend one specific approach for evaluation. This paper describes program elements which are important in developing EAP evaluations. Attention will be focused on the issues of definition(s), the importance of primary prevention, intervention as a strategy, types of evaluative issues to consider, basic assumptions in EAP evaluative research, and the presentation of a model to evaluate EAPs.

DEFINITION

A definition of EAPs has not been fully agreed on by researchers and practitioners due to the various types of programs in existence. EAPs refer to a set of policies and program procedures by which a work organization legitimately intervenes in identifying and treating problems of employees that impact and have the capacity to influence job performance (Googins & Godfrey, 1987). From a formal point of view, EAPs are a set of procedures designed to identify and respond to emotional problems that inhibit worker performance. But in many respects, correcting the problem does not only improve work performance, but also the quality of life with the individual's family and friends. The context of this service is framed in primary prevention which is the foundation of the public health model.

PRIMARY PREVENTION IN EAPs

The public health model of prevention is complex, but it is important to understand this model in order to develop a strategy for planning EAP evaluations. The public health model of prevention has provided a framework for efforts in a variety of health areas that include adolescent pregnancy, alcohol abuse, heart disease, smoking, and drug abuse. Employee Assistance Programs offer a new challenge with the threat of job loss, structured with an intervention process that may correct the pattern of dysfunctional performance.

In public health, three levels of prevention are utilized to analyze health issues: (1) primary prevention which includes the interpretation or cause of a condition within the environment. Primary prevention generally involves increasing the resistance of populations susceptible to a condition or breaking the causal chain; (2) secondary prevention involves early discovery of a condition and giving prompt treatment to prevent the recurrence of a condition, and (3) tertiary prevention is designed to delay or minimize consequences of a condition. Advanced rehabilitation services generally fall in this category. By utilizing intervention techniques (i.e., the epidemiological model), the appropriate strategy may be implemented at the appropriate level (Battle, 1985; Gilbert, 1982).

EAPs address relationships and roles within the workplace. One of the major problems faced in industry is the influence of alcohol. Prescribed rules and norms of behavior serve as standards against the impact of alcohol. Manifestations of the problem may appear in poor attitude or the production of inferior products. At the point of intervention, the occupational social worker must decide on what strategy to use and at which level to intervene. The most important aspect for occupational social workers to note in understanding levels of prevention is that common factors may be identified when individual cases are aggregated. For example, each case is unique but there are common elements and aspects of phenomenon (e.g., drug and alcohol abuse may lead to family disruption). Models of prevention are guides to preventive interventions but also provide a means to evaluate the success of the effort. Preventive interaction should lead to a significant change in the incidence and/or prevalence of the problem. For example, deteriorating job performance as a means of early identification has led to a reliance on prevention and intervention as a tool and increased the need for EAP involvement.

INTERVENTION AS A STRATEGY IN EAPs: SOCIAL WORK'S ROLE

Prevention has been primarily a public heath concern, and its transference into the workplace has been slow. However, the relationship between the workplace and economics, and the value of a sound intervention strategy is clear. Further, health promotion and cost containment are linked to the rationale behind many EAPs.

In conceptualizing social intervention, social workers generally focus on the person and the environment in an effort to achieve congruence between the individual's needs, resources, demands, and opportunities of the environment (Pincus & Minihan, 1972). This broad focus draws social workers into contact with virtually every human problem. EAPs focus on broad extrinsic problems but their focus rests with the ability of the host or individual to function in a structured setting. Consequently, there is need for a conceptual approach which provides a systemic method for analyzing problems that may manifest in such diverse ways as lost opportunities or systemic discrimination. Employee Assistance Programs are designed to instill stability and consistency in the workplace – in other words positive work characteristics that enhance the workplace. Current proactive models in social work are influenced by a blend of systems theory and the problem solving approach. Of particular note is the strong predisposition for individualizing problems. By "starting where the client is," social workers often find that such phenomena as unemployment or alcohol abuse may become obscured by the rich detail of individual life patterns. The result is an inability to step back and examine broader causal patterns. Occupational social workers are attempting to expand the traditional focus on problem amelioration to one which includes preventive intervention strategies in the context of workplace stability. Social workers wear many hats in workplace settings, as they are concerned about individual intrinsic characteristics and the maintenance of the external workplace. In the final analysis, EAPs must be assessed in the context of organizational climate and effectiveness.

TYPES OF EVALUATIVE QUESTIONS TO CONSIDER

The evaluative questions that administrators and program directors ask most frequently can be grouped into four main categories.

Appropriateness

Questions on appropriateness focus on the importance of the specific problems selected for day-to-day operations and the relative importance of polices and standards. Employees are not machines and their attitudes and behavior are important. An appropriate question for this issue, is: what type of changes do EAPs bring about?

Adequacy

Ideally, objectives are oriented toward elimination of potential problems which give rise to the program, but various constraints may necessitate reducing the scope of an objective from a focus on a complete solution of a problem. In order to accomplish the above, it is important to know why some EAPs work better than others.

Effectiveness

Performance in the workplace differs from one department to another and one organization's programs may differ in their effectiveness; that is in the extent to which pre-established objectives are attained as a result of activity. Again behavior, attitude, and performance are linked. EAPs have received great exposure but what evidence exists about the effectiveness of EAPs?

Efficiency

Program efficiency is defined as the cost in resources of attaining objectives. The efficiency of a program may be unrelated to its effectiveness, adequacy, and appropriateness.

These four evaluative issues may be addressed before a program begins or at some point after it has been in operation. If these questions are asked before the program begins, these questions serve as the ideas for the planning process. They can be phrased as asking whether the EAP has important objectives, whether the activities proposed are likely to attain the objectives, and whether the cost is reasonable.

When these questions are asked in regard to an operating program, they constitute an evaluation of performance. Questions will then focus on the EAPs' cost, overall effectiveness, and objectives.

Despite the high praise EAPs have received over the past years, very little quantitative research has been conducted to verify their program effectiveness. Much of this dilemma may be attributed to program design and resources. However, the programmatic and policy implications of not having an established body of knowledge on the success and effectiveness of EAPs becomes an increasing problem as the field seeks respectability. Should these programs be viewed as extensions of the prevention public health model?

A PROPOSED MODEL TO EVALUATE EAP's EFFECTIVENESS

Most evaluations of human service and health programs are designed to determine whether the program is effecting any change and assess the quality of services provided. Essentially, this is an issue of the quantity and quality of service that is directed toward an established need in the workplace and community.

Consistent and routine evaluations should provide information on which to base program decisions regarding modification, expansion, or even discontinuation. A rational evaluation strategy should be designed early, and be implemented throughout the life of a project. In many cases, programs are only evaluated after they have been operating a long time. In some instances, evaluations occur with the implementation of a poor design frequently made on the basis of highly subjective opinions. Resources for evaluations are often unavailable and program managers are sometimes threatened by an assessment of their own organizations.

Regardless of these potential problems, evaluation methods should be utilized as soon as possible. The best scenario is to build the evaluation process into the program early. In its simplest formulation, evaluation research involves the development of objectives and the subsequent measurement of progress towards them. The basic structure that can be used to assess EAPs is described in Figure 1.

In order to define the objectives, it is necessary to understand issues that the program is designed to address.

Over the past several years the Family Service Association (FSA)

Figure 1

Types of Objectives

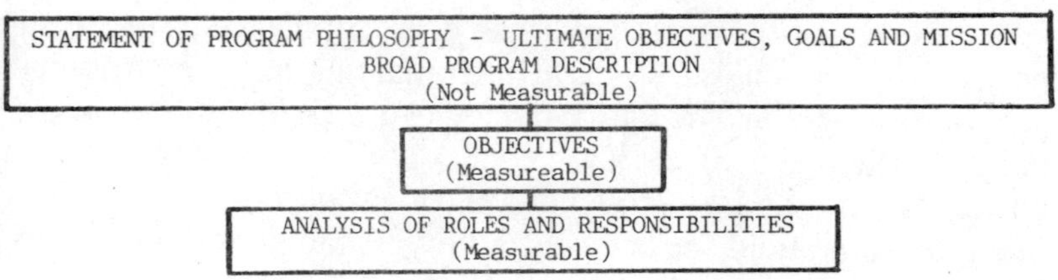

of Metropolitan Toronto has implemented EAPs in over 12 companies. Prior to the beginning of the counseling program, FSA officials offered consultation to management and union in the creation of policy documentation for EAPs (Wright, 1985). The author will utilize their administrative plan to highlight the evaluation model proposed.

Statement of the Problem – Objectives, Goals, and Mission

Typically this statement is the shortest and really provides a very broad-based approach to the kinds of services provided. This statement sets the tone for the delivery of service or in many respects, the philosophical base of the program. It is difficult to evaluate this because it varies in depth and scope. The following components may be contained in this part of the model.

1. Personal problems that are faced by employees – some rationale is given to where they should turn for help;
2. Human problems are addressed that include marriage, family difficulties, financial problems, and work related issues;
3. Confidentiality is strictly enforced; and
4. Much attention is given to the quality of the worker's life.

It is critical to comprehend intrinsic and extrinsic factors that influence the workers' total environment. In the final analysis, this section sets the tone for the program and service.

Policy Statement

This section follows in a natural progression and overall philosophy of the program. Policy statements are an important foundation to the design of the objectives and the actual delivery of service. Several precautions must be adhered to which include: who is the service designed for (i.e., employees only or members of the immediate family); no personal information should be given out without written consent of the employee; and professionals involved in the delivery of service must maintain a neutral role in matters affecting the relationship of the company, its employee representative group, and the employee.

These are only a few of the important factors about which EAPs must be concerned. This section can be evaluated and is critical to the overall structure of the program design.

Objectives

The related literature uses words like objectives, goals, mission, purpose, and aims interchangeably. For clarity and in keeping within the confines of a working definition, an objective is a situation or conditions of people or environment which responsible program personnel consider desirable to attain. In order to evaluate the program or service, the statement of an objective must specify the following:

(a) what is the nature of the situation or condition to be obtained;
(b) to what extent is the quantity or amount of the situation or condition to be obtained;
(c) what is the particular group of people or portion of the environment in which attainment is desired;
(d) where is the geographic areas of the program; and
(e) the time that the desired situation or condition is intended to exist (Deniston, Rosenstock & Gettin, 1968).

Program objectives are defined in broad terms in EAP programs. Objectives in EAP programs can be evaluated but they require a clear understanding of the overall philosophy of the program.

Objectives in EAP evaluations must include specifics such as implementation dates, number of employees to be trained, date of completion—in other words, information that can be measured from the standpoint of accountability.

Ideally, each activity which is planned as part of the program should relate to a stated program objective. Each activity should be both appropriate and feasible in terms of stated objectives and the resources and time available. It is quite possible to develop work plans which include activities which would lead to attainment of a particular objective just to find out these activities are too costly or time consuming.

Probably the greatest source of confusion and difficulty in both planning and evaluating is lack of clear understanding between an activity and objective. In short, activities consume program time and resources whereas objectives do not (James, 1961).

Many EAPs measure success in terms of positive functioning, for instance, improved job performance, a cost saving, or sobriety. In a review of the literature Kurtz, Googins, and Howard (1983) found measures grouped in four major classes:

1. change in drinking behavior—a measure of the degree to which a person has achieved an abstinent or sober state;
2. change in work performance—a measure of the degree to which the employee has improved job performance;
3. change in cost reduction—a measure of savings realized through improved work performance; and
4. change in penetration—a measure of the extent to which a program reaches the target population of given organization.

The important consideration in these four types of measures is change over time. Each measure addresses different types of mechanisms of change. Overall, the obvious program goal is to assist employees either to alter or change life-style behaviors that have led to negative patterns in their life-style, at home, on the job, or intrinsic characteristics that influence the individual. Probably the most important characteristics to consider are the formation of role and responsibilities within the EAP program.

Roles and Responsibilities

Program elements within EAPs vary. A particular program should at least include the following elements; the steering committee, the trainer, the counselor, supervisory/management, personnel, the union, the occupational physician and the employees. Each group plays a key role in the actual delivery of services to employees who participate in the EAP program.

The program should include a detailed description of the resources (personnel and material) available to accomplish the objectives. An estimate of the adequacy of the resources should be made in program planning. This would involve a judgment about the quality as well as the quantity of persons and material to be used.

These important factors should be decided by the steering committee.

The development of research questions and client variables are based from roles and responsibilities that emerge from a direct service model that includes several important groups. A very brief description of each group will be presented.

1. The Steering Committee generally plays a major role in planning the program in collaboration with management and other professionals. After actual implementation of the program, the steering committee assumes overall management of the program.
2. The Trainer works in collaboration with the counselor and the committee to deliver the program at all levels of the company. These programs are designed to explain how to use the service as either a recipient or a referral agent.
3. The Counselor offers a broad base approach to treatment services for a total range of psychosocial problems. The counselor can be available on site and at various agency office sites.
4. Managers and Supervisors are expected to support the program and provide sufficient information where necessary to employees as deemed appropriate.
5. The Union is very active at both the senior and plant flow level. Senior union officials will help plan and support the program and encourage members to use it.
6. The Occupational Health Department provides a number of supportive services to the program. For instance, a multidisciplinary team approach may evolve and information services may emerge as a mechanism for employee convenience between the two services. This relationship can only work with cooperation between the two groups.
7. The Employees' responsibility is to acquaint himself/herself with the program and utilize the service as needed. (Wright, 1985)

In order to develop appropriate research questions, the overall program plan must be taken into consideration. Every program plan includes three major assumptions.

1. The use of resources as planned will result in the performance of planned activity. In the case of an EAP, management wants to see appropriate production level and employee stability.
2. By performing planned activity there will be attainment of desired work objectives. In the case of EAPs, by addressing drinking problems, family disruption and loss of time on the job, social functioning will be enhanced.
3. The overall assumption that sub-objectives be attained before the program objectives be attained is open to question. Employee Assistance Programs must have a level of cooperation between management, union, and employers.

A variety of evaluation types can be considered. The concern over determining whether a program was actually implemented as intended, is the major focus of "process evaluations." Standards of "good" practice are defined and attempts are made to determine if they have been applied. Process evaluations, sometimes called progress evaluation, formative evaluation, or developmental evaluation are quite useful in alerting program staff about weaknesses. Impact or outcome evaluations address whether the program, service, or delivery system works with respect to some alternative condition or program. Impact is measured by changes brought about in those employees and organization units participating in the program.

Design Issues

The selection of a research design and type of research (process, impact, and outcome) depends on the intended purpose. Evaluative research of an EAP should include the following:

1. control group;
2. retrospective and prospective analysis; and
3. a comparison group.

The importance of comparing one group receiving the service versus another group not receiving the service is mandatory. The notion of a control group will help support appropriate findings. Previous experience (retrospective) is important in making projections (prospective) in the delivery of services.

Formulating the research question and appropriate variable(s) selection may be elementary in theory but in practice this is a demanding task. Program objectives and goals are generally not neat and accommodating as one would expect. Nor are outside circumstances as passive and unimportant as one might anticipate. The evaluation must consider the following problems:

1. Program goals are frequently not clear, somewhat ambiguous and hard to comprehend. In many respects, goals are a long list of incompleted thoughts.
2. Programs not only fulfill expectations of the general goals, but they also accomplish other important tasks. The evaluator must become familiar with these unexpected consequences that influence or impact program activity.
3. Programs are a combination of elements that impact change. Some elements are necessary while others are not important. It becomes important for the evaluator to separate meaningful information from that which is meaningless. Consequently, it is critical to understand the program before the evaluation process begins so the evaluator will be able to identify and separate out the elements that matter.
4. The evaluation questions as developed ignore the issue of why the program succeeds or fails.

The selection of variables is critical to the type of research performed. For example, impact evaluations address whether the program, service, or delivery system works with respect to some alternative condition or program. In addition, they are alert to any unexpected effect of the program, either positive or negative. There is a very broad variety of impact variables (questions) that can be examined. The following variables are appropriate for this type of study (impact evaluation):

1. Level of productivity (Is there an appropriate level?)
2. Number of absences (When does it become excessive?)
3. Accidents (What are the circumstances that lead up to this problem?)
4. Medical claims (When do they become excessive?)
5. Success (How is or how should success be measured?)
6. Alcoholism referrals (How many referrals is too many?)

These variables must be clearly defined as well as operationally clarified before the evaluation process begins.

Documentation

To a great extent, the findings from the evaluation will be directly related to how well information was recorded and documented. Documentation is a subjective process. For instance body language, facial expressions, and cultural differences play major roles in documentation of information. Content from EAPs may be collected based on how many people use the EAP, type of treatment they need, and the level of cooperation based on absenteeism rate after their treatment. To a great extent, you can only document qualitative information that includes characteristics and frequencies. You cannot assign impact to the type of treatment received. Consequently, measurement, reliability, and validity loom as major concerns.

Measurement, Reliability, and Validity

Measurement is very important because it represents precise procedure in understanding relatively specific variables. For instance, social class can be determined according to such indicators as income level, occupation, a combination of occupation and education, the respondents' perceptions of their own class position, or relationship to the means of production. Each of these indicators reflects differences in ideological perspectives and theoretical positions. But researchers must select indicators that are relevant to the purposes of the evaluation (Rutman, 1977). By scientifically measuring change in EAPs, it will eliminate concern that improvement occurred as a result of extrinsic factors.

Reliability is concerned with how much of the variation in the measured phenomenon is due to inconsistencies in measurement, rather than in the phenomenon being measured. Reliability is a good way to assess the value of a measure. If the measure is reliable it may provide program administrators a good indication whether any changes that show up during the treatment program are due to actual changes in the problem, changes in the instrument, or changes in the observer's way of observing the problem (Bloom & Fisher, 1981).

Validity refers to the degree to which the instrument succeeds in what it purports to measure. With validity, there is concern with the "meaning" of the measure which in turn is determined by the "purpose" for which the measure was designed. While reliability is a necessary condition for validity, it's not sufficient to ensure validity. For instance, do job performance measures really measure job performance, or other factors? Even though there may exist a job performance measure that consistently and with relatively high repeatability, measures absenteeism and tardiness and is a true indicator of job performance, it may not be very useful.

If researchers who evaluate EAP programs take into consideration the importance of measurement, reliability, and validity, their findings will be considered valid and generalizable.

CONCLUSIONS

As the EAP field matures, it will receive broader respect for its activities and accomplishments. The field has utilized philosophical principles of public health, human services, and business. Accomplishment can be measured or determined through appropriate documentation of services provided. In other words, evaluative research can play a major role in educating the public in this field. Research protocols must be developed to evaluate these programs so practice issues can be better understood and services can be provided in a reasonable manner. The key to this field is appropriate documentation of services provided. The future of this exciting field must rely on collaboration of various professional groups associated with EAPs and a continued base of credibility. Anecdotal accounts and grandiose claims will not provide the base that is needed for success. It is an opportunity in which perceived effectiveness which is felt by those in the EAP field can be translated in terms of reliable and reasonable findings.

REFERENCES

Battle, S. (1985). Applying the public health social work model: Principles of the epidemilogical approach. *Families at Risk: A Public Health Social Work Perspective*, MCH-00014-27, 122-132.

Deniston, O., Rosenstock, I. & Gettin, V. (1968). Evaluation of program effectiveness. *Public Health Reports*, 83, 323-335.

Gilbert, N. (1982). Policy issues in primary prevention. *Social Work*, 27, 293-296.

Googins, B. & Godfrey, J. (1987). *Occupational Social Work*, New York: Prentice-Hall, Inc.

Googins, B. (1983). Can change be documented? Measuring the Impact of EAPs. In Klarrich, S., Francek, J. & Moore, C. (Eds), *The Human Resources Management Handbook*, New York: Prager Special Studies.

James. G. H. (1961). Administration of community health services. *International City Managers Association*. Chicago Press.

Kurtz, N., Googins, B. & Howard, W. (1986). Measuring the success of occupational alcoholism program. *Journal of Alcohol Studies*, forthcoming.

Pincus, A. & Minihan, A. (1972). *Social Work Practice: Model and Method*, Itasca, IL: F. W. Peacock.

Ricci, R. & Hall, T. (1985). An Approach to the evaluation of human service program. *Families at Risk: A Public Health Social Work Perspective*, MCJ-0014-27, 111-116.

Rutman, L. (Ed.) (1977). *Evaluation Research Methods: A Basic Guide*. Sage Focus Edition.

Steele, J. (1970). Glossary of evaluative terms in public health. *American Journal of Public Health*, 60, 1548-1549.

Wright, D. (1985). Policy and procedures; The essential elements in an EAP. In Klarreich, S., Francek, J., & Moore, C. (Eds.) *The Human Resources Management Handbook*, New York: Prager Special Studies.

Evaluating Employee Assistance Programs: Obstacles, Issues and Strategies

Pallassana R. Balgopal
Michael A. Patchner

SUMMARY. Employee Assistance Programs (EAPs) are rapidly growing, and with this growth the goals of these programs also have broadened. There is increasing recognition that EAPs should be evaluated for their effectiveness in achieving these goals. The evaluation process poses a number of problems. This paper presents key issues to be considered for such evaluations—including the major obstacles encountered, and possible solutions to overcome them.

Employee Assistance Programs' (EAPs) main goal is to assist employees with current difficulties which affect their functioning on the job and at home. Sonnenstuhl and Trice define EAPs as "job-based programs operating within a work organization for the purposes of identifying 'troubled employees,' motivating them to resolve their troubles, and providing access to counseling or treatment for those employees who need these services" (1986, p. 1).

It is assumed that employees' problems are private unless they cause job performance to deteriorate. For when that happens, the personal problems become a matter of concern for the company, as it is protecting its valuable asset—the trained employee (Busch, 1981). EAPs respond to problems by taking into account both the productivity and financial effects on the company and also the hu-

---

Pallassana R. Balgopal, DSW, is Professor of Social Work and Michael A. Patchner, PhD, is Associate Professor of Social Work at the University of Illinois, 1207 W. Oregon, Urbana, IL 61801.

man cost factors on the employees, such as job, dignity, and sense of well-being. Therefore, it is not surprising that both the worker and the company may benefit from early identification and remediation of problems.

Employee Assistance Programs have grown rapidly and changed radically in the 1980s. In the United States in 1950, there were fewer than 100 such programs, whereas in 1987 their number has increased to over 10,000 (BNA-Special Report, 1987). With this growth, the goals of such programs also have broadened. Initially, the focus was on working with employees with alcohol and drug abuse problems. Now, many of these programs have expanded their scope to work with employees with family difficulties, financial and legal problems, interpersonal conflicts with fellow employees, and such. The programs which are emerging as "broad brush" are also more holistic and their emphasis is on wellness and the healthier workers rather than just on problem or troubled employees.

Although EAP goals, structures, and types of personnel vary, Erfurt and Foote (1977) have formulated the following service delivery components:

- identification of the employees who need assistance, and the referral of these employees to the program.
- intake into the program, and the evaluation of the employee's problems.
- counseling of the employee by the program staff, or possible referral for treatment.
- professional diagnosis and treatment for employees referred to an outside agency.

In addition to promoting the health, morale, and productivity of employees, EAPs also aim to strengthen the relationship between groups of employees, management, labor unions, and local community groups. With these goals in mind, it is important to evaluate if EAPs are effectively achieving them.

Evaluation research generally focuses on both processes and products. However, literature in this field usually addresses only the product as reflected in the dollars saved. To justify the existence of these programs, administrators and managers have tended to evaluate their cost-effectiveness rather than the personal benefits for the workers utilizing these services. According to Spicer and his colleagues (1983), the growth in EAPs has not been accompanied by an increase in the evaluation of these programs. Although there are several major studies of alcohol-focused EAPs, there are minimal data on the broad-brush model. It is still common in the literature on this field to find surprising statements based more on interesting assumptions than on fact. This issue is further compounded by the absence of systematic application of practice theory to the EAP activities.

The focus of this paper is to present key issues to be considered for evaluating the EAPs. The discussion is preceded by a brief description of these programs. Subsequently, the major obstacles encountered in the evaluation process, and possible solutions to overcome them, are discussed.

INGREDIENTS OF AN EFFECTIVE EAP

The issue of EAP effectiveness has been extensively discussed. Dickman (1985) suggests the following 11 "ingredients" of an effective EAP. These succinctly stated dimensions have heuristic value for both practitioners and evaluators, and are worth noting. Furthermore, they are included here because the evaluation of these ingredients independently or as a group may provide the effectiveness of an EAP from the dual perspective of service delivery and utilization.

1. Management Endorsement – Management endorsement and active involvement from the highest level of the corporate structure is necessary if an EAP is to be successful.
2. Labor Endorsement – Labor endorsement is crucial when the industry involved is union organized.
3. Policy Statement – Every industry utilizing an EAP needs a clear policy statement of the intentions and philosophy of that program.
4. Confidentiality – All employees have the right to ask for help

for their problems and to know that their problems will be kept in strict confidence.

5. Supervisor and Labor Steward Training – It is recommended that training occur at least once per year, and some of the suggested content for such training are: alcoholism awareness; family and other problems; drug abuse; referral procedures; importance of early interventions; and enabling behavior.
6. Financial Aspects and Insurance Coverage – When employees are clear that participating in the EAP may cost them something but that it won't break them, they will be more apt to accept a referral or to refer themselves. Therefore, company insurance coverage is an essential part of the program.
7. Professional Personnel – The EAP coordinator requires knowledge and expertise in many areas, as well as the needed access to competent resources. Some of these areas are: alcoholism and substance abuse; marriage and family counseling; general emotional problems; financial and legal problems; and basic interviewing and counseling techniques.
8. Broad Service Components – The EAP must be able to helpfully respond to a wide variety of employees' problems and needs.
9. Accessibility – Employees need to be able to access EAP sites quickly, conveniently, and in a confidential manner.
10. EAP Awareness – To be effective, the EAP needs constant marketing at all levels of the organization.
11. Program Evaluation – It is crucial for the organization and the EAP to know if the program is working and if it is doing what it purports to do. (pp. 39-52)

RESEARCH ISSUES IN EAP EVALUATIONS

Jerrell and Rightmyer stated that there is little theoretical guidance for developing or evaluating EAP programs. They propose, "Such conceptual models would prove most useful in the specification of evaluation strategies which are parsimonious, systematic, and rigorous, yet flexible enough to be implemented in diverse programs" (1983, p. 263). Suchman (1967) suggests that research on programs can be conducted to evaluate effort (i.e., what was done), performance (i.e., what were the results of what was done), impact or adequacy of performance (i.e., how effective was the program in assessing the total need), efficiency (i.e., is the program justified by its costs and are there less costly methods to achieve the same result), and process (i.e., which components of the program made it successful or unsuccessful).

Program evaluations rely on the use of social science research methodologies as the means for conducting such studies. Myers (1984) defines eight steps that he sees as essential for conducting any evaluative study. These include: (1) selecting a subject; (2) defining the variables; (3) defining a hypothesis; (4) reviewing the research; (5) choosing a research method; (6) scaling the research data; (7) checking the validity; and (8) showing the findings. These steps not only reflect clarity, but also have value to implement a systematic evaluation of the ingredients of EAP programs discussed earlier.

There are a number of methodological issues that a researcher must also deal with. As indicated by Sonnenstuhl and Trice (1986), job performance is difficult to assess. Sick days, job retention, number of grievances, number of visits to the medical departments, use of sickness and accident benefits, and the like may not be reliable measures of actual job performance. Further, performance standards often vary across and within organizations and occupational groupings. Another methodological problem is that when an evaluation relies on cost benefit data, these data are increasingly being estimated and the estimates are often based on assumptions rather than on objective accounting procedures (Jerrell & Rightmyer, 1983). Also, it must be recognized that the interpretation of a "successful" outcome can differ depending on who is doing the evaluation.

OBSTACLES AND SOLUTIONS

As discussed above, EAP evaluations raise a number of issues. In addition to these issues, an evaluator needs to be cognizant of certain obstacles frequently encountered. These obstacles and possible solutions are presented only in general terms, as they will differ from setting to setting.

Confidentiality

There are a number of obstacles that a researcher will encounter in conducting an EAP evaluation. Perhaps the most difficult issue is that of confidentiality and employee privacy. Because of societal values about many problems such as alcoholism, marital and family conflicts, emotional problems, employees are hesitant to seek assistance from EAPs. Employee reluctance is further compounded if they are not guaranteed that the data shared by them will be kept completely confidential. Such preservation of confidentiality is absolutely essential for not only client protection, but also mandated by the code of ethics of many helping professions.

While preserving the confidentiality and respecting the privacy of the employees, the evaluation process should be conducted openly. That is, EAP staff should meet with supervisors and explain the purpose and goals of such evaluations. Also, such evaluations should be written about in an EAP newsletter or memo. It should be clarified that evaluation results will not reveal the personal identity of any employees using the EAP services. Informed consent forms and release of information forms should also be obtained without coercion. Evaluators should be well-grounded in the field of program evaluation so they may alter their research designs, methodologies and if needed, change the focus of the research to protect their subjects.

Research Design

To evaluate the effectiveness of interventions and service delivery strategies, a true experimental design with a control group is preferred. However, such designs are difficult, if not impossible, to implement. Also in any evaluative process it is unethical to randomly assign persons to a control group while other individuals in an experimental group are receiving services. Even a comparison group of non-EAP users often cannot be incorporated into the research design because an individual in the comparison group may accidentally be perceived by a supervisor, fellow worker, or someone else as an EAP client. Therefore, it is mandatory to protect all persons who are included in such studies. Unfortunately, these precautions by some EAP personnel, who are generally understaffed and overworked, are perceived as additional chores, and resist participating in evaluative research involving rigorous methodologies. There is no easy solution to overcome this barrier except that the benefit of such research has to be conveyed as payoffs for all – the employees, employer, and to the EAPs for improving their mission.

Data Collection

Collection of data for evaluating EAPs poses a major dilemma of who should be entrusted with this responsibility. Reliance on outside researchers poses the following constraints: (1) The issue of protecting employee confidentiality and privacy is exacerbated; and (2) There is no guarantee that the EAP staff will fully cooperate with the external researchers in facilitating the data collection process because their commitment to the research may be lacking. On the other hand, if the data collection activity is implemented by the EAP staff themselves, their general lack of research skills (Sonnenstuhl & Trice, 1986) further complicates the evaluation process due to time limitations and staff needs for training. EAP staff may be hesitant about the evaluation outcome and concerned that the results may not positively reflect on their programs. Thus, these dynamics may not only bias the research, but may also impede this endeavor.

According to Akabas (1987), studies conducted by EAP staff have tended to be limited to basic information, lacking in follow-up data on the long-term impact, thus only scantily providing cost/benefit information. Califano (1987) also confirms the importance of collecting follow-up data especially to ensure whether the employees availed themselves of the recommended services. To address this dilemma of maintaining objectivity and integrity of the evaluation, it is essential that the EAP staff, who do not possess adequate research skills, obtain the professional help they need and cooperatively plan and conduct the evaluation. Those EAP staff with adequate research skills should not be hesitant to obtain outside consultation.

Data Base

EAPs have yet to collaborate with each other in developing data bases for their activities such as utilization rates, treatment results, and cost-benefit issues (Gould, 1987). Lack of such data prohibits studies on significant issues such as: comparisons of in-house and out-of-house EAPs; broad brush and limited focused EAPs; performance indicators; cost-benefit issues; and the overall impact on the quality of life at the workplace.

Due to confidentiality and privacy issues, systematic collection of qualitative data regarding clients' perceptions of services and the impact of the program on their personal situations and work are seldom collected. The only sources for such data have been generally through testimonials and anecdotal writings. Although EAPs are increasingly developing a holistic approach, data from co-workers, supervisors, and family members need to be collected.

Data Types

Evaluative research of EAPs should be based on both qualitative and quantitative data. In supporting these dual data sources, Sonnenstuhl and Trice state that "Qualitative field methods are appropriate for developing descriptions of programs and for generating insight and theory. Quantitative methods are most appropriate for testing generated theory" (1986, p. 57).

Practice Theory

The growing emphasis on the health and wellness approach within the EAP movement has resulted in viewing the employee as a whole person from a systems perspective. Differential strategies of interventions are utilized for addressing employee needs. These interventions are based on various practice theories such as brief therapy, crisis interventions, family and group therapy, but many EAP personnel have not systematically addressed the efficacy of these theoretical approaches and the impact upon the employees' needs. This gap has resulted in fragmented data for evaluating the effectiveness of these interventions. Similarly, this absence of anchoring in a theoretical framework affects the EAPs' evaluation from an organizational perspective.

This lack of anchoring in a theoretical framework poses uncertainty regarding the replicability of successful strategies implemented within these programs. This weakness is confirmed in Korr and Ruez's conclusion that "unlike mental health programs that have produced an abundance of data on utilization of services, EAP evaluations have frequently given data on outcome with little or no attention to process" (1986, p. 37). Albert and his colleagues also support this position. According to these authors, an EAP evaluator "–should address the question of the match between treatment interventions, clients, and various occupational settings" (1985, p. 180). Also, EAP researchers should build their study on the findings of their colleagues (Spicer et al., 1983).

Research Site

In addition to the confidentiality issue, other factors may confront a researcher in conducting an EAP evaluation. First of all, there may be an uncooperative administration. Despite the fact that most EAPs have a number of persons involved in the management and overall administration of their program, these persons may have different goals for the EAP and may have different purposes for the evaluation. Another obstacle may be that a program has diffuse goals and activities which make monitoring difficult and thus yield indefinitive evaluation results. An EAPs' different goals and priorities are often determined by the employer's reasons for establishing such programs. According to Curran and Kiefhaber, there are four possible motivating factors:

1. "selfish altruism"–the belief that rehabilitating employees saves employers money in the long run;
2. recognition of legal responsibilities an employer may have for employees' mental health;
3. the increasing awareness and acceptance of mental illness in America; and
4. an increasing focus on employees' job performance rather than on personal problems. (p. 10)

The lack of an explicit role of the evaluator in this instance may also be problematic. As indicated earlier, evaluators may be internal staff or hired from outside of the organization. There are advantages and disadvantages that come with each. For example, having internal evaluators may lead to the easier facilitation of data collection, yet they may also have some biases because of their overlapping roles within the organization. External evaluators are usually more objective, but they may also be less sensitive to the subtle influences of employee behavior.

CONCLUSIONS

In the previous discussion, major issues confronting the evaluation of EAPs are presented. Although the list of obstacles is not an exhaustive one, and the solutions are presented only in general terms, it is reasonable to conclude that success of the EAP movement depends greatly upon solid evaluative evidence of their effectiveness in improving the quality of life for the employees, and that such programs are cost-effective for the employers. In this regard, EAP evaluators will need to focus on the following areas: (1) The 11 ingredients proposed by Dickman (1985) need to be examined individually or as a group; (2) Cooperative research should take place between different EAPs in similar settings. For example, EAPs are being increasingly established in institutions of higher education, and there is significant disparity in these programs concerning their focus, mission, structure, etc. It may be well worthwhile to evaluate the effectiveness of these different programs; (3) Evaluations should be focused on examining the effectiveness of differential strategies of interventions (i.e., which types of interventions are best suited for particular problems). Therefore, EAP personnel need to be solidly grounded in theoretical frameworks; and (4) Women and minority workers have been historically discriminated against at the workplace. Thus, EAPs need to evaluate these employees' needs and develop services and intervention strategies accordingly. Finally, an EAP evaluation should be seen as a team effort. This effort should first and foremost define the purpose of the evaluation and what its payoffs are.

REFERENCES

Akabas, S. "Views of the Experts," in *Employee Assistance Programs: Benefits, Problems and Prospects*. Washington, DC: Bureau of National Affairs, Inc., 1987.

Albert, W. C., Smythe, P. C. & Brook, R. C. "Promises to Keep: An Evaluator's Perspective on Employee Assistance Programs," *Evaluation and Program Planning*, 8:1985, pp. 175-182.

BNA Special Report. *Employee Assistance Programs: Benefits, Problems and Prospects*, Washington, DC: Bureau of National Affairs, Inc., 1987.

Busch, E. J. "Developing an Employee Assistance Program," *Personnel Journal*, 60:1981, pp. 708-711.

Califano, J. A. Jr. "Views of Experts," in *Employee Assistance Programs: Benefits Problems and Prospects*. Washington, DC: Bureau of National Affairs, Inc., 1987.

Dickman, F. "Ingredients of an Effective EAP," in J. F. Dickman, W. G. Emener, Jr. & W. S. Hutchinson, Jr. (Eds.), *Counseling the Troubled Person in Industry*, Springfield, IL: Charles C. Thomas Publisher, 1985.

Erfurt, J. C. & Foote, A. *Occupational Employee Assistance Programs for Substance Abuse and Mental Health Problems*, Ann Arbor, MI: ILIR, 1977.

Gould, G. M. "Views of the Experts," in *Employee Assistance Programs: Benefits, Problems, and Prospects*. Washington, DC: Bureau of National Affairs, Inc., 1987.

Jerrell, J. M. & Rightmyer, J. F. "Evaluating Employee Assistance Programs: A Review of Methods, Outcomes and Future Directions," *Evaluation and Program Planning*, 5:1983, pp. 255-267.

Korr, W. S. & Ruez, J. F. "How Employee Assistance Programs Determine Service Utilization: A Survey and Recommendations," *Evaluation and Program Planning*, 9:1986, pp. 367-371.

Myers, D. W. *Establishing and Building Employee Assistance Programs*, Westport, CN: Quorum Books, 1984.

Suchman, E. A. *Evaluative Research: Principles and Practice in Public Service and Social Action Programs*. New York: Russell Sage Foundation, 1967.

Sonnenstuhl, W. J. & Trice, H. M. *Strategies for Employee Assistance Programs: The Crucial Balance*. Ithaca, NY: ILR Press, 1986.

Spicer, J., Owen, P. & Levine, D. *Evaluating Employee Assistance Programs*, Center City, MN: Hazelden Foundation, 1983.

Evaluating Organizations Through an Employee Assistance Program Using an Organization Development Model

Donald W. Cole

SUMMARY. This article describes one of the first accounts of an Employee Assistance Program (EAP) staffed by a social worker in industry in the United States. The author was the social worker employed in this EAP (called the Industrial Social Work Project) which was originally motivated by a vice president's concern over employee turnover. The article describes in detail how the EAP was operationalized and used to evaluate the organizational culture by using an organizational development model which involved five overlapping phases. These were: (1) orientation/information gather-

---

Donald W. Cole, DSW, ACSW, RODC is thought to be the first full-time, fully trained industrial social worker in the United States. He studied at Case Western Reserve University, Smith College, Boston University, Columbia University, the University of Rhode Island, the University of Zurich in Switzerland, and Newark College of Engineering and received his doctorate from Washington University in St. Louis. Licensed as a psychologist by the State of Ohio, Dr. Cole is also a Registered Organization Development Consultant. He has designed and presented more than 200 management development programs for some 30 companies and other organizations. He is President of The Organization Development Institute, publisher of *The Organization Development Journal*, editor and publisher of *Organizations And Change* (a monthly newsletter for O.D. professionals) and *The International Registry of O.D. Professionals*. Having written a book on *Professional Suicide* he has become very interested in "world suicide" and has been the chief organizer for 8 World Congresses on that subject. A 15 day free examination copy of *Professional Suicide* can be obtained by writing to Dr. Cole, c/o The O.D. Institute, 6501 Wilson Mills Road, Suite K, Cleveland, OH 44143. Telephone: 216/461-4333.

ing; (2) individual treatment; (3) research on cultural change; (4) team building and O.D. projects; and (5) O.D. management training. The main contention of this article is that organizations do in fact contribute to the "professional suicide" of employees, and those who plan to evaluate EAPs are remiss not considering the organization context of such programs and their possible impact on employees.

This article is about one of the first, if not the first, industrial social work program in the United States staffed by a full-time, fully trained social worker. There had been some earlier attempts to utilize social work within an industrial environment, but as far as I have been able to determine, these earlier efforts were either staffed by part-time social workers or by people not fully trained in social work.

McGraw-Hill has published a book on this project entitled *Professional Suicide* (1981) as this was the title originally given to the project by management. The term "professional suicide" was chosen because it was thought the problems were things that employees did to themselves. But, the project was really not about "professional suicide," it was really about "organizational murder." We found that these problems were not so much the result of something which people did to themselves but the result of an organization that did not know how to manage and nurture creative people. And, interestingly enough, these were the very people on whom the future life of the corporation depended.

This article is about an Industrial Social Work/Employee Assistance Program that evolved into an Organization Development project. At the time I thought our findings were only appropriate to the departments where I was working or to the corporation in which the project took place. But, later I worked in a major consulting firm and visited many of the Fortune 1000 companies and I found similar problems there. As a result, I cannot help wondering how many EAP programs might not be more helpful to clients and to management if they had an Organization Development component. In my day, social workers were trained in community organization. To my social work friends I sometimes describe Organization Development as community organization practiced in an industrial setting rather than in a geographical or community setting.

The evolution from an Industrial Social Work/Employee Assistance Project to an Organization Development program was not unique to us. John Edmonstone with the Trent Regional Health Authority in the U.K. reports on how he was hired to "provide tea and sympathy to the shell shocked victims of the corporate environment" and eventually moved from that into an Organization Development project (Cole, 1982).

I. THE HISTORY OF THE TERM PROFESSIONAL SUICIDE

In 1963, when I was Director of the West Office of Cleveland Family Service, our psychiatrist consultant asked me if I would be interested in working in industry. I said, "No, my career plans were to head a social agency" (as my father had done before). He said, "As a favor to me, won't you at least go and talk to them because I think you will be intrigued with what they have to say." So, I said I would go and talk to them. And I was intrigued with what they had to say.

I met with the Vice President and General Manager of a major division of a Fortune 100 aerospace corporation. The former was an unusually sensitive man. Much later I learned that early in his career, he and his wife had been very good friends with a male social worker and his wife. He had begun to notice that although the organization which he headed was hiring large numbers of bright creative people, in three to five years they would leave. This seemed to happen in several ways. Some would:

1. Quit their jobs for other jobs considered to be far beneath their capability;
2. Become disruptive and do things for which they must have known they would be fired;
3. Quit working and retire on the job; and
4. Fail to keep up with the rapidly changing technology and allow themselves to become out-moded.

During the course of the study, three more types were discovered:

(1) Those who developed physical complaints of a classically psychosomatic type such as headaches, ulcers, and backaches. (Alcoholism which is readily identified by the community as a form of professional suicide was infrequently found among this group of middle class managers, engineers, and scientists; possibly because individuals who try to solve their problems with alcohol rarely got promoted to this level, or at least had enough experience in masking this problem so that they were rarely discovered.)

(2) Some, after having been highly productive and creative in the past, were placed in jobs where for various reasons they were grossly underutilized. Unable to resolve these problems with their boss and unwilling to quit, they would quietly begin to deteriorate under the constant pressure of being regarded as inadequate by their peers.

(3) And, some unable to slow down or lose weight or stop smoking under doctor's orders, seemed headed for actual physical suicide.

Assuming that these problems were things that people did to themselves, the term "professional suicide" was coined by the Vice President. And, a number of things had been tried to correct this. One of the first things was to hire a team of industrial psychologists. They tested a lot of people and two file drawers had been filled with the results of their tests. But, nothing seemed to change very much. Later the corporation hired a survey research company to come in and do an attitude survey of everyone. They had produced 26 volumes of results. But, the Vice President was already very busy, and, what was he going to do with 26 volumes of results? When I finally joined the organization, they were sitting on the floor of his closet. Eventually, the Vice President met my friend the psychiatrist and asked him what he would suggest. The psychiatrist said to hire someone trained to understand the relationship between the problems of your people and the environment you create for them, someone like a social worker.

The choice of a social worker (myself in this case) was a unique decision. In the division of skills on the traditional orthopsychiatric mental health team, it was the psychiatrist who was the medical/

neurological expert, the psychologist who was the testing expert, and—while time has tended to blur these differences somewhat—it was the social worker who was the sociocultural environmental expert. On this basis, the social worker was the most logical of the mental health professionals to work on these kinds of problems. In Europe there had been many social workers employed by industry. However, in America, industry had not used social workers in this capacity and at this time they were not recognized as a resource for solving management problems.

II. SOCIAL WORK "ON-THE-JOB"

Because of the dependence on government contracts, widely fluctuating employment levels, and management's lack of awareness and support for the project, this assignment was recognized as a risky career choice. However, the Vice President had a persuasive argument for it. He said,

> Knowing the length of time it takes to be of significant help to the underprivileged and to the traditional social agency/clinic population, you can, if you want, spend the rest of your life working with them. Or, we offer you the opportunity of working with bright, motivated, highly educated people—people who would rarely go to a social agency or a clinic for help, but who, with relatively smaller amounts of your time could have a significant impact on society.

I wish I could say we were smart enough to anticipate all the problems that this project would encounter. In an organization where the professional suicide of bright, dedicated people had become obvious enough to need a project to study it, difficulties could be expected. We were aware that if there were adverse fluctuations in the business or if the project were to become sufficiently misunderstood by higher management, it could be suddenly terminated, and we were prepared for this.

In the design of the project, the psychiatrist was to be made available to employees on a regular continuing basis. He was to function on a consulting basis from outside the organization, where he would be less subject to the strains, and/or stress of the organization and where he would be available to provide some greater measure of objectivity to those involved in the project. It was also hoped that he might provide to those associated with the project, some measure of protection against their own professional suicide.

While management did have a humanitarian concern for its employees, it was felt that changes in individuals' attitudes and behaviors would lead to increased effectiveness on the job. Thus, it was sophisticated self-interest rather than improved mental health per se, that provided the budget justification for the establishment of this industrial orthopsychiatric mental health project. Because organizations are composed of people, there was an assumption of this project that many problems in the organization resulted from the unsolved problems of only a few people dispersed throughout the organization.

In retrospect, we found that this seven year project was divided into five overlapping phases (see Figure A-1). Although each phase had a major emphasis lasting about one year, most of the activities overlapped one another. Phases I and II were essentially diagnostic phases during which the problems of those committing professional

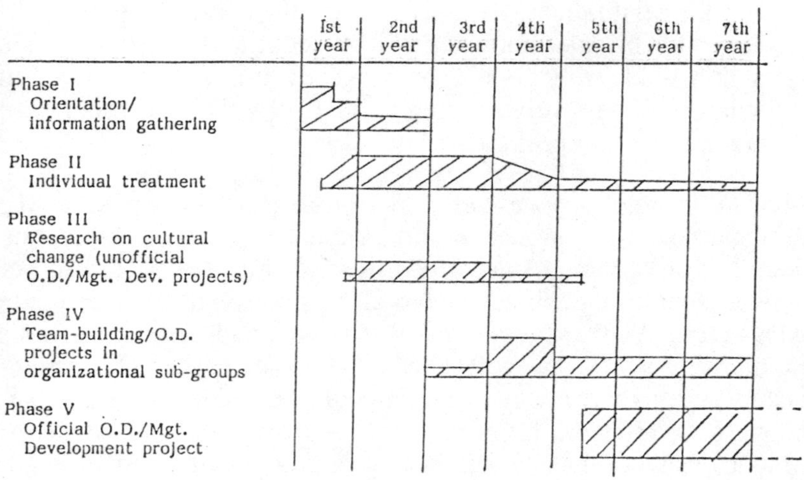

Figure A-1: Phases in the Industrial Social Work/EAP Behavioral Science Project on Professional Suicide

suicide were analyzed. Phase III was a research phase during which the expectations of management were explored. Finally, phases IV and V were essentially treatment phases during which Organization Development and Management Development efforts were made to improve the problems in the psychological environment of the organization. Although this research study was originally established to reduce the incidence of professional suicide within the organization and was referred to as "A Study of Professional Suicide," a more positive sounding official title was developed called "The More Effective Utilization of Creative Talent."

III. PHASES OF THE INDUSTRIAL SOCIAL WORK/EAP

Phase I was an orientation information gathering phase with some of the key people in the organization. Some 180 people (mostly managers and engineers) received at least one interview of about two hours focusing on the ways in which they felt their usefulness to the organization might be increased.

Phase II was an individual psychotherapeutic treatment phase during which managers and engineers were seen individually. There was a tendency on the part of management people to see organizational problems in terms of individual personality difficulties. And, there was an implicit assumption that organizational problems were in the final analysis individual problems. An obvious advantage of this assumption was that a "problem" individual could be quickly identified and removed without the need for any organizational change other than the fixing of blame on the individual. For example, one problem encountered was the reluctance of managers, engineers, and scientists to accept the "medical-sickness model." It was important to their self-image and to their future organization effectiveness that they see themselves and be seen by others as competent. The role of being a client or a patient was not seen by many of them as being helpful. A significant step in the suicide process often came when co-workers or the personnel department convinced an individual that he had a "problem." A commonly observed result of this "convincing" (in a highly competitive environment) was further deterioration and further progress toward professional suicide. As a result, people much preferred to seek help in collaborative ways such as bull sessions of indeterminate length, usually outside office hours—either over lunch or late into the evening. Efforts to use traditional professional and mental health methods such as the 50 minute hour were largely unsuccessful. In this respect the project had to evolve techniques similar to those developed for working with street corner gangs.

Nevertheless, during the second year of the program, 128 individuals were seen with some 175 different problems. The majority of these individuals were managerial-supervisory people (67 manager-supervisors, 46 other salaried, 2 hourly workers, and 13 spouses). The program was only publicized to manager-supervisors, partly for fear that one person would become swamped if the program became widely known. Nearly three-fifths of those seen were self-referrals (74), the balance coming from immediate supervisors (18), personnel people (10), and friends (9).

Phase III which overlapped the activities of the first two phases was an effort to influence the psychological tone of the organization. During Phases I and II, it had become increasingly obvious that professional suicide was to some extent a result of pressures generated by the organizational climate. Because of my extensive training and experiences as a social worker in the psychotherapeutic psychoanalytic method, it took awhile for me to hear what people were telling me. They were bright and well-educated. For the most part they came from stable families with parents who cared for them. They were hard workers, as 60 to 70 hour work weeks were common. And, they had been taught to accept responsibility for things in their life that went wrong. Eventually I began to hear what they were telling me. And, what they eventually began to tell me was that it was the job which was driving them nuts. In Phase III a small group research project was developed to test out whether the assumptions that management had for its workers were realistic. Our plan to test management's managerial assumptions in small groups was not shared with management because it was felt this would be too threatening.

Phase IV emphasized team-building. Because of the difficulties encountered in trying to change the psychological/managerial environment by individuals working alone, emphasis was focused on creating a more positive environment at the department level. Through departmental meetings and the educational efforts of department heads, an effort was made to develop and to build an environment, where the creative achievement initiatives of workers could find greater expression than had been traditionally provided for.

Phase V marked the start of an official Management Development Program. This was an organization-wide Organization Development/Management Development cultural change program designed to teach managers interpersonal competence skills and help them build an environment where employees would be strengthened for difficult tasks rather than being demoralized for them. We also found that the managerial model that managers carried in their heads about the ways in which a corporation should run was no longer the way in which the corporation actually was run. And we talked about the evolution of management styles going in the corporation. We found four different management styles in the company, each of which required a somewhat different response from the employee.

IV. HOW ORGANIZATIONS CONTRIBUTE TO PROFESSIONAL SUICIDE

A tendency towards blaming the victim is not uncommon. Most organizations spend a considerable amount of money recruiting high achievers. After they are hired, however, most of these people are left pretty much on their own. Management recognizes that machinery needs preventive maintenance and periodic overhaul, but it is only gradually coming to appreciate that employee knowledge and skill must also be maintained.

When employees are recruited, they are often made promises about the rewards for hard work. If they give their all, they are told, some day you might be president or at least a general manager. After awhile, though, some of these workers find that they are working harder and harder and their careers are going nowhere. Gradually, disillusionment sets in.

The personality structure of those who get caught up in the "professional suicide" process can best be described as "entrepreneurial." These are people with strong achievement needs and a strong desire for accomplishment. They are primarily concerned with end results and have less concern for the means by which such results are achieved.

In contrast to the typical bureaucrat, who has well-developed survival skills and is expert at sensing which way "the wind is blowing," those prone to "professional suicide" have little interest in the development of survival skills. Instead, they become single-mindedly committed to an objective and often alienate their bosses and the organization in their drive to achieve this goal.

People who end up committing "professional suicide" or being "killed off" have usually reached a point in their career where they are no longer motivated by any of the common fears. They are not much influenced by the fear of survival, the fear of social disapproval, or the fear of the "Big Boss." They are confident in their ability to survive, whether in this organization, some other organization, or on their own.

Such people do not want to be told how to do their job. Professionally secure, they believe that it is their responsibility to get a certain job done and they do not welcome direction on when, where, or how to do it. Standard operating procedures are often jettisoned as they seek better and quicker ways to reach their objectives. This creates problems for bureaucratic organizations that want not only a standardized end product but also a standardized way of getting it.

The fact that these people are creative and hard working does not protect them indefinitely. Traditional managers who are used to expecting conformity usually find ways to squeeze them out, fire them, or bury them.

The results can be viewed as "suicide," since these people do court their own fate by refusing to conform to the traditional organization and the traditional management style. Or, it can be looked at as a kind of organization "murder," because the organization has not yet learned the management skills necessary to sustain this kind of worker.

Professional suicide and other kinds of emotional problems in the workplace are preventable. Organizations can avoid many of these problems by:

(1) Employing Organization Development (O.D.) professionals to review the way people are working together and being managed. At least some of these O.D. people should be external to the organization. Sole reliance on internal resources tends to create corporate "in-breeding" in which the organization produces an image of change while in fact perpetuating traditional values, policies, procedures, and problems.

(2) Creating a Management Development program to improve interpersonal competence skills and cooperative/collaboration skills. Many bright employees get "killed" in the cross fire between two managers or because they do not get adequate supervision or mentoring.

(3) Making real use of a performance evaluation system so that employees have an opportunity to find out where they stand. For example, open job posting indicates a commitment to openness in the organization while allowing employees to seek other opportunities without having to leave the organization.

V. IMPLICATIONS

A number of studies have shown that mental health resources in the United States are too few, and mental health problems too numerous to be influenced very soon through a one-by-one approach (Albee, 1961). The value of an environmental-cultural mileau therapy approach to the prevention and correction of mental health problems has been demonstrated in mental hospitals, residential treatment centers, and residential schools, but little has been done to apply these learnings and techniques on a community wide basis, whether it be a geographical community or an industrial community. The implications of this study for community mental health evaluation and planning of prevention programs lie in demonstrating the value an environmental approach can have on improving human effectiveness and arresting human deterioration and professional suicides. I think this has especially important implications for developing and evaluating Employee Assistance Programs.

REFERENCES

Albee, George W., *Mental Health Manpower Trend*, Basic Books, New York: Joint Commission on Mental Illness & Health, Action for Mental Health, Science Editions, Inc., New York, 1961.

Cole, Donald W., *Conflict Resolution Technology*. The O.D. Institute, Cleveland, OH, 1983.

Cole, Donald W. and others, *Improving Profits Through Organization Development*, The O.D. Institute, Cleveland, OH, 1981.

Cole, Donald W., *Professional Suicide*, McGraw-Hill, New York, 1981.

Cole, Donald W., "Global Organization Development: The Application of Organization Development Technologies to Global Problems," *The Leadership and Organization Development Journal*, Vol. 5, No. 4, 1984.

Cole, Donald W., "Organization Development and Its Implications for Innovative Management in the 1990's," *The Organization Development Journal*, Cleveland, OH, Vol. 5, No. 2, 1987. (A paper presented at the 1986 International Conference on "Innovation and Management in the 1990's" in Carlsbad, Czechoslovakia, October 20-24, 1986 under the auspices of the Czechoslovakia Academy of Sciences.)

Cole, Donald W., "Professional Suicide or Organizational Murder?" *Northeast Training News*, November, 1979.

Cole, Donald W., "The Challenge to British OD from the Germans," *The Leadership and Organization Development Journal*, Cranfield, England, Vol. 3, No. 1, 1982.

Formative Evaluation of EAPs by Studying Role Perceptions and Organizational Cultures

Eli Teram

SUMMARY. This article argues that formative evaluation is the most appropriate strategy for the current developmental stage of Employee Assistance Programs (EAPs). Since most EAPs entail multiple interventions and have poorly defined success criteria, the utility of summative evaluation in this field is limited. A method for conducting formative evaluations is outlined. It involves the combination of quantitative and qualitative strategies: using a questionnaire to compare the perceived (actual and desired) role of EAP workers by significant groups in the organization; and, then by studying the organizational culture in which these programs are imbedded through interviews with key informants. Examples from a study in Israel demonstrate the usefulness of the suggested approach.

The emergence of Employee Assistant Programs (EAPs) in North America is a relatively new development (Googins, 1975, p. 466). Since most of these programs were established in an era of increased accountability, and because of their relationship to cost-conscious for-profit organizations, one would expect EAPs to generate many evaluation research studies in the literature. Two recent articles (Knott, 1986; Steidinger, 1986) suggest, however, that this expectation is premature; in fact, researchers in this field seem to be still searching for identity, direction, methodologies, and information.

Eli Teram, PhD, is Assistant Professor, Faculty of Social Work, Wilfrid Laurier University, Waterloo, Ontario, Canada N2L 3C5.

This article provides an overview of a framework for one way of conducting formative evaluation of EAPs. First, it makes the case for formative evaluation as the most appropriate strategy for the current developmental stage of EAPs. Second, it demonstrates the use of concepts from role theory by using a study of EAPs conducted in Israel (Teram, 1977). Finally, it suggests that quantitative data must be supplemented by qualitative exploration of the organizational culture in which EAPs operate in order to enhance its relevance.

At the outset, it must be emphasized that, while this chapter is based on an empirical study, no attempt is made to describe the full details of this study. Instead, emphasis is placed on selected methodological issues relevant to the author's assumptions, experiences, and findings. Thus, those findings related to organizational cultures, are presented for demonstrating the kind of insights the proposed approach may yield. This planned deletion of detailed research findings seems more appropriate for a volume attempting to advance evaluative research of EAPs. It is also hoped that this deletion will help illustrate the main assumptions and arguments put forward.

I. THE CASE FOR FORMATIVE EVALUATION

Despite some impressive attempts by social scientists to develop strategies for assessing the impact of programs (for a recent review see Rossi & Freeman, 1985, pp. 185-319), the usefulness of these strategies for producing meaningful evaluative data is questionable to a great extent (for a comprehensive critique of the rationale underlying these strategies see Lincoln & Guba, 1985). The inclusion, in this text, of quantitative studies which attempt to evaluate the impact of EAPs is certain. To be sure, such investigations, and the proponents of summative evaluations, usually incorporate a clearly identified impact model which allows for quantitative and outcome-oriented evaluations. These studies also usually include a research design which attempts to control for the numerous threats to external and internal validity. Further, some of these investigations usually advise their readers about the limitations of their designs, emphasizing practical and methodological constraints and the current state of EAPs as the obvious explanations for such imperfections.

Without getting into ontological, epistemological and/or methodological arguments, which may question the utility of summative evaluations, the case for formative evaluations of EAPs is based on two main components that characterize most EAPs: (1) they usually have multiple interventions, and (2) they usually have poorly defined success criteria.

Most EAPs attempt to assist employees in a variety of ways, ranging from providing basic concrete assistance to counselling individuals who have very complex psychosocial problems. This mixture of "hard" and "soft" benefits, and their simultaneous provision to the same employees, makes the identification of a clear outcome-oriented model which defines interventions difficult, if not impossible. In this regard, I would propose that the greater the variety of interventions and services provided to employees, the greater the vagueness of defining the impact and outcome of such interventions.

There are of course service components of EAPs, and sometimes entire EAPs, with a relatively narrow problem focus and an easier to define outcome, such as alcoholism or drug abuse counselling (with the outcome being abstinence at best or zero absentee days at worse). As far as the evaluation of these programs is concerned, however, it seems more logical to examine them in the context of similar programs dealing with similar problems rather than within the context of an individual EAP. Thus, a program aimed at curtailing drug abuse by providing interventions to its employees may be considered an "EAP," only within the context of understanding its individual origins and philosophy. The evaluation of this program would, however, be better designed and understood within the context of the knowledge about the impact that similar programs aimed at curtailing drug abuse are having.

Even EAPs with clearly defined interventions and proposed impacts do not escape the difficulty of reaching agreement about what the success criteria for the program are. For example, should an employee coming out from a program dealing with alcoholism be considered a success even if abstinence is accompanied with declining productivity? Or, do improved family relationships constitute success for an EAP when the treated worker refuses to work overtime, in order to be with the now reunited family? These are only two examples of the types of questions surrounding the ultimate objectives and successes of EAPs. One does not necessarily have to accept Edward's (1979) account of the transformation of control mechanisms in the workplace in order to acknowledge the possibility that EAPs may serve the interests of employers more than the needs of the employees. The existence of such doubts regarding the actual purpose of EAPs, whether justified or not, is sufficient to provide justification for the position that the objectives and success criteria of many EAPs need reexamination and perhaps redefinition. Without such considerations, I am convinced that summative evaluation studies are bound to lead to more questions than answers.

By itself, the issue of agreeing on consensus objectives and success criteria for EAPs may be an important part of a planning process which may contribute to the development of better programs. Nevertheless, such issues should be raised as an integral part of any systematic formative study rather than considered at the outset of a summative evaluation. In the latter case (which is the norm), there is always the risk that success criteria will be defined arbitrarily without taking into consideration the views of all involved parties (e.g., EAP coordinators, administrators, union, nonunion staff, and EAP evaluators). This risk is related to the fact that summative research cannot be conducted without clearly defined success criteria, and EAP evaluators are not always in a position to wait for consensus about this issue to emerge. Formative studies, on the other hand, are sensitive to input from all involved parties and oriented to using conflicting ideas in order to improve the design and operation of the evaluated programs. In these types of studies, the resolution of the debate whether the success of EAPs should be determined by the measurement of production related variables, health and welfare criteria, or anything else, is not of paramount importance. Instead, the emphasis is on identifying differing perspectives in an attempt to respond effectively to immediate program needs, resources, and contingencies. One way to examine EAPs and their relevance to their needs and problems is through focusing on the actual and desired role perception of workers within these programs.

II. ROLE TAKING AND THE EVALUATION OF EAPs

The taking of organizational roles is a complex process which entails role expectations, role-sending, and in many cases, role conflicts and ambiguity (Katz & Kahn, 1978, pp. 185-221; for a more recent review see Jackson & Schuler, 1985). The relevance of these concepts for understanding EAPs relates to their emphasis on the multiplicity of role expectations and the difficulty to respond simultaneously to conflicting and unclear expectations. Equipped with these concepts, the study on which this paper is based compared the actual and desired role of social workers (the EAP workers) in EAPs as perceived by: (1) union leaders; (2) personnel managers, and (3) the workers themselves (Teram, 1977).

To find out what the perceptions were of these three groups, respondents were presented with a structured questionnaire. The questionnaire was constructed from a list of 51 tasks originating from three sources (Atherton, Mitchell & Schein, 1971a, 1971b; *The Book of Professions and Occupations in Israel*, 1968; *Task Analysis Inventory*, 1973). Respondents were then asked to specify for each task: (a) to what extent they perceive EAP personnel are engaged in the task; and (b) to what extent they perceive the EAP personnel should be engaged in the respective task. Respondents scored their perception on two ordinal scales ranging from "0 to 7": where "0" indicated the worker is not, or should not be, engaged in the task; and "7" indicated that the worker is very much engaged, or should be engaged, in the task. The questionnaire was first pretested using a small number of respondents ($n = 7$). It was felt that a larger number would have exhausted the otherwise small sample of EAPs in this population. This pretest led to a number of changes, namely: a few tasks were deleted because they seemed not relevant; two new tasks were added; two were combined into one; and some tasks were redefined. This pretest and its outcome are described in order to highlight the types of problems one may expect when constructing similar questionnaires. Since future questionnaires must be updated and geared to address local programs, their objectives, and needs, there is no point in providing the details of these revisions. Despite the time spent in pretesting, or perhaps because of its limited scope, three more tasks were excluded from the final data analyses, as one was found to be irrelevant, and the other two were considered unclear by a number of the actual respondents.

Each questionnaire took about 30 minutes to complete and was followed by a semi-structured interview. The questionnaire provided a sound basis for the subsequent interview primarily due to the curiosity of the respondents regarding the perceptions disclosed by the other study participants. For example, some of them found the whole process useful as an opportunity to review their EAP.

It should be noted that the study was not constructed, nor the data analyzed, with the intention of examining individual personnel or EAPs. As an exploratory study in a new field (in 1970s Israel) the analyses focused on comparisons between the perceptions of the three previously mentioned groups: social workers, personnel managers, and union leaders. It attempted to identify the major tasks occupying social workers in EAPs (who were the main personnel of such programs), and the perceptions of these three groups regarding the future development of their programs. The analyses also focused on the gaps between actual and desired roles, again as an intergroup comparison. Descriptive statistics and one way analysis of variance provided effective tools for rendering these comparisons.

With a different focus, and some minor revisions, the method and instruments of the original study may provide a useful way for conducting formative evaluations of EAPs. The inquiry about actual and desired roles of EAP workers, through a concrete list of tasks, provides a basis for thinking about and allows the generation of "usable knowledge" (Lindblom & Cohen, 1979) without putting heavy demands on the time of informants. Similarly, there is little cost involved for those collecting the data. In retrospect, the lists of tasks can be easily constructed, shortened, lengthened, or revised based on specific program needs, problems, resources, and contingencies. Further, data can be collected on an ongoing basis (e.g., from employees who use the programs, or from those who make referrals) and may be useful for longitudinal analysis. Alternatively, data can be collected periodically to provide "snap-shots" about the state of the program and its development. In either case, the focus on actual and desired role perceptions, and the gap between them, provides input for thinking about an EAPs deficiencies and benefits. In addition, new ideas for program development can be tested by adding innovative tasks to the list on the questionnaire.

One should not forget that the questionnaire is about role taking perceptions which do not necessarily reflect reality. For example, the identification of significant differences between what EAPs try to do (e.g., through examining the actual time and resources devoted to the performance of certain tasks) and the way they are perceived is valuable information, reflecting either on the marketing of the program or the organizational culture in which it is imbedded. Action in the form of providing information to correct distorted comparative perceptions is one simple way to deal with such findings. If this corrective action is not effective, one has to pursue the origin of the distortion through further qualitative methods.

III. THE QUALITATIVE EXPLORATION OF ORGANIZATIONAL CULTURES

Even if there is no quantitative evidence for disagreements between comparative groups regarding the role of EAP workers, it is important to qualitatively understand these programs within the context of the organizational culture in which they operate. Unlike structured questionnaires, which focus on very specific and discrete information, personal interviews may be open-ended and provide an opportunity for respondents to naturally and spontaneously reflect on EAPs. One of my most memorable interviews from the Israeli study was with a union leader who at first refused to meet with me. Being a "true Marxist," he considered universities part of the oppressing establishment and my study was perceived as servicing "the interests of capitalists." He agreed to be interviewed only after mediation by a mutual friend who was a member of the Israeli Communist Party. When we met he insisted that we talk "openly," surrounded by his co-workers around a large table in the factory's lunch room. For almost an hour, he tried to open my eyes to putting this industrial social work business in the context of power, control, exploitation, and Marxist ideology. The workers around us listened attentively, occasionally suggesting that he illustrate his points by outlining certain relevant events and examples. Later, the personnel manager of the same factory provided me with examples about the kind of "troubles" caused by the union. The social worker, still optimistic, was not sure he was going to gain the trust of this union at all.

Unions and workers do not have to be guided by Marxist philosophy in order to pose obstacles for EAPs' workers. Unfortunately, when the relationships between management and workers are characterized by mistrust, the introduction of EAPs may add another cause for suspicion. This is particularly true when management does not realize that the EAP is not a tool for limiting the power of the union or for rewarding and/or punishing workers. In another example, management informed the union executive that with the hiring of a social worker, the former could not leave work to deal with the personal problem of employees. Other personnel managers stated very adamantly that their EAPs should prefer workers who make important contributions to the organization over those whose problems are more severe. One of them suggested that the assistance to employees is a bonus that should be limited only to "good workers."

Such misconceptions about EAPs are not necessarily the product of actions or statements of the kind exemplified in the above paragraphs. Sometimes, the location of the social worker's office, or the association of EAPs with personnel departments, unions, or management is sufficient to originate concerns which may limit the use of the programs. The most common and troublesome source of concern, the possibility that personal problems, shared with social workers, would have negative effects on chances for promotion, does not have to be based on facts in order to limit the utilization of the EAP. Similarly, the allegation by one union leader that one of the social worker's psychosocial reports had been used to help management fire an employee, does not have to be true in order to create certain perceptions about the program. To use another example, intrusion into leisure time activities, formerly organized by the union, may not only create shaky beginnings for an EAP, but may also lead to employees perceiving the program as "political." This perception is bound to continue a long time after the honest or naive error has been corrected.

In Israel, where a very small number of workers are not unionized, much of the culture of organizations is developed around the relationships between managements and unions. Thus, it is logical that EAPs in these settings must be understood in the context of these relationships. But organizational cultures and their impact on EAPs expand beyond the relationships between these two groups (for the complexity of organizational cultures see Frost, Moore, Louis, Lundberg & Martin, 1985). As well, with time, all EAPs are bound to develop an image reinforced by horror stories or glorious tales. If we want to increase the number of the latter and reduce the former, we should take the collection of these stories as a central activity of evaluation research. Sometimes, as in the case of many of the examples in this article, there can be nothing done to correct such distorted images without transforming the whole organizational culture. In other cases, a responsive EAP may lead to the desired change in such cultures. Whatever the case, as this study showed, there is need for qualitative information that supplements the knowledge gained through the use of quantitative methods.

IV. CONCLUDING REMARKS

The study of role perceptions can provide cost effective usable knowledge for EAPs, especially in their developmental stages. The listing of relevant tasks, which is by itself a useful evaluation exercise, is not a complicated process. This list can be also easily revised in order to find out the response to new developments or to test new ideas in a comparative sense. The focus on actual and desired role perceptions induces thinking about EAPs by both providers and users. Respondents' suggestions of additional tasks may also originate innovations and alterations of current operations.

Supplementing the narrowly focused data about role perceptions with information about the culture in which the EAP is imbedded expands knowledge beyond the boundaries created by tightly constructed quantitative instruments. As this study showed, the rationale for subsequent qualitative exploration of organizational cultures can come from the findings about role perceptions. Major gaps between the perception of different groups, either regarding the actual or desired role for EAPs' workers (or both), can be detrimental to the utilization of these programs. Sometimes, these differences suggest there is a need to improve the communication between the EAP and its users, or potential users. In other cases, perception gaps, or distorted perceptions about EAPs, cannot be addressed without gaining the trust and cooperation of key groups, and/or leaders. It is my opinion that the vitality of EAPs depends on understanding the organizational culture within which these groups operate and the ability to provide programs in a way which does not alienate the creators of this culture—and from my own experience, qualitative methodology provided me with more insight into thoroughly understanding and exploring this issue. Try it, you may like it!

REFERENCES

Atherton, C. R., Mitchell, S. T. & Schein, E. B. (1971A). Locating points for intervention. *Social Casework*, *52*, 131-140.

Atherton, C. R., Mitchell, S. T. & Schein, E. B. (1971B). Using points for intervention. *Social Casework*, *52*, 223-233.

The book of professions and occupations in Israel (Vol. 1) (1968). Jerusalem, The Institute for the Improvement of Labour and Productivity. (Hebrew).

Edwards, R. C. (1979). *Contested terrains: The transformation of the workplace in the 20th century*. New York: Basic.

Frost, P. J., Moore, L. F., Louis, M. R., Lundberg, C. C. & Martin, J. (1985). *Organizational Culture*. Beverly Hills: Sage.

Googins, B. (1975). Employee assistance programs. *Social Work*, *20*, 464-467.

Jackson, S. E. & Schuler, R. S. (1985). A meta-analysis and conceptual critique of research on role ambiguity and role conflict in work settings. *Organizational Behavior and Human Decision Processes*, *36*, 16-78.

Katz, D. & Kahn, R. L. (1978). *The social psychology of organizations* (2nd ed.). New York: John Wiley & Sons.

Knott, T. D. (1986). The distinctive uses of evaluation and research: A guide for the occupational health care movement. *Employee Assistance Quarterly*, *1*(4), 43-51.

Lincoln, Y. S. & Guba, E. Y. (1985). *Naturalistic inquiry*. Beverly Hills: Sage.

Lindblom, C. E. & Cohen, D. K. (1979). *Usable knowledge: Social science and social problem solving*. New Haven, CT: Yale University Press.

Rossi, P. H. & Freeman, H. E. (1985). *Evaluation: A systematic approach* (3rd ed.). Beverly Hills: Sage.

Steidinger, J. (1986). The current state of evaluation practices in employee assistance programs, San Francisco. *Employee Assistance Quarterly*, *1*(4), 51-65.

Task analysis inventories: A method for collecting job information (1973). U.S. Department of Labor, Manpower Administration.

Teram, E. (1977). *Actual and desired role perception of organizational social workers in Israel*. Unpublished master's thesis, Tel-Aviv University, Tel-Aviv (Hebrew).

EAP Benefit and Cost Structure Analysis: A Suggested Estimation Method

Hide Yamatani

SUMMARY. This presentation is a review of basic estimation methods geared for assessment of service benefit and cost structure of employee assistance programs (EAPs). The methodologies specify how various benefit and cost items can be organized and measured in dollar figures in order to translate effects of the EAP and operating cost distribution patterns. Based on the calculations, EAPs may assess cost saving patterns and avoid becoming a financial liability to the company. The estimation of benefit/cost ratios can be utilized for establishing program accountability and planning purposes. The methodologies presented in this chapter are at an introductory level. They are geared for EAP personnel and social work students interested in EAPs who have minimal familiarity with cost and benefit structure analysis.

Social programs in community settings tend to be evaluated by professionals with educational credentials and often direct work experience in the field of social work including consultants from schools of social work, program staff evaluators, and administrative agencies (Tripodi, 1983). However, based on the author's experience in working with business organizations, the merit of industrial social work programs may be more appropriately judged by experts with educational credentials and job experiences in fields other than social work; particularly individuals with business and educational

---

Hide Yamatani, PhD, is Associate Professor, and Director of Data Management Systems, School of Social Work, University of Pittsburgh, 2201 Cathedral of Learning, Pittsburgh, PA 15260.

backgrounds and administrative experiences in areas such as personnel management, corporate finance/planning, operations research, product promotion, and marketing. Additionally, social service programs in industrial settings tended to be judged by three major groups: (1) service clients (e.g., employees with personal problems, customers in need of assistance, and corporate policymakers); (2) social service workers themselves who are directly familiar with the service needs of various worker clients and others associated with the company; and (3) administrators devoted to measuring accountability of the industrial social work program (Yamatani, 1987). Although a comprehensive program evaluation requires involvement of all three groups, the so called "bottom line merit" tends to be established more directly by the latter group of corporate administrators.

Consequently, in addition to knowing how to deliver social services to the problemed workers, clients and other individuals associated with the corporate environment, industrial social workers should be familiar with basic administration and management theories and methods pertinent to business and industrial environments. The viability and strength of an employee assistance program (EAP) could be determined more directly by the industrial social workers who are capable of integrating social work with business concepts. Overdependence on corporate experts may result in an underestimation of the merit of the EAP due to their unfamiliarity with social work concepts and theories and scope of the benefits associated with the service system.

EAP workers, for example, should be knowledgeable of how to examine the cost and benefit structure of their service system. They should be able to exchange ideas with personnel managers, corporate planners and administrators, describe their program performance in reference to business concepts and theories, and suggest ideas related to future planning or reorganization of EAP based on benefit/cost assessments translated into dollar figures. However, based on a review of major social work journals (*Social Work, Journal of Council of Social Work Education, Social Work Research and Abstracts, Social Service Review, and Social Service*

Research), during the past 10 years, only few articles had incorporated business concepts and theories in the evaluation of social service programs in business and industrial settings.[1]

Therefore, this presentation is a review of basic estimation methods geared for assessment of program benefits and cost structures. The methodologies specify how various benefit and cost items can be organized and measured in dollar figures in order to translate effects of the EAP and operating cost distribution patterns. Based on the two major estimations, the benefit/cost ratio can also be calculated for assessment and planning purposes. Therefore, familiarity with basic benefit and cost structure analysis should help enhance the professional relationship between EAP and corporate administrators, avoid unwarranted underestimation of the utility of EAPs, strengthen program capability, and significantly increase the viability of the company.

It should be noted that the methodologies presented in this chapter are at an introductory level. They are geared for EAP personnel and social work students interested in EAPs who have minimal familiarity with cost and benefit structure analysis. Although most parts of this presentation utilized mathematics, the figures used are basic and relatively simple. A more advanced form of cost analysis, which employs macroeconomics, accounting, and statistical methods, is available for those interested in advanced methodologies.

ESTIMATION OF BENEFITS ATTRIBUTABLE TO EAPs

The total benefits attributable to EAPs can be divided into two major categories: (1) tangible; and (2) intangible benefits (Dunn, 1981). The tangible benefit is represented by measurable (estimatable) effects of the EAP directly related to its program objectives, e.g., savings effected by the EAP as a result of changes in the work behavior of the employee or increased sales due to customer satisfaction. The intangible benefits include positive changes effected by an EAP which are indirectly related to EAP objectives and often too difficult to translate into dollar figures. For example, the EAP may have improved quality of community living by helping the company to stay competitive and remain a successful business organization. Further, a lower unemployment rate due to successful business organizations, for example, may have lowered rates of domestic violence and crime, and improved education, health and transportation services in the community. In this presentation, however, the benefit concept will be limited to the estimation of savings directly attributable to EAP due to changes in the work behavior of the program clients. Specifically, the following three major areas will be addressed: (a) rate of absenteeism; (b) work performance; and (c) savings in health insurance cost reduction.

Reduction of Absenteeism and Cost Saving

EAP clients could be observed in regard to a change in the extent of absenteeism pre- and post-EAP intervention (Starr & Byram, 1985). Although there are no formulae available (based on the author's review of literature) for the assignment of length for pre- and post-periods, the suggested criteria for measuring change may be based on a 3 to 12 month pre-EAP intervention period compared against a 3 to 12 month period subsequent to the EAP intervention. The selection of the length of study period may vary with the type and seriousness of the problem as well as the individual's behavioral pattern. For example, the suicidal death of an elderly parent and a worker's drug addiction may have a significantly different "crisis" period and a different effect among different types of individuals. Thus, there is no single formula that will provide an optimal length of measurement period applicable to all of the EAP clients.

The estimated savings to the company due to the reduction in absenteeism is typically calculated based on the number of days of reduction in absenteeism multiplied by the workers' daily cost of wage and fringe benefits (Spicer, Owen & Levine, 1983). The author suggests, however, to use the *net* number of days of reduction in absenteeism multiplied by the workers' daily cost of wage and fringe benefits. The net number of days of reduction in absenteeism could be derived by subtracting the average number of reduction days in absenteeism of non-EAP client workers from the EAP client workers. This calculation allows a general adjustment for factors unrelated to the EAP but may have had a direct association with a change in absenteeism of the entire work force (e.g., a new work incentive program, change in administrative or supervisory personnel, pay increase or reduction, union sponsored strike, etc.). Without such adjustment, the absenteeism rate for the EAP client workers may be: (1) overestimated in cases involving company wide positive changes; or (2) underestimated in cases involving increased absenteeism rate due to factors unrelated to EAP intervention during the study period. The accuracy of the calculation should increase as the workers' absenteeism rate is adjusted individually among company locations, departments, and divisions instead of relying on a company wide absenteeism rate.

Thus, if the average reduction in absenteeism was 10 and 3 days during the selected study period among EAP and non-EAP clients, respectively, the average net reduction in absenteeism among EAP client workers would be equal to 7 days. Additionally, if the EAP workers' average wage and fringe benefits equalled $210 per day, the average saving per EAP clients is equal to 7 times $210 or a total of $1,470. Consequently, if the total number of EAP clients is 125, the total savings is equal to 125 times average saving ($1,470) or equal to $183,750.

The final results should indicate that the magnitude of the saving is positively associated with the number of EAP clients, the extent of reduction in absenteeism, and workers' salary and fringe benefits. Additionally, as suggested earlier for deriving a net absenteeism rate, the estimation accuracy may be improved if the workers' salary and fringe benefits could be calculated individually among company locations, departments, and divisions and then aggregated in order to derive the final total savings.

Savings Due to Change in Job Performance

The savings due to changes in work performance may be measured by incorporating a performance rating produced by the employer organization. Should such a job performance rating be unavailable or unreliable, the EAP should conduct its own observation. As suggested previously, the job performance rating should be measured in reference to the individual's performance level prior to the service intervention period and compared against the performance after the intervention is completed. To conduct such measurement, the author suggests using two major groups for information solicitation: (1) immediate supervisor(s); and (2) the individual workers themselves. Information from both groups of individuals may be necessary for obtaining accurate data and for establishing cross-validation of the derived ratings. If there are significant variations among the ratings, the EAP may be forced to reinvestigate such cases. Otherwise, the mean or median of the ratings can be utilized as the final figure representing the change in performance ratings.

It is possible that the workers may be individually observed in order to measure the extent of change in job performance (Shain, 1980). If a company already has developed such a measurement system, it is recommended that the EAP utilize it as the major measurement technique and as a source of cross-validation. Based on the author's experience in measuring worker performance, however, the individualized observation over the study period (in some cases as long as 2 years) tends to be timely and costly.

Similar to the previous section, the change in work performance should be measured in reference to the net percent change by adjusting it, by subtracting the value of the percent change among non-EAP workers. The range of net job performance change should include negative to positive ratings with zero (0) indicating no change. The derived net change rating should then be multiplied with the number of days worked during the selected time period, times amount of his/her daily wage plus fringe benefits.

For example, if in an EAP client, workers on average improved work performance by 7% during the year compared to other non-EAP workers with an average of 2% improvement, the net job performance improvement is equal to 5%. Thus, if the total number of EAP clients was 125, the average number of work attendance was 205 days, and the average salary plus fringe benefits equalled $210, the total savings is equal to 125 times the average work performance improvement (5%) times the average number of work attendance days (205) times the average salary plus fringe benefits ($210) or equal to $269,062.50.

The selection of the worker's wage and benefits as the major criteria for assessing the monetary value of absenteeism and work performance is a relatively conservative method since it is based entirely on the cost of replacing or substituting the individual worker. Although the minimum utility of workers is equal to the total cost of the worker to the company, the actual utility may be much higher (Levine, 1985). In other words, if a company selects to hire an employee, say at $31,000 per year for salary plus fringe benefits, the company, by employing the worker, should earn the $31,000 plus an additional amount as net profit. Hence, the actual utility of the worker depends entirely on the net profit attributable to the employee. Thus, the value of the worker based on the total cost of the employee, necessarily depends on the assumption that workers are easily replaceable or readily substituted. Should such an assumption not apply (e.g., in the case of highly specialized workers or a company that depends on the creativity of the individual workers), the value of the worker may be calculated in reference to the actual utility of the worker based on the total cost of the employee plus the company's portion of the profit attributable to the employee. Obviously, loss of "hard to replace workers" means a greater financial deficit to the company than what was offered as the worker's salary plus fringe benefits.

Savings Associated with Health/Medical Insurance

Similar to the previous sections, the change in the use of health/medical care may be measured by observing the pre- and post-service intervention period for each client worker and noting the net change in the health/medical care cost for the company. Those using health/medical care include workers who utilized the company's benefit program, such as medical treatment, short-term disability, and worker's compensation due to job related accidents or physical/mental illnesses (Spicer, Owen & Levine, 1983). Although it tends to be a time-consuming task, the health/medical department in the company should be able to produce or assist in identifying the difference in the cost for each EAP client.

Additionally, the change in the annual total cost of health/medical care due to the general reduction of benefits utilization by the company work force should also be included in the estimation. Similar to the previous case, the cost saving must also be differentiated based on factors directly associated with the EAP verses other factors such as institution of a company-wide nonsmoking policy or physical exercise and weight reduction programs. Thus, as described above, the derived average reduction in health/medical care services among EAP clients must be adjusted by subtracting from it the average reduction among their counterpart workers.

For example, if the average reduction in health/medical services equalled \$4,375 and \$1,500 for EAP clients and non-EAP workers, respectively, the average net savings among EAP clients is equal to \$4,375 minus \$1,500 or \$2,875. The derived figure should then be multiplied to the total number of clients. Thus, if the total number of EAP clients is 125, the total savings in the health/medical care is equal to the average net saving times the number of EAP clients (125) or \$359,375.

Based on the above calculations, the grand total saving attributable to the EAP operation can be presented as follows:

Total Savings Due to EAP:

a. Absenteeism Reduction = \$183,750
b. Work Performance Improvement = \$269,062.50
c. Health/Medical Service Reduction = \$359,375
d. Grand Total Saving = (a + b + c) = \$812,187.50

The average cost savings per worker is equal to grand total saving (\$812,187.50) divided by the total number of clients served (125). Thus, based on the suggested strategy and these hypothetical figures, the average savings per worker during the selected study year is equal to \$6,497.50.

In contrast to the above calculation method, if the grand total savings can be partialed out in reference to those clients successfully terminated from the EAP and divided by the total number of those individuals, a much higher level of average savings should be derived for the selected sample. EAP staff, as well as their company administrators, may find such figures to be indicative of the extent of savings among successfully terminated worker clients as well as the maximum potential of the EAP service system.

It should be obvious that not all EAP benefits are measurable based on the suggested method. The positive changes in areas such as worker's self-esteem, motivation, confidence, and loyalty to the company management may strengthen the work environment with desirable effects on not only the individual worker but also on other employees and supervisors as well. Such beneficial effects are quite difficult to estimate in dollar figures. An employee with serious personal problems without access to EAP intervention may continue to escalate the cost to the company—over and beyond the average cost of the troubled employee fortunate enough to receive EAP intervention. As discussed earlier, there is no perfectly accurate calculation method for deriving the cost and savings effected by EAP—methods that are reasonable in their requirements of resources and staff time needed to conduct the assessment. The suggested estimation method should, however, generate helpful findings regarding the EAPs worth.

COST STRUCTURE ANALYSIS

Cost element structuring allows an assessment of cost distribution patterns associated with the implementation of an EAP program. Based on this method, the total direct costs incurred by a program should be categorized into two major groups: (a) fixed costs; and (b) variable costs (Anderson, Sweeney & Williams, 1982).

Fixed Costs

The fixed cost is an expense item that will not change even if the number of persons served by the EAP increases or decreases during a program period (Anderson, Sweeney & Williams, 1982). The fixed cost items include such expenses as overhead; space rental; utility; insurance; new equipment; equipment maintenance contracts; a fixed budget for conferences/workshops, and travel; and administration costs over and above the EAP staff and director's salary. In a number of cases fixed costs may be published in the company on a scheduled basis by the corporate accounting or budget office for each department and sometimes at the level of divisions and offices.

If such a cost report is not readily available in the accounting or budget offices, the total costs of each item may be estimated by the EAP. The suggested calculation involves the selection of an appropriate denominator and the multiplication of the relative size of the EAP by the total costs of various line items. For example, if the total office space utilized by the EAP is X square foot and the total square foot of the company is Y square foot, the relative size of the EAP (based on a square footage as a denominator) is equal to X divided by Y. Additionally, if the total property insurance cost of the company is Z dollars, the relative cost of the EAP's property insurance cost is Z multiplied by the relative size (X/Y). If the administrative overhead is not available in reference to the EAP operation, the total cost of salary and fringe benefits expended during the selected year should be multiplied to the relative personnel expenditure of the EAP compared to the company's grand total expenditure for personnel (excluding total expenditure of administrative overhead). In this case, the personnel expenditure is the common denominator from which the administrative overhead for the selected program is derived.

It should be noted, however, that the cost calculations involve estimations based on what is believed to be the most reasonable denominator as a criteria. Thus, based on the suggested method, the fixed cost assessment tends to be, at best, a general estimation. However, even if the accounting or budget offices publish fixed cost distribution reports on a regular basis, EAP offices should also calculate it on their own (at least estimate it) for an important purpose of cross-validation. Without such validation efforts, EAPs may unfairly suffer from overestimated fixed cost expenditures without the knowledge of the program office.

Variable Costs

The variable costs are expenses related to the operation of the program (Anderson, Sweeney & Williams, 1982), such as staff training, staff salary and fringes, supplies and materials, and travel related directly to client service, and costs associated with the temporary removal of workers from work stations and offices in order to provide services. All of the cost items must be what the company had to expend during the selected program period. Thus, costs incurred by staff which were not reimbursed by the company (e.g., uncovered costs associated with the use of the staff's automobile, purchasing of office related equipment and materials, etc.) should not be included. It is expected that all of these cost items change positively with the number of clients—the higher the number of clients, the higher the total variable cost.

The variable cost calculation is often the most accurate account of the amount and rate of the program expenditure for the service implementation. It is also these budget items that are more readily available within the EAP. Thus, a number of studies may be carried out by just concentrating on the variable cost patterns among various components which comprise the EAP, such as its annual program objectives (as long as they are stated in a measurable form), and different service programs (e.g., prevention, delivering services to problemed workers, and follow-up services). Additionally, cost distribution can be calculated in reference to the type of clients served (e.g., workers suffering from alcohol and drug dependency, poor physical health, mental/emotional illness, marital problems, difficulties with family members, financial, and legal problems, etc.) in order to assess the extent of the match between the cost distribution and service needs as well as success rates.

Thus, hypothetically, if the fixed and variable costs were \$110,000 and \$160,000, respectively, the grand total cost of operating the EAP is equal to \$270,000. Additionally, if the total number of clients served equalled 125, the average variable cost would be equal to \$160,000 divided by 125 or \$1,280. Based on such estimations EAPs should be able to generate a table of EAP cost distribution in a following manner:

Total EAP Operational Cost:

a. Total fixed cost = \$110,000
b. Total variable cost = \$160,000
c. Grand total cost of operating EAP = (a + b) = \$270,000
d. Total number of clients served = 125
e. Average variable cost per client worker = (b/d) = \$1,280

As indicated above, the derived total variable cost can be used to calculate the average variable cost per worker by simply dividing the cost by total number of clients as indicated above. Based on the fixed cost, the relationship will be such that the number of clients are virtually unaffected and, therefore, the higher the number of clients, the lower the fixed cost per client worker. On the other hand, variable costs should associate positively with the number of clients. Thus, in general, increasing number of clients leads to higher variable costs, and vise versa.

BREAK-EVEN POINT ANALYSIS

Break-even point analysis is a balance between the total cost of the program operation and its total savings effected to the employer organization (Connor, 1982). Based on the derived costs (fixed and variable) and savings due to EAP, the program evaluation can be translated into specific dollar figures. The assessment of the cost and savings will generally be the benefit/cost ratio (Levin, 1985), and findings pertinent to EAP decisions regarding whether to further increase or decrease EAP variable costs in order to adjust client services and penetration rates. Additionally, the relationship pattern will allow the projection of the cost/benefit ratio based on selected variable cost level or number of workers served. The questions such as "given the EAP's operational cost, how many clients do we need to served in order to break even?" can be answered based on this assessment.

Benefit/Cost Ratio

Based on the above figures, the EAP's benefit/cost ratio can be calculated by dividing the grand total savings by the grand cost of the EAP operation:

Benefit/Cost Ratio = (Total Savings)/(Total EAP Operational Cost)

If the total savings is greater than the cost of the EAP operations, the result will be a figure greater than 1. On the other hand, if the derived figure is less than 1, the EAP is a financial liability to the company due to its higher cost of operation compared to its savings. Thus, based on the derived figures in the previous sections, the benefit/cost ratio is equal to grand total savings ($812,187.50) divided by the grand total operational cost of the EAP ($270,000) or equal to 3.0. The derived figure 3.0 could be interpreted as "there was $3 return to the company for each dollar expended for the EAP operation during the study period." It is expected, however, that the EAP will initially show figures less than 1 until the program is well-grounded in the company setting.

Break-Even Point

Based on the fixed and variable costs, and savings attributable to EAP, the break-even point analysis will generate the number of client workers required to use the program in order to avoid its becoming a financial burden to the company (Connor, 1982). The author suggests the consideration of two possible major assumptions under which this calculation would be completed: (1) break-even point analysis based on an assigned amount of variable cost; and (2) break-even point analysis based on a flexible amount of variable cost. In the first case, a company may have already allocated a given budget for the EAP and, thus, the program may select to expend all of the allocated budget. In the second case, the EAP is capable of adjusting the variable costs for the program operation. In such a case, the program evaluator may select to derive an answer based on no restrictions regarding the amount of variable cost.

Break-Even Point (with assigned variable cost)

By using the total EAP operational cost and the total savings per client worker, the minimum number of clients necessary for the EAP for the selected year can be calculated. Assuming that the derived variable cost is inflexible due to the budget allocation for a given fiscal year, the break-even point (assigned variable cost) is equal to the grand total cost of the EAP operation divided by the total savings per client. The derived figure will generate how may client workers will be needed to prevent the company from suffering a financial loss do to EAP operation. For example, based on the previously defined figures the break-even point calculation would be as follows:

Break-even point (number of clients needed) = (Grand Total Cost)/(Average Savings)
= (270,000)/(6,497.50)
= 41.55 (or approximately 42 clients)

Since the actual number of the clients needed is slightly over 41, the number of the clients needed should be the next whole number 42. Thus, based on the given cost and savings structure, the absolute minimum number of clients needed for the EAP for the year (based on the assumption that the allocated variable cost budget will be completely expended), is equal to 42 clients. Any additional clients beyond the number becomes revenue generating. The above relationship pattern can be shown by plotting the total fixed cost, total variable cost, and total savings as follows (see Figure 1).

The figure contains a vertical axis (called the Y axis) indicating the dollar amount and horizontal axis (called the X axis) indicating the number of EAP clients. The previously derived calculations can be graphed by, first, locating the total number of worker clients

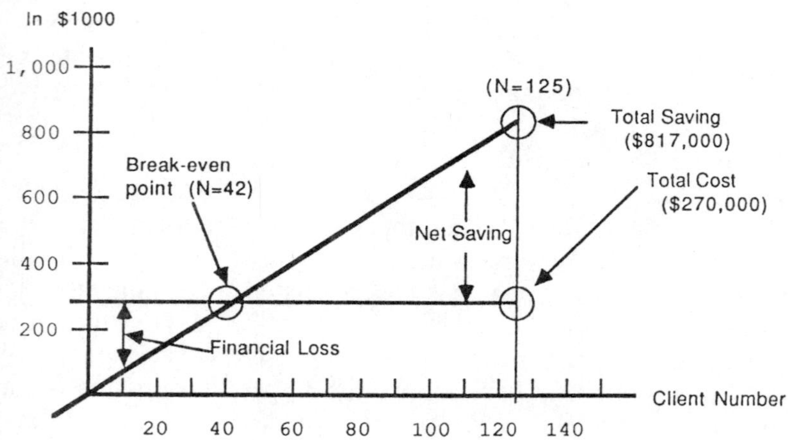

Figure 1: Break-even point based on the assumption that the allocated budget for variable cost will be completely expended.

(125) on the X axis and drawing a straight vertical line; second, plot two points – reflecting the total EAP operational cost ($270,000) and total savings attributable to EAP ($812,000). From the first point, a horizontal line should be drawn indicating the total EAP cost. A line indicating the amount of savings can be drawn from the second point to the corner of the graph (the point indicating zero values for both X and Y axis).

The location of the intersection between the two lines indicates the break-even point which reflects the necessary number of EAP clients (42) on the X axis. The net savings generated by the EAP is the area beyond the 42 on the X axis and between the savings and total cost lines (indicating increasing net savings as the number of client exceed past 42). In contrast, the area up to the 42 on the X axis and between the savings and total cost lines indicate the extent of financial loss attributable to the EAP operation.

Break-Even Point (with flexible variable cost)

Based on the assumption that the variable cost is under the complete control of the EAP administrator, there will be a new break-even point with a different number of client workers. The derived figure will generate not only the minimum number of client workers needed, but also the necessary minimum budget for the variable cost that insures against the EAP becoming a financial liability. The calculation method in this case requires the total fixed cost ($110,000) be divided by the difference between the average savings ($6,497.50) and average variable cost ($1,280) as follows:

Break-even point (number of clients needed) = (Grand Total Fixed Cost)/(Average Savings – Average Variable Cost)
= (110,000)/(6,497.50 – 1,280)
= (110,000)/(5,217.50)
= 21.08
= approximately 22 clients.

Based on the derived number of clients, the minimum total variable cost necessary for the EAP can be calculated by multiplying the derived number of clients (22) with the average variable cost ($1,280). Additionally, the derived minimum variable cost and the total fixed cost ($110,000) can be summed in order to calculate the minimum total budget necessary for operating the EAP.

Break-even point (minimum total variable cost) = (Minimum number of clients) × (Average Variable Cost)
= (22) × (1,280)
= $28,160;

thus,

The minimum total budget necessary for operating the EAP = Total Fixed Cost + Minimum Total Variable Cost
= 110,000 + 28,160
= $138,160.

Because the total budget must be equal to or less than the total savings attributable to EAP, the accuracy of the calculation can be quickly checked by multiplying the average savings attributable to the EAP ($6497.50) by the minimum number of clients needed (22) and comparing it against the derived total budget. Thus, ($6497.50 × 22) = $142,945 is slightly over the derived total budget of $138,160 (by $4,785). The slight overestimation is due to the rounding off of the minimum number of worker clients to the next higher whole number (from 21.08 to 22).

The above relationship pattern can be illustrated graphically in a similar manner as shown in Figure 1. In this case, however, the fixed cost will be the horizontal line instead of the total budget as in Figure 1 (Anderson, Sweeney & Williams, 1982). The total savings should be plotted as previously and a line should be drawn through the point equal to X = 0 and Y = 0. Additionally, a line should be drawn between the total cost and the point of X = 0 and Y = fixed cost (see Figure 2).

The intersection between the total savings and total budget lines indicate the break-even point. Based on the point, the number of worker clients is approximately 22 on the X axis. The area between the total cost and the fixed cost lines indicate the total variable cost. Thus, based on the graph, the relationship pattern is correctly presented – as the number of worker clients increase on the X axis, the variable cost also increases.

In either case (flexible or inflexible variable cost situations), an EAP may consider two major possibilities in order to generate the highest possible net savings: (1) lower the fixed and variable costs without changing the service quality or quantity; and (2) increase the average savings by improving the program success rate. In order to accomplish such objectives, the EAP managers may reduce the operational cost (e.g., by substituting technologically advanced equipment for variable cost factors) or by improving the efficiency of the personnel. For example, staff counsellors may be financially supported for attending workshop training and educational programs. The service quality and efficiency can also be increased by

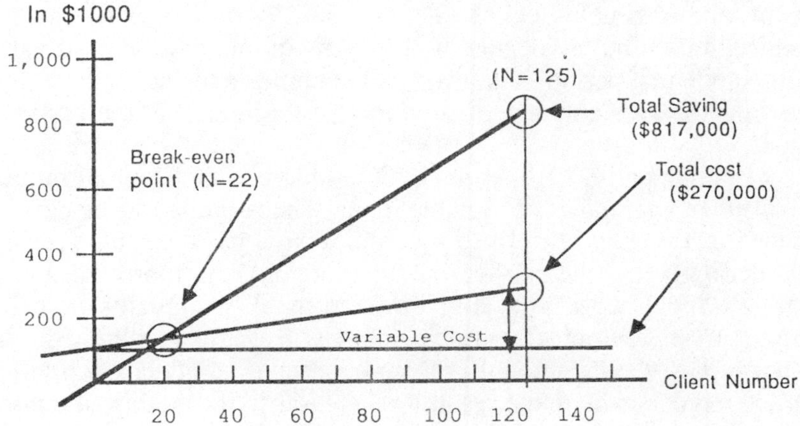

Figure 2: Break-even point with flexible variable cost.

conducting an accurate needs assessment among potential clients, and by improving the intervention effectiveness (Yamatani, 1987).

DISCUSSION

It should be noted that the above presentation on the break-even point analysis is based on the assumption that the relationship between variable cost and savings attributable to the EAP through intervention services is linear. A linear relationship implies that the association pattern between the two factors will be retained at a specific and constant rate through the range of values within the factors. Such an assumption tends to be suited for company settings with up to moderate size EAP. With large EAPs (perhaps with counsellors staff exceeding 30), a more precise measurement of the relationship pattern between the variable cost and savings attributable to an EAP can be conducted based on assumptions reflective of a curvilinear relationship pattern—without a constant rate continuing through the range of values between costs and savings (Thompson, 1985).

When units of variable and fixed inputs are progressively increased, for example, it could be expected that the quantity of program output rises rapidly at first, then more slowly, reaches a maximum, and begins to decline (Thompson, 1985). The exact change in program output associated with the use of one more unit of variable input per period is known in economic and business as the marginal service output (or called marginal product) of the variable input.

Mathematically, the marginal output curve is the slope of output function at each point of variable input. The formula for the curvilinear function can be derived by employing a basic calculus (using the derivative of the service output function). As more and more variable input is added to a given fixed input, eventually the marginal service output of variable input will begin to diminish. In other words, as the amount of a variable input is increased, a point will be reached where the resulting increases in the quality of output will get smaller and smaller. Imagine that the pattern of program outputs will be based on an EAP hiring an additional 3, 6, 9, 12, and 15 EAP counsellors. The rate of increase in the program output will more than likely get smaller and smaller at a certain point reflecting a curvilinear relationship pattern (see Figure 3).

Such a curvilinear relationship pattern is called the principal of diminishing marginal return (Thompson, 1985). As shown in Figure 3, the curvilinear relationship between variable cost and service output is increasing (i.e., increasing return to the variable input over this range). This means that the increases in output are more than proportional to the increase in variable input. Beginning at the point of diminishing marginal return (DMR)—the inflection point at which possibilities for increasing return have been exhausted and although the rate of service output is *still increasing* but at a slower rate compared to the previous level of variable input.

At a higher variable input unit, the average service output (based on the total output divided by total variable input) also increases and then begins to decline, resembling the DMR pattern. This inflection point is called point of diminishing average return. Finally, at approximately 7 units of variable input, the service output is at the peak and any increase in variable input will lead to a diminishing total return. Thus, should more than 7 units of variable input be used in conjunction with the fixed input, the quantity of service output would actually fall.

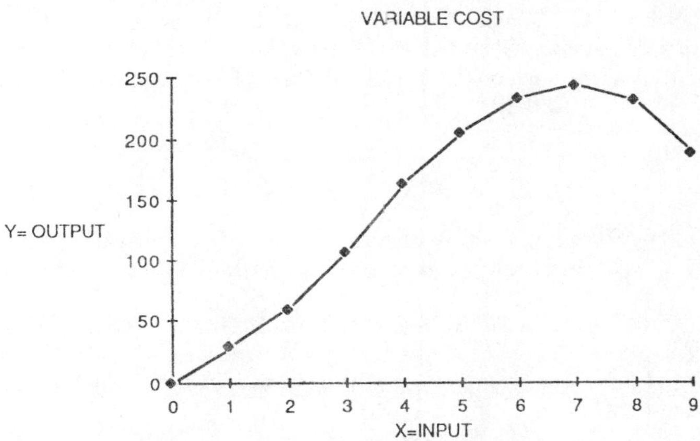

Figure 3: Curvilinear relationship pattern between variable cost and program output (EAP cost savings).

Thus, although the optimal combination of fixed and variable cost resources insures the lowest operating cost of an EAP for a given (previously determined) level of service units and quality to be delivered to the company workers, calculation results based on a linear assumption as discussed should only be taken as a useful estimate for up to moderate sized EAPs.

NOTES

1. See the following social work related journals: *Social Work*. New York: National Association of Social Workers, *Journal of Council of Social Work Education*. Washington DC: Council on Social Work Education; *Social Work Research and Abstracts*. New York: National Association of Social Workers; *Social Service Review*. Chicago: The School of Social Service Administration; and *Journal of Social Service Research*. New York: The Haworth Press, Inc. There are, however, a number of contributory articles related to topics other than savings and cost estimations of EAPs. For example, Martin Jr. G. (1985). "Union Social Services and Women's Work," *Social Service Review* 59 (2): 62-74; Akabas, S. (1983). "Industrial Social Work: Influencing the System at the Work Place," M. Dinerman (Ed.), *Social Work in a Turbulent World*. Silver Spring, MD: National Association of Social Workers, 131-141; Kurzman, P. & Akabas, S. (1981). "Industrial Social Work as an Arena for Practice," *Social Work* 26 (1): 52-60; Ozawa, M. (1980). "Development of Social Services in Industry: Why and How?" *Social Work* 25 (6): 464-470; Popple, P. (1981). "Social Work Practice in Business and Industry, 1875-1930," *Social Service Review* 55 (June 1981): 257-269; and Bradley Googins & Joline Godfrey, "The Evolution of Occupational Social Work," *Social Work* 30 (5): 396-402; Ozawa, M. (1985). "Economics of Occupational Social Work," *Social Work* 30 (5) 442-445; and Skidmore, R., Balsam, D. & Jones, O. (1974). "Social Work Practice in Industry," *Social Work* 19 (3): 280-287.

REFERENCES

Anderson, D., Sweeney, D. & Williams, T. (1982). *Management Science: Quantitative Approaches to Decision Making*. St. Paul, MN: West Publishing Company.

Connor, P. (1982). *Dimensions in Management*. Boston: Houghton Mifflin Company.

Dunn, W. (1981). *Public Policy Analysis: An Introduction*. Englewood Cliffs, NJ: Prentice-Hall, Inc.

Levin, H. (1985). *Cost-Effectiveness: A Primer*. Beverly Hills: Sage Publications.

Shain, M. (1980). *Employee Assistance Programs*. Lexington, MA: Lexington Books.

Spicer, J., Owen, P. & Levine, D. (1983). *Evaluating Employee Assistance Programs: Source Book for Administrator and Counselor*. New York: Hazelden Foundation.

Starr, A. & Byram, G. (1985). Cost/benefit analysis for employee assistance programs. *Personnel Administrator* 30 (8), 55-58.

Thompson, Jr. A. (1985). *Economics of the Firm: Theory and Practice*. Englewood Cliffs, NJ: Prentice-Hall, Inc.

Tripodi, T. (1983). *Evaluative Research for Social Workers*. Englewood Cliffs, NJ: Prentice-Hall, Inc.

Yamatani, H. (1987). "Client Assessment in Industrial Setting: A Cross-Sectional Method." *Social Work* 32 (5), Pages to be assigned.

A Framework for Evaluating Employee Assistance Programs

N. Joseph Cayer
Ronald W. Perry

SUMMARY. Particularly in the past decade, Employee Assistance Programs (EAPs) have become an integral part of the management of public sector and private sector organizations. The evolution of EAPs is briefly traced and the claims of advocates regarding their positive effects are documented. It is also emphasized that, in spite of their ubiquity, little attention has been given to devising strategies for evaluating the success or failure of EAPs. A framework is developed to guide comprehensive evaluations of such programs. A framework is developed to guide comprehensive evaluations of such programs. The framework stresses five aspects of EAP performance: effort, program performance (outcome evaluation), adequacy of performance, efficiency, and process evaluation.

Employee Assistance Programs (EAP) are crucial elements of management in contemporary society. EAPs are designed to help employees whose job performance is affected by their personal problems. Estimates of the number of employees who have problems affecting their work range widely, although figures between 5 and 20% seem to be most common. The difficulty in accurately estimating the number stems, in part, from the fact that there is no clear definition or standard by which the problem can be measured. Similarly, there are no clear standards by which the effectiveness of EAPs can be assessed. As a result, the purpose of this paper is to elaborate a framework for assessing the effectiveness of EAPs.

N. Joseph Cayer, PhD, and Ronald W. Perry, PhD, are both affiliated with the School of Public Affairs, Arizona State University, Tempe, AZ 85287.

BACKGROUND

Employee Assistance Programs are an extension of alcohol abuse programs which many industries and government jurisdictions set up years ago. In recent years, "substance abuse" has replaced "alcohol abuse" as a more descriptive term for people who are impaired by the use of drugs, including alcohol. Drugs of all kinds have become a major issue in the United States, and numerous proposals for dealing with the problems are extant. Employee Assistance Programs represent one alternative for dealing with the problem in the work setting.

While EAPs often are associated with substance abuse problems, they also encompass much more. In recent years, they have evolved to deal with all types of personal problems individuals have which may affect performance, and many EAPs include service for the whole family of the employee. Problems other than substance abuse which are covered by some EAPs include marital problems, emotional distress, job stress, and sexual dysfunction and anxiety. In short, as long as the problem affects job performance, it may be included in the EAP.

EAPs have emerged as part of "good management" and out of the humanizing of the workplace which is a hallmark of the growth of organization theory in the 1960s and 1970s (Denhardt, 1984; Stewart & Garson, 1983; Harmon & Mayer, 1986). EAPs are justified as good management because they are expected to save money and increase organizational productivity. Because of the numbers of employees estimated to have personal problems which affect work performance, estimates of the cost to industry have been immense as well. In 1984, for example, it was claimed that employers incurred nearly $200 billion in costs associated with personal problems related to work performance (Myers, 1984). Avoidance of those costs through proactive programs to help individual employees before they have to be disciplined is generally touted as good management.

Humanizing of the workplace began with the landmark Hawthorne Studies of the 1920s and the development of Human Relations in management. Human Relations focused on the psychological well-being of employees and used social group norms and support to complement formal management. Because they became more manipulative in practice, many employees saw through many Human Relations' efforts. During the 1960s and 1970s, however, individual rights and the personal growth of individuals became important elements of our political and social culture. Employee rights and treating employees with dignity were extensions of those concerns. Organizational humanism focuses on the compatibility of the individual and the organization, specifically the work organization (Argyris 1973a, 1973b; McGregor, 1960). The individual is viewed as a whole person who has needs and a life outside the organization. Thus, it is impossible for the individual to function inside the work organization with no reference to his/her life outside. Training programs dealing with the human side of management burgeoned during the late 1960s and early 1970s. Managers became aware of the human beings who were their employees and were encouraged to take interest in the whole person. Employee Assistance Programs are consistent with such a perspective. They are much easier to develop in an atmosphere in which the organization is sensitive to the employee as a complex human being.

While there has been phenomenal growth in Employee Assistance Programs, research on them has been extremely limited. Most research has focused on private sector EAPs and is primarily descriptive or promotional without much rigor in evaluation methodology or design. In the public sector, there is even less written on EAPs, and almost no evaluation materials are available.

Employee Assistance Programs are found at all levels of government. The federal government encourages EAPs through efforts of the Office of Personnel Management. Alcoholism programs are required by *Public Law 91-616*, and employees must have the opportunity for rehabilitation before they can be terminated for alcoholism related job performance deficiencies. While the law applies only to alcoholism, its spirit carries over into development of general EAPs.

State and local levels also have a variety of programs although they are not as extensive as those at the national level (Beyer & Trice, 1978; Johnson, 1985; Kemp, 1985). While programs are established, they do not seem to be evaluated, at least as indicated by published research. In periods of retrenchment, it would seem natural that programs which cannot be demonstrated to have tangible benefits would be very vulnerable to cuts. Evaluation of EAPs provides a basis on which to make rational decisions about their viability. So far, people suggest that they save money by using EAPs, but there is no solid research to support the effectiveness of them (Myers, 1984). Thus, we propose a model for evaluating EAPs.

ISSUES IN EVALUATING EAPs

There are several possible approaches to evaluating Employee Assistance Programs depending upon the type of assessment desired. One tactic is to evaluate an organization's need for an EAP (cf. Burgrabbe & Swift, 1984). Another approach involves evaluating service vendors associated with an existing EAP (cf. Chiabotta, 1985). Still another perspective entails evaluating an EAP as a functioning program associated with a host organization (Rostain et al., 1980). Each evaluation approach answers specific questions about the need for or operation of EAPs. Our specific concern is with the growth of EAPs in the public sector. In this context, we expect that decisions to establish or expand EAPs will be based at least in part upon data regarding the performance of EAPs. The conception of performance that is important here encompasses a broad view of the EAP. How does an EAP fit into the host organization? Do EAPs realize their goals? Are such plans cost-effective? We acknowledge these different approaches to evaluation, but will concentrate on the more general task of creating a framework for the comprehensive evaluation of an Employee Assistance Program.

At this point, it is useful to briefly discuss two primary assumptions about EAPs and the structural characteristics of the plans that underly the development of our evaluation model. The first assumption is that EAPs should *not* be conceptualized as a special fringe benefit under the rubric of employee compensation (Hollmann, 1981:40). Instead, one should deal with EAPs in terms of human resources management and fit an Employee Assistance Program into the matrix of other personnel services. For example, one means of identifying employees who need assistance might be the performance appraisal system, since EAPs typically cite improved performance as an objective. Also, one might find that a particular work unit sends many employees to an EAP "stress reduction/coping" treatment program. This information could be used to either inform the selection process to include stress tolerance in screening, or to begin a process of job redesign in an effort to minimize structural sources of stress. This example shows the potential value of connecting EAPs with performance appraisal, selection, and job design. A consequence of our assumption that EAPs should be integrated into the personnel process is that our evaluation model demands attention to the fit of the EAP into the organization's management structure.

One structural characteristic of EAPs that has implications for evaluation is that they provide a variety of specific (but distinct) services. A 1980 survey of ASPA member organizations showed that more than 90% of those with EAPs offered alcohol rehabilitation, drug abuse counseling, emotional counseling, and family/marital counseling (Ford & McLaughlin, 1981:32). Other programs commonly offered as employee assistance include financial, legal, and career counseling. The EAP then, may be represented both as an office in the organization with an employee assistance function *and* as a collection of diverse services some of which may be rendered by organizational staff and some by outside vendors.

From an evaluation standpoint, both of these characterizations are important. A primary justification offered for EAPs is that they improve employee performance and consequently improve organizational productivity. The specific services are aimed at treating individual's problems and thereby affecting (presumably improving) job performance. A comprehensive evaluation must, therefore, examine each type of service rendered to determine whether treatment objectives are met. In the aggregate, all of these services combine to form the Employee Assistance Program which, in itself, has the objective of improving organizational productivity. Consequently, an evaluation model should address changes in aggregate measures of productivity as well. Our evaluation framework will reflect this implicit distinction between the EAP and the services offered.

The two assumptions discussed above serve to clarify our definition of the phenomenon to be evaluated. We will treat employee assistance as a process that is ongoing within the organization and that is integrated with other types of personnel services. We also acknowledge that EAPs involve an organizational component (at a minimum, an assessment office attached to personnel department). Furthermore, they may also entail an external component or components in the form of vendors who may control one or more of the specific treatment services offered by the EAP. These assumptions begin to set minimum evaluative performance expectations for the EAP vis-à-vis the operations of the host organization. They also alert the evaluator to the importance of multiple audiences in understanding the performance of EAPs. These audiences include management, vendors, treated employees, and untreated employees. The following section builds upon these assumptions and lays out the rudiments of a comprehensive evaluation model for EAPs.

A COMPREHENSIVE EVALUATION FRAMEWORK

From a policy research standpoint, evaluation is often conceived as primarily outcome or summative evaluation—designed to determine if a program meets its goals. Weiss (1972) has pointed out that this is a deceptively simple conception of the evaluation. The deception stems from the implication that goals and outcomes may be specified in a straightforward manner. Indeed, to specify the goals of a program one must appreciate its full context and operation; as some important goals may be implicit, unstated, or not subscribed to by the operators of a given program. In addition, a given program may produce a variety of "outcomes" along a variety of dimensions well beyond the objectives that could be derived from an organizational or legislative goal-type statement.

The issues mentioned above commonly arise in the context of policy-related evaluations where a single organization is charged with the delivery of a service or the dissemination of a message. Even here, one must acknowledge the importance of process or formative evaluation as a means of providing information to help the evaluator understand the outcome evaluation. Process evaluation focuses upon how the program functions—not "whether" goals are met but "what" is done to attempt to meet them. As part of process, the evaluator must document what organizational and procedural devices we create to achieve stated objectives. Thus, process evaluation answers the question of "why" relative to outcome evaluation – e.g., if the program achieved its objectives, our process evaluation supplies clues regarding why that occurred.

Put another way, process evaluation supplies information on the context in which a program operates. We wish to argue that understanding "process" is critical to the understanding of the performance of programs associated with public or private sector organizations. In connection with EAPs, the context in which the program operates is crucial to determining the success of its operation. In fact, our conception of EAPs as a component of the personnel process emphasizes that context may vary and principles of evaluation – what to identify as objectives and how to define performance – depend upon this organizational context. For example, a completely "in-house" EAP would be evaluated largely in terms of intraorganizational relations, while an EAP involving vendors adds an interorganizational dimension to the evaluation. Thus, it is important that a comprehensive evaluation framework contain elements of both process and outcome evaluation.

This approach raises the question of exactly what constitutes an evaluation *framework*. In general research terms, frameworks are often seen as precursors to more formal models that constitute symbolic constructions designed to represent structures or processes which prevail in the "real" world (Kaplan, 1964:256). An evaluation framework, then, may be seen as the specification of the foci and purposes of evaluation. In terms of this paper, an evaluation framework must identify the standards in terms of which performance will be assessed, define the organizational dimensions of the program, specify the units of analysis, and specify the populations from which evaluative information should be collected.

Many of these issues have already been discussed or at least alluded to in this paper. Our comprehensive framework will take the form of an elaboration of performance standards. Then, under each standard we will identify both specific research questions for evaluation and particular issues that might arise in connection with an assessment. In keeping with traditional evaluation practice, and with our concern about the importance of including process dimensions for evaluation, we shall build an evaluation framework around five performance standards: Effort, Program Performance (outcome evaluation), Adequacy of Performance, Efficiency, and Process.

Effort

In general, evaluations of program effort concentrate upon assessing the input or energy expended in goal-connected activity (Suchman, 1967:61). One is not concerned with goal achievement here; only the level of effort and commitment associated with the program. Ultimately, of course, the results of the "effort" evaluation should be connected to program performance especially when evaluators diagnose particular levels of performance. The phase of effort evaluation itself, however, is aimed only at documenting expenditures of energy and resources to be used as baseline data for other interpretation.

With regard to evaluating EAPs, the routine part of effort evaluation involves the production of a resources expenditure chart. Relative to internal organizational resources, this involves specification of the number and levels (rank) of personnel involved in managing the EAP, estimates of levels of effort (personnel hours per week), equipment and space assigned for program use, and budget. If vendors are involved in particular treatment services, one would construct similar charts for each vendor. In dealing with vendors, however, the evaluative purpose of resource charting is to insure that adequate resources are provided for services relative to the price of service.

Our assumptions about the role of EAPs in the personnel process demand that as part of effort evaluation one also assess the management priority of such programs. Two elements should be considered here. First, one should examine management's commitment to the EAP as a personnel tool. This entails examining, perhaps through a series of interviews or a self-administered questionnaire, attitudes of managers toward the EAP, their estimate of its value as a mechanism for dealing with problem employees, and the extent to which they are involved in reviews of the EAP. Second, it is necessary to examine the organizational arrangements associated with the EAP. This involves determining the location of the EAP: is it an office, a branch of the personnel department, a branch of a compensation office, or perhaps wholely handled by external vendors? Also, one should document the extent to which the EAP is integrated into the larger matrix of human resources management. The objective of all these analyses is to determine the overall resources and effort that are devoted to employee assistance.

EAP Performance

This phase of the comprehensive evaluation deals with what is traditionally called output or summative evaluation: determining if the programs under review accomplish their goals (Rossi & Freeman, 1982:20). Traditional research designs for assessing program performance rely heavily upon experimental or quasiexperimental designs of a before-after nature (Campbell & Stanley, 1966:20). While this type of design remains appropriate, our evaluative interests in EAPs require that more than one type of assessment be made.

EAPs are actually a collection of what could be called employee "treatment" services. We are, therefore, interested in all of the individual programs that make up an EAP (e.g., legal counseling, substance abuse treatment, emotional counseling, and so on). The relevant unit of analysis is the individual and each individual is typically tied to a particular program. Of course in long-standing programs, the evaluator would want to look at the effects of one person being treated in multiple programs.

Two types of questions need to be asked about treated individuals. The first is: did the program work? Did the substance abuse program, for example, result in the employee becoming detoxed and learning positive coping behaviors? This question may be assessed using the traditional before-after control group designs one associates with evaluation. The second, and perhaps more important question, is: did the treated employee's work performance improve?

The almost universal claim regarding EAPs is that they are necessary to improve performance. There are many ways in which one might operationalize performance, but there seem to be at least three important dimensions of the concept insofar as EAPs are concerned. The first dimension is employee job performance. This might be measured by standard performance appraisal techniques. A second dimension relates to their acceptance and socialization of employees into the work group. Indicators of this dimension might include absenteeism, tardiness, grievances filed by employees, grievances filed against employees, work related accidents, and supervisor assessments of cooperativeness.

The third dimension of performance, as it is discussed in the EAP literature, involves a change in the unit of analysis and focuses upon organizational measures of performance. For evaluative purposes, organization refers to the units from which EAP treated employees come. In this sense, we are concerned with the collective performance of the work unit which is normally captured under the rubric of productivity. Indicators of this dimension could include aggregate absenteeism and tardiness, health care payments and insurance premiums, time spent in grievance and termination proceedings, turnover of experienced employees, aggregate production estimates, and recruiting and training costs. The indicators mentioned in connection with all three dimensions are intended to be suggestive rather than exhaustive. The important point is that one should choose at least some indicators from each of the three dimensions of performance.

In answering the question of whether the treated employees work performance changed after their experience with the EAP, we would focus upon the indicators listed under the first two dimensions of performance just discussed. Two types of comparisons are relevant: looking at differences between treated and untreated employees and at differences between pre- and posttreatment performance of treated employees.

The results of such analyses of individual performance should be aggregated by EAP service. Thus, the evaluator compiles information on the effectiveness of each service relative to treating individuals and with regard to the impact of the treatments themselves on subsequent employee performance.

The previous analyses all deal with the behavior of individuals and their experience and treatment in EAP service components (which may be in-house or vendor operated). We have pointed out earlier that employee assistance constitutes a personnel function and that consequently it is important to assess the aggregate performance of that function. With regard to outcome evaluation, this may be accomplished by looking at indicators of the third dimension of productivity discussed earlier. These aggregate measures are designed to examine the unit-wide or organization-wide performance of the EAP. One may pursue at least three tactics for making such evaluations.

First, in organizations where EAPs are new or relatively recent, comparisons on the productivity dimension may be made between periods before and after the EAP began to operate. Second, in organizations with longer standing EAPs, one might seek structurally similar organizations without EAPs for comparative purposes. Another option in this regard would be to compare productivity in organizational units served and not served by EAPs; this requires of course, a large organization.

Finally, one can assume that as an EAP operates over time and more employees are processed, productivity benefits should increase. (The appropriateness of this assumption depends upon the accuracy of EAP advocate's claims that the programs really increase productivity.) If this is true, then over a delimited period of time – a year perhaps – one should be able to track changes in the productivity indicators. This third type of design is based upon what psychologists call an "A-B-A" logic and is somewhat complicated to implement (cf. Bushell & Burgess, 1969:145).

Adequacy of EAP Performance

The concept of adequacy of performance is a relative matter. It has its roots in the needs assessment literature and refers to the ability of the program being evaluated to address the extent of the prevailing problem (cf. Burdge, 1983:191). Put another way, we are interested in the power of the EAP to deliver employee assistance relative to the total need for employee assistance in the organization.

Clearly, estimates of "total need" are difficult to acquire and sometimes may be somewhat arbitrary. Options for estimating total need include: (1) estimating need by examining the number of employees seeking assistance in an EAP operated in a comparable organization or unit; (2) estimating need by comparing the number of employees waiting to be served with the number actually being processed through an EAP; (3) estimating need for specific programs by using standard formulae, like – for example – those which exist for calculating aggregate levels of alcohol or substance abuse in organizations; or (4) taking a probability sample of all employees and asking for self-reports of "felt" needs for particular types of assistance.

Without regard to the precise logic used for estimating need, adequacy assessments involve comparing this need to the current levels of output of an EAP. The results of such evaluations may be used in making recommendations for expanding or reducing levels of effort in connection with specific employees assistance services.

Efficiency

The concept of efficiency is largely bound up in cost-benefit or cost-effectiveness analyses of EAPs (Thompson, 1980). This involves both value judgments and technical judgments. The value judgments focus upon the extent to which the benefits of a program justify the costs. While one may pursue a variety of "objective" techniques for assessing both cost and benefit, the ultimate balancing of one over the other relies both upon the availability of resources to sustain the cost and upon the perceived value of offering the service. Cost-benefit analyses may be achieved through a variety of standardized techniques (Rossi & Freeman, 1982:291).

Technical judgments are captured in the determination of whether there is a more efficient means of obtaining the observed results. Here interest focuses upon identifying alternative paths to the same level of output and characterizing each in terms of costs. These costs might be measured in terms of budget expended, treatment and administrative personnel time, employee work time lost, and levels of personnel involvement. Once again, the objective is to determine if structural or programmatic changes may be made in the EAP that would reduce costs but not seriously alter output. This type of evaluation draws heavily upon the concept of efficiency in the sense that it is used in operations research, where the goal is to determine an optimum course of action relative to decision-maker's objectives (Ackoff, 1956).

Process Evaluation

In large part, the purpose of process evaluation is to aid in interpreting other phases of the comprehensive evaluation (Weiss, 1972). Most process evaluations begin by creating a case flow chart. Such charts resemble decision trees or fault trees in that they specify all operations (decision and contact points) associated with selecting, evaluating, treating, and reintegrating employees. Process evaluations of EAPs should address at least four issues.

Attributes of the EAP

Here we are concerned with documenting particular aspects of EAP operation. An initial concern is with the paths through which employees come to be involved with the EAP. What are the common modes of selection—employee self-selection, supervisor nomination, assignment by performance category, etc.—and how many employees enter through each mechanism? This analysis also offers cues to differential use of EAP services and to constellations of treatment programs needed by certain types of employee problems.

Another attribute of the EAP which should be explicitly examined is the effect of employee participation in EAP services on the routine production of work units. There are several aspects of this problem. First, one should document the way in which employee participation is handled. Do employees obtain EAP treatment during work hours and if so, is work made up after regular hours? If an absence from the work group is required, is the employee granted personal leave and replaced or is work simply redistributed? The primary evaluative objective is to determine if unit productivity suffers as a function of EAP use.

In sophisticated evaluation designs, one might also want to examine the effect of EAP participation on morale in the work group. In this case, interest centers upon documenting hostilities or hardships that might prevail in the work group. Such analyses would demand either interviews or self-administered questionnaires for members of the work unit.

Two final attributes of EAP performance which demand attention are the length of time employees remain in treatment and chronic EAP use. The average time required to complete any particular

EAP service correlates with both the cost of the service and the work time lost by employees. Work time lost may also be a factor in the level of work unit disruption that stems from EAP participation. By documenting time involved, one can identify potential problems stemming from such commitments and potentially develop structural modifications to mitigate them. Chronic EAP use may not be a problem in itself, although it would tend to exacerbate the problem of time away from the work unit. Since EAP participation is usually contingent upon formal assessment of employee need conducted by trained personnel, it does not seem likely that chronic use would be a manifestation of employee malingering. On the other hand, chronic use may indicate that: (1) EAP treatment services produce transient effects; or (2) that the organization may require a mechanism for reviewing employees with serious problems for retention.

Differential Treatment Results

The evaluative goal here is with identifying the consequences of treatment results. For example, are some types of employees more or less likely to constitute treatment successes? The research tactic involves comparing treatment successes with treatment failures to determine if there are differences relative to sex, age, length of employment, type of work, mode of selection for treatment, specific treatment program, or some other employee attribute. It is also appropriate to determine if a work unit containing EAP treatment successes experiences any changes in productivity, morale, or use of the EAP.

Conditions of EAP Service Success

In this context, attention is focused upon determining if the timing, location, or treatment arrangements associated with a given EAP service is related to either the number of treatment successes or levels of employee participation. In the latter case, data would be generated that could be used for structuring services in such a way that employee participation is facilitated by maximizing personal convenience. Organizational goals could also be promoted by determining which service arrangements involved the lowest levels of work unit disruption, but maintained reasonable treatment success rates. In the former case, failure rates of different EAP treatment programs could be monitored to determine the need to possibly contract with new vendors or adopt different treatment modalities which might yield higher levels of treatment success.

Specification of Treatment Program Effects

In the case of EAPs, the evaluator is interested in a chain of effects. In the first place, one expects that each treatment program will have defined positive effects upon a specific employee problem; that is, alcoholism programs will reduce employee dependence on alcohol. We have given much attention to specifying and analyzing such effects in the preceding discussions. It is also assumed that EAP participation will have a secondary effect; namely that correction of the treated problem will also result in improved employee productivity. We have already elaborated a variety of performance (productivity) indicators which might be changed as a function of EAP participation.

As part of specifying program effects, it is important to document which performance indicators tend to change the most among employees who receive EAP services. If management-defined "key" performance indicators change, then it may be assumed that the EAP function is adequately served. On the other hand, if no change is observed or if the changes occur with indicators not deemed important by management, then it is necessary to reconsider and possibly reconfigure EAP services.

Another aspect of creating an inventory of effects associated with EAP participation is specifying the full range of effects. In comprehensive evaluations, it may be desirable to document effects other than those upon productivity. For example, EAP participation may enhance employee job satisfaction or motivation. Also, there may be identifiable impacts on the work unit from which treatment successes come; perhaps higher unit morale or productivity. In part, such analyses also begin to establish the extent to which treatment effects are primarily behavioral or attitudinal or both. In some cases, management may feel that a more positive attitude toward work is as useful an outcome as improvements in productivity.

Finally, in specifying program effects, it is important to document both the immediacy and duration of effects. If a particular service renders immediate improvements in the employee which increase with increased participation, the level of disruption to the work unit may be reduced. From the point of view of management, it would seem appropriate to select programs that produce high levels of immediacy. The issue of duration of effects raises the question of recidivism. If results are short-lived, with the employee problem quickly reappearing, it would seem necessary to again determine if the problem rests with the treatment program itself—necessitating a program or vendor change—or with the employee—which may demand a retention review.

CONCLUSION

This paper proposes a comprehensive framework within which one may evaluate Employee Assistance Programs. It is understood that in achieving a degree of comprehensiveness, we have developed a very broad evaluative strategy. The resources required to conduct an evaluation with this many components are admittedly substantial. Indeed, it is likely that none but the largest organizations could afford to undertake an evaluation of the scope proposed here. The framework is useful, however, in at least two senses. First, in its full form we contend that it captures the range of evaluative questions that might be asked with respect to any EAP. Second, it is explicit enough to be amenable to selective reductions in scope to accommodate organizations unable to commit the full complement of resources to evaluation. Thus, one could select components of the comprehensive framework for an evaluation effort of smaller scope. Furthermore, the selection can be made on an informed basis by drawing on the types of questions most important to management.

REFERENCES

Ackoff, R., The Development of Operations Research as a Science. *Operations Research*, 1956, 4, 265-295.

Argyris, C., Some Limits of Rational Man Organizational Theory. *Public Administration Review*, 1973a, 33, 253-267.

Argyris, C., Organization Man: Rational *and* Self-Actualizing. *Public Administration Review*, 1973b, 33, 354-357.

Beyer, J. & Trice, H., *Implementing Change*. New York: The Free Press, 1978.

Burdge, R., Community Needs Assessment and Techniques. pp 191-214 in Kurt Finsterbusch, Lynn Llewellyn & Charles Wolf, *Social Impact Assessment Methods*. Beverly Hills, CA: Sage, 1983.

Burgrabbe, J. & Swift, J., Evaluating Your EAP: A Practical Approach. *EAP Digest*, 1984, 4, 13-16.

Bushell, D. & Burgess, R., Characteristics of the Experimental Analysis. pp 145-174 in Robert Burgess & Donald Bushell, *Behavioral Sociology*. New York: Columbia University Press, 1969.

Campbell, D. & Stanley, J., *Experimental and Quasi-Experimental Designs for Research*. Chicago: Rand McNally, 1966.

Chiabotta, B., Evaluating EAP Vendors. *Personnel Administrator*, 1985, 30, 39-43.

Denhardt, R., *Theories of Public Organization*. Monterey, CA: Brooks/Cole, 1984.

Fitz-Gibbon, C. & Morris, L., *How to Design a Program Evaluation*. Beverly Hills, CA: Sage, 1978.

Ford, R. & McLaughlin, F., Employee Assistance Programs: A Descriptive Survey of ASPA Members. *Personnel Administrator*, 1981, 26, 29-35.

Harmon, M. & Mayer, R., *Organization Theory for Public Administration*. Boston: Little, Brown, 1985.

Hollman, R., Beyond Contemporary Employee Assistance Programs. *Personnel Administrator*, 1981, 26, 37-41.

Johnson, A., Municipal Employee Assistance Programs: Managing Troubled Employees. *Public Administration/Review*, 1985, 45, 383-390.

Kaplan, A., *The Conduct of Inquiry*. San Francisco: Chandler Publishing Company, 1964.

Kemp, D., State Employee Assistance Programs: Organization and Services. *Public Administration Review*, 1985, 45, 378-382.

McClellan, K., The Changing Nature of EAP Practice. *Personnel Administrator*, 1985, 30, 29-37.

McGregor, D., *The Human Side of Enterprise*. New York: McGraw-Hill, 1960.

Myers, D., Measuring EAP Cost Effectiveness: Results and Recommendations. *EAP Digest*, 1984, 4, 23-25.

Roman, P., Employee Assistance Programs in Australia and the United States. *Journal of Applied Behavioral Science*, 1983, 19, 367-379.

Rossi, P. & Freeman, H., *Evaluation: A Systematic Approach*. Beverly Hills, CA: Sage, 1982.

Rostain, H., Allan, P. & Rosenberg, S., New York City's Approach to Problem-Employee Counseling. *Personnel Journal*, 1980, 21, 305-325.

Sonnenstuhl, W. & O'Donnell, J., EAPs: The Why's and How's of Planning Them. *Personnel Administrator*, 1980, 25, 35-38.

Starr, A. & Byram, G., Cost/Benefit Analysis for Employee Assistance Programs. *Personnel Administrators*, 1985, 30, 55-62.

Stewart, D. & Garson, G., *Organizational Behavior and Public Management*. New York: Marcel Dekker, 1983.

Suchman, E., *Evaluative Research*. New York: Russell Sage Foundation, 1967.

Thompson, M., *Benefit-Cost Analysis for Program Evaluation*. Beverly Hills, CA: Sage, 1980.

Weiss, C., *Evaluation Research*. Englewood Cliffs, NJ: Prentice-Hall, 1972.

Assessing Employment Assistance Programs: Evaluation Typology and Models

Dong Soo Kim

SUMMARY. There is a great need for better understanding of an overall evaluation scheme of EAPs. The author presents four types or phases of EAP evaluation: (a) intervention planning; (b) program monitoring; (c) impact assessment; and (d) economic efficiency. Under this typology, seven common models of evaluation methods are elaborated with some procedural references: (1) need assessment; (2) program development; (3) utilization analysis; (4) outcome evaluation; (5) net effect assessment; (6) cost-benefit analysis; and (7) cost-effectiveness analysis.

INTRODUCTION

The emergence of Employee Assistance Programs (EAPs) is relatively a new system of supports for workers by various organizations, based upon the fundamental recognition of the interrelationship between personal problems and job performance. A review of the historical development of EAPs indicates that not only the number and scope of EAPs has increased drastically in the past decade, but also that EAPs have become an integral part of the corporate world (Googins & Godfrey, 1985; Trice, 1986; Walsh, 1982). The literature on the subject suggests that, through the evolution of EAPs, their purpose has been changing somewhat, from programs

Dong Soo Kim, PhD, is Professor at Norfolk State University, School of Social Work, Norfolk, VA 23504.

for "improving productivity" to a more comprehensive "employer benefit" (McClellan, & Miller 1987; Spicer, 1987; Steele, 1982).

One of the most inviting features of EAPs is the alleged fit of altruism and economy. Early EAPs had their major thrust from humanitarian motives, and over time it became apparent that the humanitarian reasons for EAPs could be reinforced by cost savings. There is ample evidence which support the idea that EAPs make good business sense (Decker, Starrett & Redhorse, 1986; Scanlon, 1983). For example, the U.S. Postal Service boasts an annual savings of more than $2 million through their EAP; the National Institute on Alcohol Abuse and Alcoholism conservatively estimates a $5.78 return on every $1.00 invested in an EAP. However, monetary savings may not be the only or a primary reason for business and industrial organizations' acceptance of EAPs. Environmental, social, and other benefits may be equally important, especially in view of the fact that some EAPs may not result in economic gains for management. Some reports indicate that EAPs are not effective in achieving set goals, economic or noneconomic, and there seems to be great need for more research in the field of EAPs (Beavers, 1984; Groeneveld et al., 1985; Jerrell & Rightmyer, 1982; Roll & D'Aonzo, 1970; Walsh, 1982).

Questions on whether a project or program is needed, how it operates, whether it performed, why it worked the way it did, and for what results, etc. are related to an applied social research field called program evaluation. The purpose of program evaluation is to provide information necessary to improve intervention services for human needs (Posavac & Carey, 1985: 5-29). Most program planners and administrators do acknowledge the need and importance of a systematic evaluation of their EAPs. Yet many may not have knowledge of the overall conceptual framework for their evaluations, let alone specific research techniques required in each step of an evaluation (Albert, Smythe & Brooke, 1985; Omara-McCabe, 1985; Steidinger, 1985; Weinberg, 1984). Also, many empirical studies reported tend to focus on very specific variables and relationship or use narrowly conceived research designs (Jorrisch, 1986; Krucher, 1986; Price, 1986; Putnam & Stout, 1985).

The author in this paper will present four typological categories of EAP evaluation in terms of need, process, outcome, and efficiency, with various evaluation models. More specifically, the purpose of this paper is to elaborate each of the above four phases of evaluation as applied to employee assistance programs, with (a) conceptual and practical framework; (b) appropriate methodology and models; and (c) study exemplars in the field. In view of the dire need for systematic and comprehensive evaluation in the area of EAPs, this paper should help enhance evaluation rationale and strategy in the field.

PROGRAM EVALUATION

A program evaluation is a broad area of research activity devoted to collecting, analyzing, and interpreting vital information on the need, implementation, and impact of a given program for the purpose of some improvement and/or justification of the intervention efforts. Such evaluations are undertaken for policy development and program planning, for management and administrative purposes, for requirements of fiscal or legal accountability, and for other perceived practical needs of organizations such as improvement of productivity and/or reduction of certain problems.

There are generally four types of evaluations: (A) intervention planning; (B) program monitoring; (C) impact assessment; and (D) economic efficiency. Each has its respective evaluation purpose and specific questions. The intervention planning is the first type or stage of evaluation for program design and development in conformity with intended goals. Critical questions, here as formative research, are concerned with (1) how to define the extent and distribution of the problems or target population, and (2) whether the proposed intervention is a suitable means of resolving or reducing the identified problems with reasonable chances of success.

Program monitoring is a systematic, ongoing assessment of implementation of the intervention program. The important questions in this stage of evaluation are related to (1) whether intervention efforts are undertaken according to the program design, and (2) whether program is reaching the specified target population. The impact assessment is a very important stage of evaluation in regard to program effectiveness in terms of measuring the extent to which a program affects real differences in a desired direction. Using various evaluation methods and preset criteria of success, this phase of evaluation addresses the question of (1) whether the program actually produces change toward the desired objectives and/or intended direction, and (2) whether some or all changes can be attributed to some alternative process other than the program. The economic efficiency is the tangible way of calculating economic efficiency of the program in terms of cost-benefit or cost-effectiveness analysis. Here questions are raised as to (1) how much each service unit costs or how the total costs and benefits compare, and (2) whether the program is an efficient use of resources compared with other approaches (Rossi, Freeman & Wright 1979: 18-51).

While each of the above types or stages of evaluation is distinctive in its own purpose and approaches, they occur generally in a sequential order and are basically cumulative. For example, impact assessment is meaningful only when implementation actually took place, and efficiency analysis is possible only when a program has been found to be efficacious.

The comprehensive evaluation refers to a study which encompasses monitoring, impact, and efficiency analyses. While the existing programs have certain difficulties and limitations as to evaluability, practical considerations of what, if not all, types of evaluations can be undertaken may be determined by logically following the stage and state of a given program as depicted in Diagram 1.

EAP PLANNING

Research for EAP planning may be conducted under different names such as exploratory evaluation, need assessment, formative evaluation, or planning research. During this stage or phase of evaluation, the crucial issues are to define the nature, extent, and location of the specific problems to which EAP will be addressed. This requires finding the best method to identify the target population which exhibits the problems in the organizations. Also needed here is to develop an intervention program designed to reach them and to alleviate their problems. This means assessing whether the proposed intervention model can be a suitable delivery system to the target population for the desired change. There are several studies on planning, developing, and implementing EAPs with varying degrees of success (Barach, 1986; Lesser & Cavaseno, 1986; Teingeer, 1981). Specially Sholoette (1983) offers a useful checklist for

Diagram 1 Evaluation Scheme of Employment Assistance Programs (EAPs)

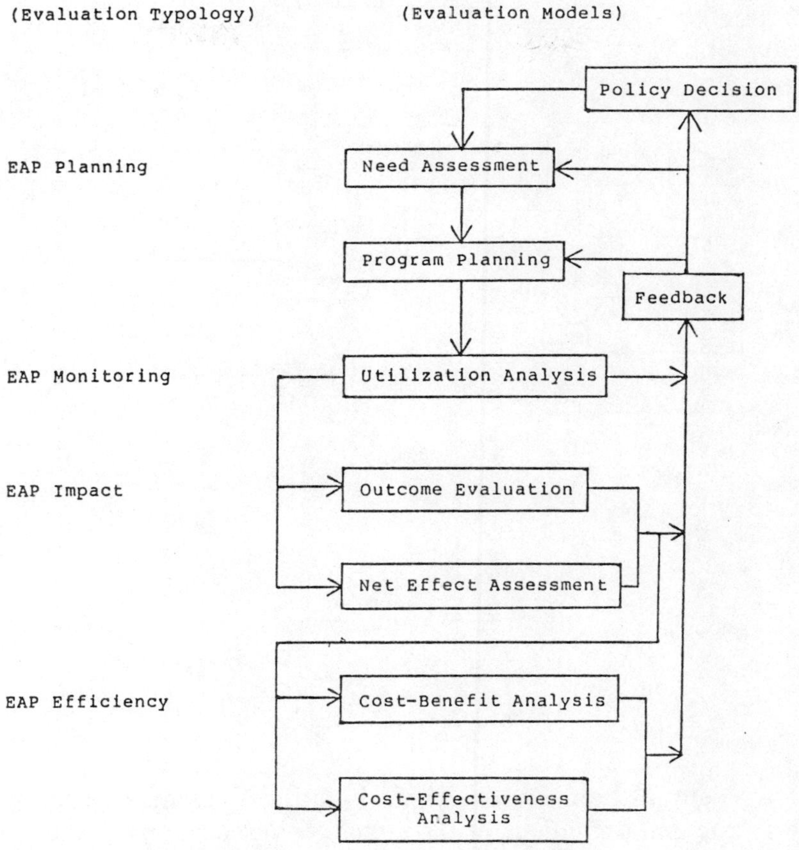

preprogram analysis and assessment. The general procedure of the planning research is shown in Diagram 2.

Need Assessment

This is a process of verification and mapping out the extent and location of the problems to which the program would be directed. Employees who have such problems will become the target population. Need assessment has varying perspectives and many methods

Diagram 2 General Process of EAP Planning

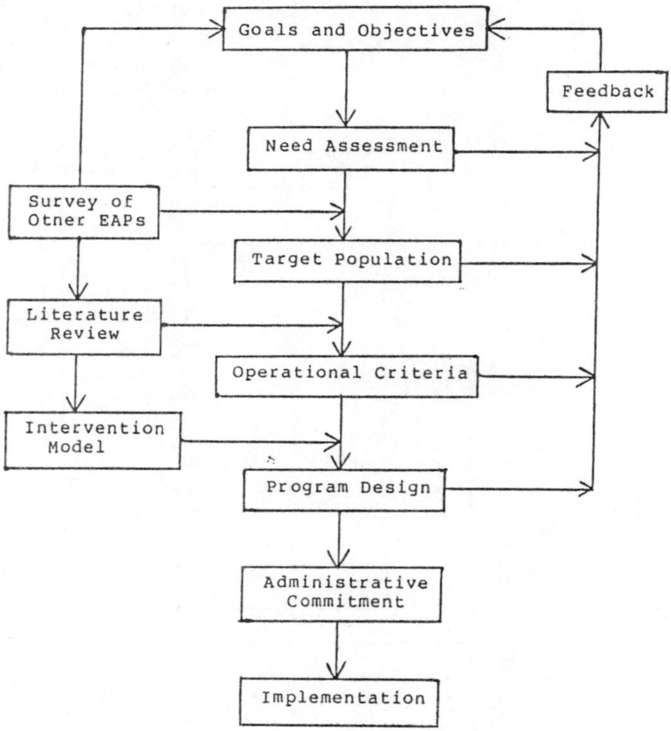

for its identification. Some technical clarifications may be useful for operational definitions of the target population. "Population at need" refers to individual employees who currently manifest given problem conditions and it may afford precise criteria for a reliable and valid screening technique.

However, "population at risk" are those employees who are likely to develop such conditions. "Incidence" indicates the number of new cases of a particular problem in an organization during a specified period of time, whereas "prevalence" means the number of existing cases. "Rates" or percentages are a convenient way of assessing incidence or prevalence in terms of proportion per set employee population. Specifying rates by certain employee characteristics such as age, sex, race, organizational unit, job classification, etc. can produce useful data for precise targeting and programming.

There are several accepted procedures for assessing needs. These procedures are based on different approaches to various sources of relevant data—key informant, community forum, rates-under-treatment, social indicators, and survey, with corresponding advantages and disadvantages for each (Need Assessment Approaches, 1977: 19-49).

In the case of EAP planning, however, the use of employee performance records and some specific incidence statistics maintained by the organization may be the best approach. They may include documented indications of absenteeism, tardiness, accidents, known alcoholic or drug abuse, low productivity, disciplinary action, and other disruptive work behavior. While an anonymous survey in the organization and some social indicators in the region can be used or supplemented, they tend to be unreliable or blur the true need of a specific organization.

Program Development

Once the needs are determined and goals are set, a specific intervention program may be developed for the purpose of reaching and helping the identified target population. Program development here is the design of specific intervention and rehabilitative activities based on the information, analyses, mandates, and recommendations. In this transition from the general and value-oriented goals to more detailed activity-oriented processes, practicality and specificity are very important evaluation criteria. The program should be designed to be most effective in light of the size, nature, and characteristics of the target population. Here an intervention model should be based on some implicit or explicit hypothesis about the relationship between intervention and changed behavior of employees. The hypothesis may stem from experimental studies, logical theories, clinical impressions, or predictive statistical associations. Since many organizations tend to adopt an EAP in a prescribed package model, it is important to carefully examine the hypothetic causal assumption, manipulability and feasibility of intervention programs according to specific needs and characteristics of the organization. For example, the proposed program should be analyzed as to whether services can be sufficiently and practically rendered, manipulated, and controlled with some reasonable assumption of their impact, Certain EAPs may lack the above factors due to technical limitations, workers' rights, lack of proper training or aftercare, and/or the organizational policy and, if so, such a program needs to be modified or not be selected. In short, an intervention program should be assumed to produce sufficient changes in a desired direction among the target population (Rossi, Howard, Wright 1979: 82-120).

EAP MONITORING

Monitoring is an evaluation process to check on congruence between program design and program implementation on a continuing or regular basis. Two important issues in this process are whether the program has reached the target population and whether the program has been actually delivered to them as designed. In the case of EAP monitoring, both questions are related to employee participation in the program from the initial referral to the follow-up services. Some studies report monitoring process on referral, compliance, and information management of EAPs (Jorrisch, 1986; Krucher, 1986; Long, 1983; Price, 1986). The general process of EAP monitoring is depicted in Diagram 3.

Utilization Analysis

The first tangible measure of success or failure of the EAP in any organization is the extent to which the target population actually uses the program as designed in the program planning stage. After all, poor participation in the program as well as nondeliverance or incorrect deliverance of the program may make a well-planned EAP meaningless and its outcome invalid. Actual participation and utilization of the target is especially important in cases where program acceptance is voluntary and self-referral is the more common practice of EAPs.

Specific measures of program participation or utilization are "coverage," "bias," and "attrition." Coverage means the extent

Diagram 3 General Process of EAP Monitoring

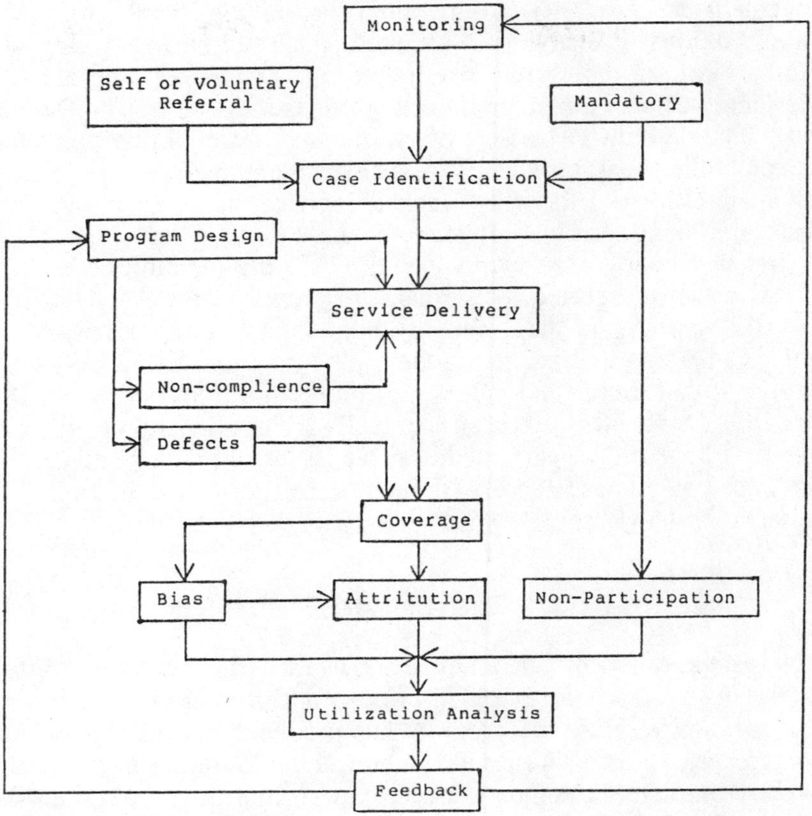

to which the program enjoys widespread target population participation as specified in the program design and it is usually indicated in terms of percentage or proportion of over- or underserved population. Bias is differential utilization patterns by subgroups of the target population and is usually measured by ratio among different subgroups. Attrition means dropouts from among the program users and is measured by the rate of participation reduction over time.

Monitoring these measures and especially information about program nonparticipants and dropouts on an ongoing basis may render important data not only on the current state and status of the EAP, but also on corrective measures and direction by means of feedback mechanisms. Feedback from monitoring allows timely program modifications, if change is warranted. For example, analyzing information from monitoring may point to a faulty EAP program design and/or noncompliance of a program specification. The former may include built-in barriers or problems of accessibility and adequacy of the program as intervention efforts and the latter, problems of availability or eligibility, lack of service standardization, and arbitrary changes of the delivery system.

Usual data sources for monitoring EAPs are (a) direct observational data, (b) service record data, (c) service provider data, (d) program participant data, and (e) data about eligible nonparticipants. Collecting and analyzing these data tend to overlap from one source to the other and often, comprehensive monitoring would need data from all sources. Since EAP services depend heavily on person-to-person delivery methods, the issues of privacy and confidentiality may require careful protective considerations in monitoring evaluation (Rossi, Howard & Wright 1979; 123-179).

EAP IMPACT

Impact assessment is to analyze and evaluate the outcomes of the intervention efforts as intended effects, and it attempts to answer the question whether the program has produced real results as expected. Assuming a causal linkage between EAP inputs and participating employee changes, impact assessment tries to establish whether EAP works, how well it works, and with what evidence. In addition to demonstrating the efficacy of the program, it can also assess the magnitude of the effect and some unintended and undesired impacts as well. The result or outcome means a change in the level of a measurable variable, such as noticeable changes of identified problem behavior of employees. In EAP impact assessment, two outcome evaluation methods are used: overall outcome evaluation and net effect assessment. The former is to assess the gross change found in a group after the EAP intervention, regardless of its true sources, whereas the latter is to assess the results only attributable to the EAP intervention, free and clear of the effects of other concurrent processes. Changes in employees' behavior can always happen "naturally" with or without the EAP intervention and/or with other interventions and influences. Here any observed outcome may be due to EAP efforts, plus some contamination resulting from other sources of changes such as "history" (learning a lesson from special life events), "maturation" (growing old and wise), "self-selection" (high motivation to participate and to improve), "test effect" or "Hawthorne" effect (being referred to and watched over), etc. They offer alternative "competing explanations" of the results and become sources of invalidation, which may in turn discount the total outcome of the EAPs (Campbell & Stanley, 1966).

The choice of specific outcome measures for evaluating impact is very important, significantly coloring the degree or nature of the result. Since EAPs usually have specific treatment goals with measurable criteria such as reduction of absent days, medical claims, and number of accidents, etc., its reliability and validity may not be so much of a problem as the research design for controlling extraneous variances. There are many studies indicating effectiveness of EAPs in specific goal achievements (Jorrisch, 1986; Morgan-Janty, 1982; Nadolski, 1987; Price, 1986). The outcome assessment procedures are shown in Diagram 4.

Outcome Evaluation

These overall outcome evaluations are approximate methods for assessing EAP impact using nonrigorous research methods and often based on slim data. This is a "nonexperimental" approach to outcome evaluation and common classic examples are "single-group designs" with one set or two sets of observations. The EAP participant group is evaluated after or before-and-after receiving services. Such evaluation may give an overall estimate of what changes have occurred during and after the EAP intervention, but it is not possible to attribute all or some of these changes exclusively to the EAPs intervention. This type of design has no real means of controlling or ruling out contamination by other influences, which

Diagram 4 General Process of EAP Impact Assessment

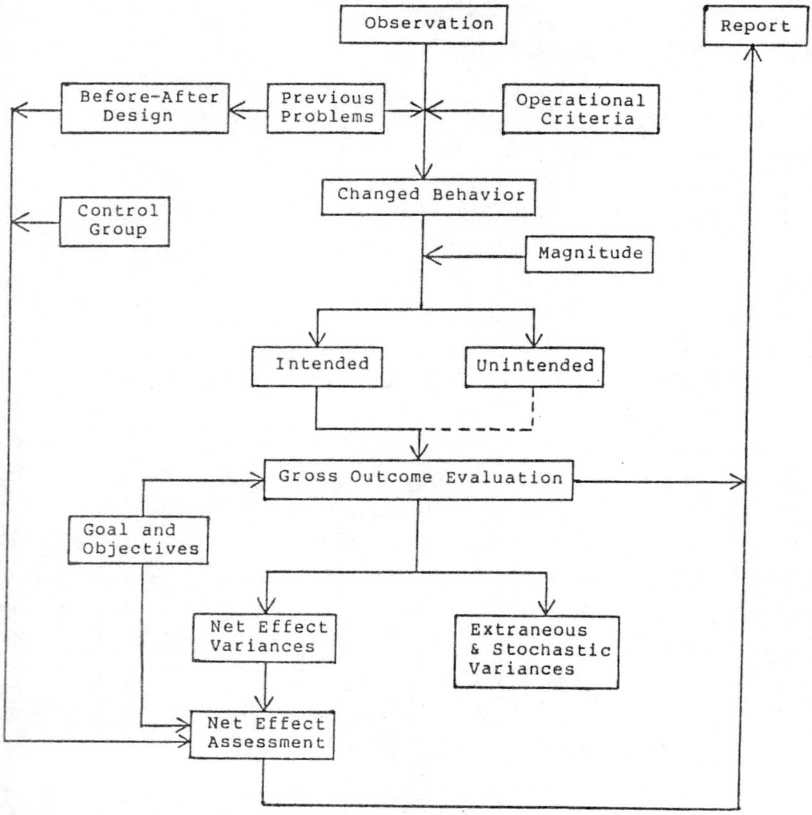

constitutes "threats to internal validity" (Posavac & Carey, 1985: 173-203).

These approaches sometimes rely on judgmental or expert assessment to varying degrees of careful examination of a variety of existing or collected data. For example, program data on participants, participants' own ratings, use of outside experts and/or administrators' assessment may be utilized to assess overall changes, If clear objective criteria are not prescribed, such judgmental or expert assessment tends to become an impressionistic subjective appraisal.

While this type of evaluation cannot measure the true effects of the EAPs, it is nevertheless, a useful and often the only practical means to assess the outcomes, requiring less technical sophistication, time, and resources. It may be sufficient for evaluation purposes for most EAPs in small organizations with limited budgets.

Net Effect Assessment

These assessments are more rigorous approaches to the precise measurement of the net effects of EAPs based on randomized controlled experiments of similar designs. Such designs ideally utilize experimental and control (or comparison) groups, random assignment, and two or more observations, usually before and after the EAP treatment. Here the net effects are defined as the gross outcome, subtracted by impact of other variables, plus or minus "stochastic effects," namely, fluctuating variances due to chances. In a typical randomized experimental design, net effects are measured as in Table 1.

Net effects of the EAPs are then the difference in scores on outcome measures before and after intervention for the EAPs (experimental) group, minus differences for the unexposed (control) group, plus or minus stochastic effects. Randomization achieves "equivalence" of experimental and control groups, and being equivalent in all aspects, any difference in changes between the two groups accounts for a real net impact introduced by only the EAPs. Such sophisticated designs are to control and eliminate all possible changes due to extraneous influences other than the EAP treatment itself.

In most organizations, however, assigning employees to EAP treatment or nontreatment at random is almost impossible, raising many ethical, logical, and cost problems. Thus as alternatives,

Table 1 Outcome Measures in a Randomized Experiment

	Before EAPs	After EAPs	Differences
Experimental Group	E1	E2	E = E2 - E1
Control Group	C1	C2	C = C2 - E1

Net effects of EAPs = E - C

"quasiexperimental" methods are used, which use constructed controls by matching group, controls by longitudinal comparison, statistical adjustments, or other similar designs (Campbell & Stanley, 1966). Although these approximations to true experiments have some limitations, they represent feasible methods for measuring net effect assessment of EAPs with validity in most organizations.

EAP EFFICIENCY

In any intervention program, putting limited resources to optimal use is a very important administrative decision. EAPs also require economic efficiency which merits support or continued support out of many competing needs and other approaches of organizations. Even in the planning stage, ex ante analyses must favorably show their worth on the basis of anticipated estimates of costs and benefits, and in the impact assessment stage, ex post analyses need to be undertaken to justify the costs of the EAPs by the magnitude of established net outcomes. EAP efficiency here means that the specified approach and program produce the most favorable impact on the most target employees for the same expenditure and that the benefits somehow outweigh its costs. Benefits are the net outcomes or, in some cases, gross outcomes, derived from EAPs, both tangible and intangible. Costs are the total resources put into EAPs, both direct and indirect. In order to measure the EAP efficiency, the benefits and costs of the EAPs must be compared. There are several studies indicating the economic efficiency or lack of it in EAPs (Decker, Starrett & Redhorse, 1986; Scanlon, 1983) (see Diagram 5).

Cost-Benefit Analysis

This is a widely used efficiency evaluation technique on the basis of total monetary inputs and outputs in an intervention project or program. In this analysis, the benefits and costs have to be translated into a common measure, usually monetary values, for a straighforward comparison. Thus all resources invested in the EAPs are computed in dollar costs, covering all allocated personnel, facil-

Diagram 5 General Process of EAP Efficiency Measurement

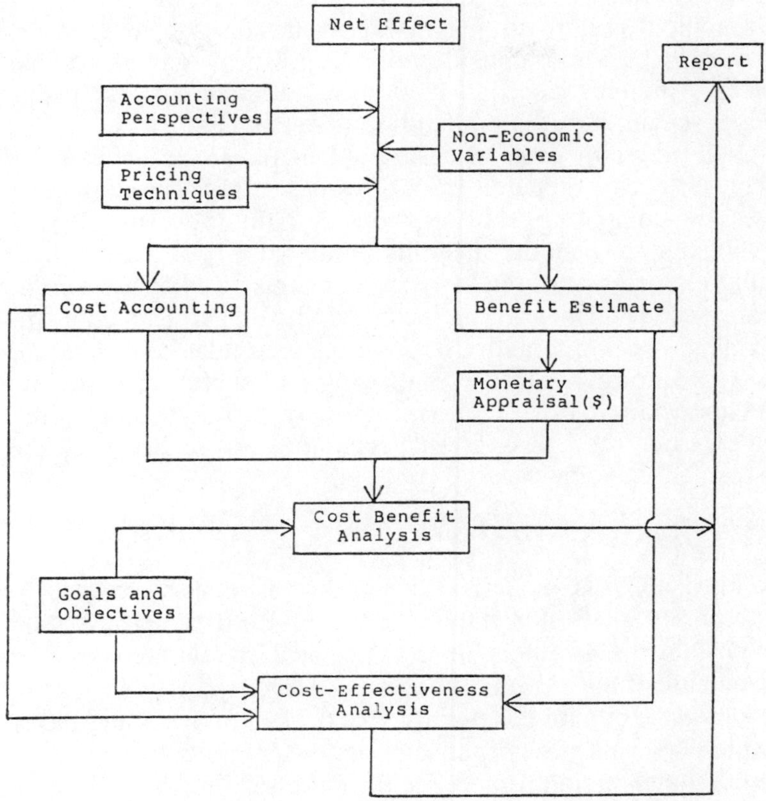

ities, materials, equipment and participant inputs, etc. Also, all benefits accrued such as decrease of absenteeism and accidents, increase of productivity, reduction of health claims, recruitment and retraining costs, etc. have to be tabulated and priced in dollar amounts. Some considerations should also be given in the process of calculating monetary values of benefits and costs of the EAPs. There are several different accounting perspectives, depending on the question of "whose" costs and benefits. In the case of the EAPs, there are at least three major perspectives: the individual employees, the organization, and the community or society at large. One component may be calculated at a cost from one perspective while the same as a benefit from another perspective. Realistic pricing methods require not just market values of each component, but also distributional considerations, political values, "shadow prices," indirect or secondary effects, "discounting," adjusting future costs and benefits to the present values, etc.

Once all components of costs and benefits are realistically calculated, both are compared from one or several accounting perspectives by computing a benefit-to-cost ratio (benefits divided by costs), the net benefits (benefits minus costs), or some other formula (internal rate of return), etc. Since this analysis has a common denominator, namely, a monetary unit, it has clear comparative meanings when alternative approaches are under consideration for resource allocation. However, pricing all benefits of EAPs in precise monetary terms is often extremely difficult. Therefore this analysis may be a less useful technique for the EAPs efficiency assessment in some cases.

Cost-Effectiveness Analysis

This analysis is much the same as the cost-benefit analysis, yet it is a more realistic technique for the EAP efficiency assessment, where benefits are intangible. Often benefits of intervention programs cannot be specified in monetary terms. EAPs, for example, may produce certain beneficial impacts on employees and the organization in terms of work satisfaction, better intercolleague relationships, higher morale, good health, enriched life, as well as more tangible benefits such as productivity. Cost-effectiveness analysis requires quantifying program costs and benefits, but benefits do not have to be calculated into monetary terms, as with cost-benefit analysis. Instead, the EAP effectiveness in reaching the set goal is compared to the monetary value of the resources put into the program (Levin, 1975). Thus, it allows the comparisons and rank-ordering of programs in terms of their costs for achieving set goals or different degrees of the goals. While this analysis uses the same principle and methods as the cost-benefit analysis, the EAP efficiency here, due to the lack of a common denominator, is assessed by a relative comparison of costs for the same or similar benefits, where efficiency is a function of minimal costs. Or in some cases, the relative efficiency of the EAPs can be demonstrated by more benefits for the same costs.

CONCLUDING REMARKS

EAPs are broad and legitimate human services for employees as their personal, marital, emotional, and behavioral-medical problems have been known to affect their work performance. These programs are rapidly growing in the worksites everywhere. The Association of Labor & Management Administrators and Consultants on Alcoholism, the professional organization of EAP field, now claims about 4,000 organizational members (Googins & Godfrey, 1985). This phenomenal growth requires careful evaluative scrutiny from administrative, legal, and fiscal perspectives for their legitimacy and validation.

At the same time, evaluation is among the fastest-growing activities in applied social research as the need for reliable and valid data, timely feedback, and rational decision-making ever increases in all social intervention projects and programs. Then the surging interest in evaluation of EAPs at this point is not an accident but a natural and inevitable thing. Yet many program managers of EAPs do not have skills or time to embark on any systematic evaluation of their programs and many evaluators do not have the knowledge or opportunity to manage EAP activities sufficiently to assess their process or outcomes. Most evaluation reports are so much concerned with specific aspects or components of EAPs that they tend to help lose sight of the totality, context, or framework of the evaluation.

The present author has tried to provide readers with the overall scheme of EAPs evaluation in terms of typology and models without burdening them with technicalities and protocols. First, need, process, outcome, and efficiency of EAP evaluation were presented by the incremental sequence or phases of (a) intervention planning; (b) program monitoring; (c) impact assessment; and (d) economic efficiency. Under this, seven distinctive evaluation models were elaborated: (1) need assessment; (2) program development; (3) utilization analysis; (4) outcome evaluation; (5) net effect assessment; (6) cost-benefit analysis; and (7) cost-effectiveness analysis.

This framework would offer readers the overall EAP evaluation structure so that they can evaluate their evaluation need, state, and focus for EAPs. The typology and models presented here, however, should not be taken as fixed norms but as useful schemes. Scheme as a conceptual tool has value of only practical utility as applied to the real tasks in the field.

REFERENCES

Albert, W.C., Smythe, P.C. & Brook, R.C., "Promises to Keep: An Evaluator's Perspective on Employee Assistance Programs." *Evaluation Program Planning*, 8(3):175-182, 1985.

Barach, J.M., An Assessment of Program Development in Employee Assistance Programs within a Public School Setting. Unpublished EdD Dissertation, Seattle University, 1986.

Beavers, C.H., An Evaluation of the Impact of an Employee Assistance Program on Alcohol Abusing Employees. Unpublished PhD Dissertation, Georgia State University College of Education, 1984.

Campbell, D.T. & Stanley, J.C., *Experimental and Quasi Experimental Design for Research*. Chicago: Rand-McNally, 1966.

Decker, J.T., Starrett, R. & Redhorse, J., "Evaluating the Cost-effectiveness of Employee Assistance Programs." *Social Work*, 31(5): 391-393, 1986.

Ettinger, R.G. III, Evaluating A Community Mental Health Center's Implementation of An Employee Assistance Program. Unpublished PhD Dissertation, California School of Professional Psychology, Fresno, 1981.

Googins, B. & Godfrey, J., "The Evolution of Occupational Social Work." *Social Work*, 30(5): 396-402, 1985.

Groeneveld, J., Shain, M., Brayshaw, D., Keaney, J. & Laird, L., "Cost Effectiveness of EAP: Testing Assumptions." *Employees Assistance Quarterly*, 1(1): 75-87, Fall 1985.

Jorrisch, M.R., Variables Affecting Compliance to Treatment in an Employee Assistance Program. Unpublished EdD Dissertation, University Of Louisville, 1986.

Jerrel, J.M. & Rightmyer, J.F., Evaluating Employee Assistance Programs: A Review of Methods, Outcomes and Future Directions." *Evaluation Program Planning*, 5(3): 255-267, 1982.

Krucher, K.J., The Relationship Between Supervisors' Interpersonal Need Structure and Use of Employee Assistance Programs. Unpublished PhD Dissertation, Florida State University, 1986.

Lesser, J.G. & Cavaseno, V.H. "Establishing a Hospital's Employee Assistance Program." *Health and Social Work*, 11(2): 126-132, 1986.

Levin, H., "Cost-Effective Analysis in Evaluation Research." pp. 89-124 in M. Guttentag & E.L. Struening (eds.), *Handbook of Evaluation Research*, Vol. 2. Beverly Hills: Sage Publication, 1975.

Long, R.J., A Management Information System and Evaluation Scheme for the University of Texas Employee Assistance Programs. Unpublished DrPH Dissertation, The University of Texas H.S.C. at Houston School of Public Health, 1983.

McClellan, K. & Miller, R.E., "EAPs in Transition: Purpose and Scope of Services." Unpublished Paper, Council on Health Costs, Charlotte, NC, 1987.

Morgan-Janty, C.J., A Process Evaluation of Employee Assistance Programs in Wisconsin. Unpublished PhD Dissertation, The University of Wisconsin, Madison, 1982.

Nadolski, J.N., "Evaluation of an Employee Assistance Program." *Journal of Occupational Medicine*, 29(1): 32-7, 1987.

National Institute of Mental Health, Needs Assessment Approaches: Concepts and Methods, Washington, DC: GPO (DHEW Publication, No. (ADM) 77-472.

Omara-McCabe, E.J., Employee Assistance Programs Aimed at Alcohol Abuse: Evaluating the Evaluations. Unpublished EdD Dissertation, Fairleigh Dickinson University, 1985.

Pell, S. & D'Alonzo, C.A., "Sickness Absenteeism of Alcoholics." *Journal of Occupational Medicine*, 12: 198-210, 1970.

Perkins, D.N.T., "Evaluating Social Interventions: A Conceptual Scheme." *Evaluation Quarterly*, 1:642-645, November 1977.

Posavac, E.J. & Carey, R.G., *Program Evaluation: Methods and Case Studies* (2nd Ed.). Englewood Cliffs, NJ: Prentice-Hall, 1985.

Price, C.E., Employee Assistance Programs: Toward A More Effective Model. Unpublished EdD Dissertation, The George Washington University, 1986.

Putnam, S.L. & Stout, R.L., "Evaluating Employee Assistance Policy in an HMO-based Alcoholism Project." *Evaluation Program Planning*, 8(3): 183-194, 1985.

Rossi, P.M., Freeman, H.E. & Wright, S.R., *Evaluation: A Systematic Approach*. Beverly Hills: Sage Publications, 1979.

Scanlon, W., "Trends in EAPs: Then and Now." *EAP Digest*, 3(4): 38-41, 1983.

Sholette, R.L., "Pre-Program Analysis and Assessment." *EAP Digest*, 3(4): 17, 1983.

Spicer, J., The EAP Solution: Current Trends and Future Issues. Center City, MN: Hazelden Educational Materials, 1987.

Steele, P.D., "Characteristics of Employee Assistance Programs Throughout the United States." U.S. Public Health Service, National Institute on Drug Abuse (No. 271-76-4413), 1982.

Steidinger, J., Assessment of the Current State of Evaluation Practices in Employee Assistance Programs. Unpublished PhD Dissertation, California School of Professional Psychology, Berkeley, 1985.

Trice, H.M., Organizational and Occupational Dimensions of Employee Assistance Programs: A Review and Critique. Society for the Study of Social Problems, 1986.

Walsh, D.C., "Employee Assistance Programs." *Milbank Memorial Fund Quarterly/Health and Society*, 60(3): 492-517, 1982.

SECTION III: CASE EXAMPLES OF EAP EVALUATIONS

Employee Assistance Program Evaluation in a Federal Government Agency

R. Paul Maiden

SUMMARY. Demonstrating the efficacy of an Employee Assistance Program is an equally important endeavor in public and private sector work organizations. This paper discusses the cost-benefit and cost-effectiveness evaluation that was conducted by the U.S. Department of Health and Human Services Employee Counseling Services program. Further, it details the components of the 30 month project relative to evaluation design, data collection proccesses, and strategies used to maintain employee privacy while analyzing personnel data. Results of the evaluation are also presented.

Employee Assistance Programs (EAP) have emerged as an effective method for dealing with employees whose job performance has deteriorated due to personal problems such as alcoholism, drug

R. Paul Maiden, PhD, is Chair of the Employee Assistance Program specialization at the University of Illinois, Jane Addams College of Social Work. He holds a masters degree in social work from the University of Tennessee at Knoxville and has completed a PhD at the University of Maryland at Baltimore, School of Social Work and Community Planning. Address correspondence to Dr. Maiden, University of Illinois, Jane Addams College of Social Work, M/C 309, Box 4348, Chicago, IL 60680. A copy of the final report of the USDHHS Employee Counseling Services evaluation can be requested from the Freedom of Information Office, U.S. Department of Health and Human Services, 200 Independence Avenue, S.W., Washington, DC 20101.

The author wishes to thank Thomas S. McFee, Assistant Secretary for Personnel Administration, U.S. Department of Health and Human Services and Dr. Dale A. Masi, former Director of the Employee Counseling Services program for their tutelage during his tenure at HHS.

abuse, mental illness, and family problems. One of the critical concerns of this constantly growing field is the need for comprehensive program evaluations to demonstrate the cost-effectiveness and cost-benefit of EAPs. Additionally, companies and organizations developing and implementing EAPs are demanding fiscal accountability from their programs to maintain them. Demonstrating cost-effectiveness and cost-benefit of EAPs involves the measurement of numerous variables. It also requires a financial commitment on the part of the organization to carry it out.

One of the most ambitious and sophisticated evaluations of this type was undertaken by the U.S. Department of Health and Human Services Employee Counseling Services (ECS) program. It was also the first of its kind in a federal government agency. The completion of this evaluation is remarkable because it required the cooperation and coordination of ECS programs in 16 operating units throughout the United States that were providing services to the Department's approximately 150,000 employees. ECS counselors also saw in excess of 2,500 troubled employees during the 30 month period the evaluation was conducted.

ECONOMIC IMPACT OF THE TROUBLED EMPLOYEE

Although EAPs are seen as a humanitarian endeavor, the primary motive for their development has been economic. Monetary considerations are a particularly strong driving force due to the considerable losses incurred from absenteeism, increased health care utilization and other associated costs which drive up health insurance premiums, grievances, and lost productivity. A review of the literature suggests that 18% of the working population is losing 25% productivity due to personal problems that affect their jobs (Masi, 1984). These loses are related to the following:

- Alcoholism is costing U.S. industry more than $20.6 billion in lost productivity (Royce, 1981).
- Stress related illness is responsible for an annual loss of 132 million working days (Feinstein & Brown, 1982).
- The national expenditure for mental health services accounts

for approximately 15% health care expenditures and is continually on the rise.
– One major insurance carrier, for one state alone, found an increase of nearly 115% over a five year period, out of all proportion to other health care expenditures (Masi & Maiden, 1987).

Employee Assistance Programs have emerged as a successful and cost-efficient method of prevention and intervention. General Motors, Equitable Life Assurance Society, and others have demonstrated respectable cost-benefit ratios and have shown that their EAPs are worthwhile endeavors, both economically and socially (Lanier, 1981; Manuso, 1979).

It is evident from the studies of the programs cited above as well as many others in the literature that there are economic advantages to having an EAP. Central to this is a need to demonstrate cost-efficiency to remain a viable part of an organization rather than becoming a financial drain for which there is no return on the investment. This element is equally important in public sector organizations. With ever increasing budget cuts and belt tightening, EAPs must demonstrate their economic effectiveness or fall under the budget knife.

LEGISLATIVE IMPETUS FOR FEDERAL AGENCY EAPs

In 1970, Congress passed a new historic bill that has had the most far reaching impact on the development of Employee Assistance Programs in both the public and private sectors. The Comprehensive Alcohol Abuse and Alcoholism Prevention, Treatment and Rehabilitation Act – P.L. 91-616 (more commonly known as the "Hughes Act" after its author Senator Harold Hughes) mandates alcoholism programs for federal employees. This law also assigned responsibility to the Office of Personnel Management (OPM) for developing and maintaining employee counseling programs in cooperation with the Secretary of HHS and other federal agencies and departments (Askt, 1976).

In 1972, the Drug Abuse Office and Treatment Act was passed.

Similar to the Hughes Act, it assigned OPM the added responsibility of developing and maintaining drug abuse treatment services for federal employees. In 1979, OPM issued a Federal Personnel Manual Letter directing the incorporation of the Federal Civilian Alcohol and Drug Abuse Programs into a management system dealing with a broader range of medical-behavioral problems. In addition to alcohol and drug abuse counseling, personal/emotional, marital, family, financial, and legal problems were included in the scope of service provision by the employee counseling service programs. Shortly thereafter, the Department of Health and Human Services (HHS) secretary, announced a major initiative to combat alcoholism. Like many other EAPs, the early federal government programs evolved from what were once occupational alcoholism programs to what are now described as "broad brush" programs. A significant emphasis was to encourage other federal agencies as well as state and local governments, businesses, and labor organizations to establish EAPs to deal with employee substance abuse and other problems that impaired employee performance (HHS, 1984).

The federal government's involvement in the development of EAPs was also intended to protect federal agencies from the losses incurred by troubled employees. This concern was evident in a statement made by HHS's Assistant Secretary for Personnel Administration, Thomas S. McFee upon signing the department policy for the ECS program. He noted that,

> National studies indicate about 10 percent of the work force suffer from alcohol abuse, another three percent from drug abuse, and seven percent from other emotional problems. Employee suffering from these problems are estimated to be 25 percent less productive than those who do not experience these problems. Since the average HHS employee earned about $22,000 in 1981, it can be estimated that that years loss alone amounted to $148.5 million. The human costs of alcohol abuse, drug abuse and emotional problems, although not easily measured in dollars and cents are considerable. The resulting loss of employee well-being is of great concern to the Department. (McFee, 1982)

THE HHS COMMITMENT

From the inception of the Department of Health and Human Services ECS program, the highest priority was placed on the need to demonstrate that the development of an EAP within this organization would be effective in reducing costs related to troubled employees. It was the view of the Assistant Secretary for Personnel Administration that unless this program and others like it could be shown to produce economic benefits, they are likely to be eliminated during budget cuts.

The ECS program is divided geographically among 16 operating units. Ten are based in each of the HHS regional offices and six are located in designated headquarters offices. These 16 units each provide broad based EAP services using a variety of service delivery models. Some were established as in-house professionally staffed counseling programs, while others were contracted out and still others were part of federal agency consortiums. Each unit is administered by an ECS Unit Director who is responsible for implementing and managing the program in his/her unit. Policy direction and functional management are provided by the ECS Director who is strategically located in the Office of the Assistant Secretary for Personnel Administration in Washington, DC.

DEVELOPMENT OF THE EVALUATION PLAN

One of the major priorities in the development of the ECS program was to demonstrate that it is an economically viable operation from a cost-effectiveness and cost-benefit perspective. To control for the bias inherent in an organization performing its own EAP evaluation, HHS contracted the evaluation to Development Associates Inc., an Arlington, Virginia based research and evaluation firm. They were responsible for developing data reporting procedures. Data analysis, synthesizing results, and reporting findings to the Department. Data collection from the 16 ECS units was coordinated by support staff in the ECS Director's office. After completing an extensive two year design and development process, the evaluation plan emerged with the following key features;

- Assurance of client confidentiality and compliance with privacy requirements;
- Maximum compatibility with ECS program policies and procedures;
- Minimum necessary burden to ECS units;
- Timely feedback to promote informed management decisions;
- Sufficient rigor to assure credibility of results through the collection of individual level data;
- Emphasis on outcomes in terms of cost-effectiveness and cost-benefit.

The evaluation system was made up of five components: (1) context, (2) inputs, (3) process, (4) impact, (5) outcomes. This was a variation of the Stufflebeam CIPP Model of Evaluation which was designed for the ECS evaluation to provide ongoing management feedback while building the data base for an overall cumulative evaluation (Stufflebeam & Gula, 1970).

Context evaluation is the setting in which the ECS unit operates and includes the organizational characteristics, community setting characteristics and geographical/physical characteristics.

Inputs are the characteristics of how units are set up and what they do. They include project and staff characteristics, means for allocating resources, project services, and formative inputs such as training and technical services.

Process, impact, and outcomes are the core of the evaluative process using this model. Process evaluation provides program decision-makers with information needed for: (1) anticipating and overcoming procedural difficulties, (2) making administrative program decisions, and (3) interpreting program outcomes. Toward process evaluation, ECS units were required to provide a Unit Quarterly report at the close of each quarter. The quarterly report tracked supervisory training, employee orientation/education sessions, internal marketing activities, contract and service agreement activities, and employee participation and penetration data. Some of the questions of particular relevance in this phase were: (1) What employee problems were most often addressed? (2) By what means was the ECS program being promoted: (3) What was the program's primary source of referrals?

Impact evaluation was operationally defined for the purpose of this study as changes effected on particular employees relative to personal problems such as health, work performance, coping with family problems, self-concept, etc., as a result of the program. Its purpose is to demonstrate that improvement is due to the program and not other working conditions such as pay raises, promotions, job changes, transfer of supervisor, etc. Impact phase questions were: (1) What were the criteria used by each unit in addressing treatment success? (2) What were the differences in treatment success criteria for alcohol, drug, and mental health problems? (3) How effective was each unit in achieving treatment success with its allocated resources?

Outcome evaluation was the most critical aspect of the evaluation design. Outcomes for the purpose of this evaluation were measured in terms of reductions in administrative costs to the Department of Health and Human Services. The term "worker performance measures" was used to identify where administrative costs to the department would be reduced. Selected personnel items were:

- Sick leave used (Year to Date) before and after treatment;
- Leave without pay (YTD) before and after treatment;
- Absent without leave (YTD) before and after treatment;
- Annual leave used (YTD) before and after treatment;
- Annual leave balance (YTD) before and after treatment;
- Annual leave advanced (YTD) before and after treatment;
- Sick leave balance (YTD) before and after treatment; and
- Sick leave advanced (YTD) before and after treatment.

To retrieve outcome evaluation data on employees, ECS Unit Directors secured appropriate personnel payroll items from the computer terminal in each ECS Unit personnel office and transferred them to coded data sheets. The "hard copy" retrieved from the computer containing personal identifiers were then destroyed to protect the privacy of the individual. Data sheets contained no personal identifiers. Outcome phase questions were: (1) What financial impacts were experienced by the department through the implementation of the ECS program in terms of personnel items? (2) What is the most cost-effective model, or set of components to a model in

ECS? This involved comparing one ECS Unit against another and comparing one service delivery model against another (e.g., internal vs. contracted vs. consortium).

USE OF CONTROL GROUPS

As with any research endeavor, a control group is imperative to ascertain what change is due to treatment rather than some other variable. For ECS to conclude that changes were attributable to the ECS program the HHS employee population in each of the regions, that did not use the ECS were used as a control group, using data which was already being generated in regular reports by the Regional Personnel Offices. The items for the control groups were retrieved by each ECS Unit and within each Unit by agency, sex, age, and salary level. This data was then compared to the same information collected on employees using the ECS program. This enabled analysis of data linked to the total program costs, and costs to the individual ECS Units. The department was then able to do a cost-benefit and cost-effectiveness analysis of the data. As the number of clients from each site increased, it became feasible to compare the units in terms of cost-effectiveness. Using the data generated from the various phases of the evaluation process, the cost-benefits of the program were then calculated.

CLIENT TRACKING SYSTEM

The Client Tracking System (CTS) was designed as a management information tool to facilitate assessment of the impact of the program on ECS clients, to help determine the cost-effectiveness of the program and to provide data to assist in the management of the ECS Units. The Client Tracking System was comprised of three parts: (1) Client Status; (2) Work Performance Rating by Supervisor; and (3) Personnel Data. The client status and work performance data were recorded by ECS staff from clients or their ECS records, supervisors (for employees who had been supervisor referred), treatment providers, and others as appropriate. Personnel data was accessed via computer. There were three versions each of the Client Status and Work Performance Rating by Supervisor: one for point of intake, three month follow-up, and nine month follow-up. The CTS required documentation of client data (in coded, nonpersonally identifiable form) by the ECS staff at these three points in time. The Client Tracking System was the core of the evaluation and through its utilization facilitated a continual process of data collection and analysis throughout the evaluation period.

MAINTAINING CONFIDENTIALITY

The most critical aspect of the evaluation design was insuring the confidentiality of ECS clients for which data was collected. From the inception of the ECS program the Assistant Secretary for Personnel Administration and the Director of the ECS program were committed to protecting the privacy of all employees receiving assistance from the ECS program. It was also decided that no part of the evaluation would be done unless absolute employee privacy was maintained. As mentioned previously, no data had personal identifiers. Additionally, only immediate ECS staff had access to personnel data and once the quarterly data was collected, any hard copy with personal identifiers was destroyed. A very stringent policy of handling documents was also adopted and maintained throughout the 30 month evaluation period. Transmittal of confidential client information between ECS staff members was done directly and in person unless staff were more than 60 miles apart. Under these circumstances, registered mail with restricted delivery was the only permissible method for sending and receiving ECS documents. Additionally, the packages were double wrapped with "Penalty of Law" warning labels to discourage tampering. Unit Directors were required to deliver the packages in person to the U.S. Postal Service for mailing rather than going through the department's mail room. All ECS staff were also trained in the handling of documents in their offices and record keeping systems were coded with no employees' names used throughout the documentation process. Client names and corresponding case numbers were kept in a secured location.

COST-EFFECTIVENESS AND COST-BENEFIT ANALYSIS

A critical element in evaluating the ECS program concerned the relationship between the costs of the program and the related outcomes and benefits. There are two types of analysis that can be performed on such data: (1) cost-effectiveness analysis in which program costs are compared with some quantitative measure of program output, and a cost per unit is calculated (cost per client served, cost per unit change in client status) (Rossi, Freeman & Wright, 1979); (2) cost-benefit analysis in which program costs are compared with the dollar value of program results (benefits), and a ratio of costs to benefits is computed (e.g., $5 worth of increased productivity is gained for each dollar spent on services) (Swint, 1978).

Two measures of cost-effectiveness were calculated for various ECS units: (1) the cost per client for all clients served; (2) cost per unit change in counselor ratings for those clients for whom nine month follow-up data was available. The cost per client was determined by taking all the costs of operating each ECS unit (e.g., supervisor training, employee education, etc.) and dividing the sum by the number of clients referred to the ECS program. Cost-effectiveness analysis was also calculated based on changes in counselor ratings between intake and nine month follow-up. Clients were rated on a scale from one to five on three measures of functioning (job performance, interpersonal, personal/emotional). In order to define cost-effectiveness, the cost per client of the ECS program was divided by the product of the number of clients and the mean change in ratings for those clients. The resulting value was thus expressed as the cost of producing an improvement of one point in counselor ratings for a single client.

Cost-benefit analyses are intended to compare the cost of a program with the dollar value of the resulting benefits. In the case of the ECS program, many of the expected benefits (improved interpersonal functioning, greater self-esteem, etc.) were only indirectly relevant to the HHS workplace and are also difficult to define in dollar terms. Instead of collecting data on a comprehensive list of benefits (which any EAP replicating this evaluation could choose to do), the decision was made to focus on the two measures which were directly relevant to HHS: (1) changes in leave usage by ECS clients; (2) changes in supervisor ratings of client job performance. Because these two measures were assumed to be interrelated at least to some extent, the two measures were analyzed separately rather than being added together in a single benefit measure.

Five categories of sick leave usage were examined in the analysis: (1) sick leave; (2) advanced sick leave; (3) leave without pay; (4) absence without leave; and (5) administrative leave. These categories were assumed to be most costly to the department and most used by ECS clients. Annual leave was excluded because almost all employees use all their annual leave at one time or another.

The second type of cost-benefit analysis performed, involved the use of monetized supervisor ratings. The assumption here was that a higher rated employee is more productive than the lower rated employee and that productivity can be translated into dollar values. Employees were rated on a scale with a theoretical range from −16 to +16, but of this analysis their scores were divided by 32, producing an overall theoretical range of −5 to +5. Their intake scores were then compared with the mean of their three month and nine month follow-up scores to get a change score for six month period following intake. Change scores were then multiplied by salary levels for the six month period to get a dollar value.

EVALUATION FINDINGS

The cost-effectiveness analysis yielded some promising results:

– The average cost per client served was approximately $951.
– In the most cost-effective ECS unit, there was a $9 return for every $1 spent on the program.
– One full-time counseling staff per 3,500 employees (with a range of 2,900 to 3,900) may be optimal to realize the maximum return on the dollars invested in an EAP.
– The average cost of producing on improvement of one point in total supervisor rating for a single client was $219. On a scale of +3 to −3 the average work performance rating by supervi-

sors of employees referred to the ECS programs was −2.5 at point of intake and +1.3 three months after intake.

The results of the cost-benefit analysis were equally encouraging:

- The estimated costs per clients as a whole were $991.
- The estimated dollar benefits in only six months were $1,274 per employee served.
- For every dollar spent, there was a return in six months of $1.29.
- Assuming continued improved benefits for ECS clients well after the six month follow-up, the yield of an estimated five year cost-benefit ratio would be 1:7.01.
- Ultimately, HHS should realize a $7.01 return per dollar invested in the program (HHS, 1985).

CONCLUSIONS

Based on prior experience and knowledge of EAPs, there was little doubt that the ECS program would not demonstrate, through this evaluation, to be a cost-effective and cost-beneficial endeavor. What separates this evaluation from many others that have been conducted is that it appears to be the first EAP to use control groups to distinguish the impact the program had on the population served. Further, it should be considered a major achievement that an evaluation of this magnitude, was successfully completed. Only through the continued commitment and efforts of Thomas S. McFee, Assistant Secretary for Personnel Administration; Dr. Dale A. Masi, former Director of the ECS program; Drs. Harry Day and JoAnn Willette of Development Associates, Inc. (Arlington, VA); and 16 Unit Directors and technical expertise of numerous support staff, was this possible.

Through the implementation and subsequent evaluation of the ECS program, the Department of Health and Human Services was able to demonstrate that it could also realize the benefits of a healthier and more productive work force through an employee assistance program.

REFERENCES

Askt, E. L. (1976). *Federal Legislation Relating to Alcohol Abuse and Alcoholism*. Rockville, MD: NIAAA, 7.

Feinstein, B. & Brown, E. (1982). *The New Partnership: Human Services, Business and Industry*. Cambridge, MA: Schenkman XI.

Lanier, D. (1981). "Industrial Social Work in the Computer Age." *EAP Digest*, January, 21.

Manuso, J. (1979). "Executive Stress Management." *Personnel Administrator*, November, 23.

Masi, D. A. & Maiden, R. P. (1987). "Employee Assistance Programs: The State of the Art." *Corporate Commentary*, 2(4), 1-10.

Masi, D. A. (1984). *Designing Employee Assistance Programs*. New York: AMACOM, 1.

McFee, T. S. (1982). "HHS Transmittal 82.16: Employee Counseling Services Policy Statement." Washington, DC: USDHHS, 1.

Rossi, P. H., Freeman, H. E. & Wright, S. N. (1979). *Evaluation: A Systematic Approach*. Beverly Hills: Sage Publication, 247.

Royce, J. E. (1981). *Alcohol Problems and Alcoholism: A Comprehensive Survey*. New York: Free Press, 198.

Stufflebeam, D. & Gula, E. (1970). "Strategies for Institutionalizing the CIPP Evaluation Model." (Address delivered at the Annual PDK Symposium on Evaluation Research) Columbus, OH, June 24.

Swint, J. M., Decker, M. & Larison, D. (1978). "Economic Evaluation of Industrial Alcoholism Programs." *Journal of Studies on Alcohol*, 39: 1633-1639.

U.S. Department of Health and Human Services (1985). *Evaluation of the Department of Health and Human Service Employee Counseling Services Program: Final Evaluation Report*. (Contract No. HHS-100-82-0040) Washington, DC: USDHHS.

USDHHS (1984). *Evaluation of the Department of Health and Human Service Employee Counseling Services Programs: Report #3*. (Contract No. HHS-100-82-0040) Washington, DC: USDHHS, p. 2.

A Brief Overview of Research Techniques Used to Evaluate Three Employee Assistance Programs Through the Family Service Association of Metropolitan Toronto Experience

David A. Wright

SUMMARY. This article describes three models of Employee Assistance Program (EAP) evaluations used by the Family Service Association of Metropolitan Toronto, a major provider of national EAPs in Canada. Each EAP and their subsequent evaluation is tailored to the specific needs of the different organizations. Example 1 focuses on a case by case review. Example 2 describes a method of determining how well the EAP reaches troubled employees and comments on the effectiveness of the intervention. Example 3 describes how a simple but effective user survey provides information for evaluation purposes. These three evaluation models are examples of how EAPs and their evaluations respond to the uniqueness of various organizations and their respective client groups.

INTRODUCTORY COMMENTS

The Family Service Association of Metropolitan Toronto has been involved in providing Employee Assistance Programming since 1975. Twelve years later we are a major Canadian provider with a client list that is not only lengthy but perhaps more impor-

---

David A. Wright, MSW, is EAP Director, Family Service Association of Metropolitan Toronto, 14 College Street, Toronto, Ontario, Canada M5G 1K4.

tantly very impressive in terms of the quality of the participating organizations. Starting as we did in 1975 with a few Toronto area employee populations for whom we provided broad brush full service models, we now have a national presence in Canada and provide a wide variety of different program models as a response to the various needs of our corporate and government clients.

Along the way, we have among other things gained experience in the area of program evaluation and this paper will outline the major thrust of our work in this area. Our goal is not so much to focus on the results of the studies as it is to generally describe the techniques used. Although our results were universally positive – in every case well beyond even our expectations – the more interesting story for us was the manner in which we derived evaluative information that would stand the test of both the rules of client confidentiality and academic rigour.

Our choices of the techniques we will discuss below were determined in collaboration with our EAP corporate clients and were designed to meet their unique needs at a given point in the evolution of their programs. The list is not meant to represent the full range of possibilities available to those interested in evaluation and research in the employee assistance field. I will present the three models in historical order.

EXAMPLE I

An analysis of 61 mandatory referral cases involving problem drinking: prepared by David Wright of Family Service Association of Metropolitan Toronto and Russ Pickering, Alcohol Consultant, March 1985.

Program History

This Employee Assistance Program originated in 1976. The firm, whose name will not be disclosed here, has an employee population of about 9,000 employees. Their original intention was to provide a drug and alcohol program for employees. A joint committee comprised of two union and two management officials was formed to take responsibility for the creation and monitoring of the program.

Choosing an addictions counsellor proved to be a difficult task and eventually the committee enlisted the services of both the Family Service Association of Metropolitan Toronto and Canadian Mental Health Association, who collaborated in the creation of a broad brush program. Eventually, an addiction counsellor role was added to the service and under the auspices of this position, a volunteer addiction team was created, made up of company employees who had been clients of the Employee Assistance Program or other programs such as Alcoholics Anonymous.

The counselling program dealt with a variety of case problems including marriage and family problems, most of which came to the service on a voluntary or self-referral basis. This study relates to a small, but very important part of the work of the program, those cases referred on a mandatory basis. These cases had all been referred by management because of job performance or attendance problems of such a severe nature that dismissal was imminent. As well, there were typically a host of other related personal problems.

The population of this study involves the 61 mandatory referral cases seen by the counselling services between June 1976 and year end 1983. Where, beyond the performance problems mentioned above, problem drinking was a major factor.

Methodology

The main research tool used was a questionnaire designed to organize data taken directly from the files in question. Sixty one cases were studied, recorded and tabulated on the questionnaire format.

We began by looking at the type of drinking behaviour the employee was practicing when he came to the Employee Assistance Program for the first time. Two categories were used: continual drinking and binge drinking. Next we recorded the length of time the employee had been drinking and what treatment, if any, the employee received prior to intervention by the Employee Assistance Program.

Job categories were listed to establish whether the program was reaching a good cross section of the firm. We also recorded the various community resources and services utilized by the employees.

Finally, a comparison of before and after intervention by the Employee Assistance Program was made to study the results of the intervention. One of the more critical aspects of data collection was the determination of concrete evidence of outcomes. For this purpose, we had at our disposal two sources of information. In cases treated since 1982, we had regularly recorded outcomes on the Mandatory Referral Progress Report. This report was routinely completed by the counsellor quarterly on all active mandatory referrals and included statistical reports from both the counsellor and employer. Secondly, for all the cases, we were able to access case recordings.

Description of the Sample

On December 31, 1983, 19 cases were still open and 42 cases had been closed. One interesting finding related to the closed cases was that 23 or 38% of them had previously been closed and reopened. This is a higher reopening rate than the Family Service Association average of 25% and would suggest that there is a significantly higher probability that many of the closed cases may yet require further service.

The entire sample by definition involved problematic drinking. In terms of what we called "related problems" in the questionnaire, we found that 67% of the sample showed deteriorated job performance, 74% had attendance problems, and 57% described themselves as well as having personal problems.

The job categories represented by the sample, proved to cover a broadly based group. As to how well this scatter represented the actual distribution in the firm, we noted that the 45% usage rate by employees whose major job function involved the operation of a vehicle related almost exactly to the actual ratio, while the 8.2% usage rate of staff compared poorly with the actual ratio of about 20%.

Outcome Summary

The outcomes of the interventions at the time of case closing is illustrated in Figure 1 where we noted the emergence of two clear categories of outcomes; those who improved and remained in the

THERAPEUTIC AND JOB STATUS AT TIME OF CASE CLOSURE		
Therapeutic	Still Employed	Left the Firm
Improved	41	7
Failed (Unchanged, Deteriorated)	14	88
Not Known (includes open)	45	5

FIGURE 1

employ of the firm; and those who failed and left because of resignation or termination.

Another interesting finding emerged from a study of the progress of the cases between termination and time of the study. There was a 50% increase in the improved cases in the period between case closing and the time of the study. This indicated that the gains achieved by the intervention of the program were not only maintained but continued to increase with a passage of time.

This study was made somewhat less difficult because of the focus on mandatory referral cases. In these cases, the firm was aware of the names of the group and requests for job performance particulars by our counsellors were ongoing. In Employee Assistance Program studies where the general caseload is analyzed, matching of case reports and performance files is much more difficult.

Summary

This study made a major impact on our corporate client who was clear that before the advent of the EAP and its mandatory component, many of the employees had gone on for years in a nonfunctional and dangerous manner unchecked by a system that felt impotent to deal effectively with these problems. Our study showed that in a very substantial percentage of cases, some form of resolution to the problem was found after the firm decided to proceed with a mandatory referral.

EXAMPLE II

A third party program audit completed by the firm James W. Westcott & Associates Ltd. Toronto, Ontario, May 1985.

History

This study, which was completed for the same corporate customer as Example I, is a much more extensive piece of work. I discuss it here in less detail first because it was authored by a Toronto based consultant who is currently formulating a paper about his work on this study, and secondly, because with the space available here I cannot do justice to this extremely in-depth report. Instead, I will list the titles of the major sections of the report and comment in-depth on one section that I felt broke new ground in terms of evaluation research methodology.

The Areas of Focus in the Audit

This audit was commissioned by the purchasing firm to determine not just the degree to which the concept of EAP had proven to be effective for the organization but also to determine whether we, as the providers, had operated the program on behalf of the firm in the most effective manner. These objectives will become clear from a glance at the major areas of focus which appear as follows in the table of contents of the report:

Administration of the Program

a) Compliance with the Terms of the Contract
b) Time Utilizations
c) Record Keeping
d) Staffing

The Reach of the Program

a) Overview
b) Service Provision
c) Reaching a Problem Group

Effectiveness of the Program

a) Objective Measures
b) Client Opinions
c) Opinions of those involved

Mandatory Cases

Cost-Effectiveness

A Note re: Confidentiality

I will discuss in limited detail the methodology used relative to the area above entitled Reaching a Problem Group. Hopefully, the remaining items from the table of contents will be, in themselves, some help to the reader. For some, no doubt, it will stimulate a need to know more. In that case I would refer you to the author who is, strictly speaking, the owner of this technology.

Reaching the Problem Group

The question of "program reach" relates to how well the program can be shown to reach the population in general and, the troubled sector of that population in particular.

The way we handled this is, I think, new and creative. Because it was new, the consultant first cleared the technology with both the Research and Ethics Committee of Family Service of Metropolitan Toronto (FSAMT) and the Joint Committee of the company.

Specifically, the question was to determine whether the "troubled people" in the firm were actually reaching the program. In order to determine this, the consultant and the firm first collaborated with the company in the creation of a definition of "troubled." They chose to define troubled in performance terms and noted that this was making an assumption about the connection between personal problems and job performance. Certainly, troubled or not, the firm's clear interest was in reaching the nonperformers. Poor performance was defined as all those employees with 30 plus absence days, and/or 8 plus absence incidents. Names of employees who fell into this (these) categories were readily available to the company from their computer information.

Secondly, an FSAMT secretary was provided with this rather lengthy employee list, and without any prior explanation as to the purpose of the assignment, cleared that list with the master file system of FSAMT, in order to determine whether FSAMT had opened a counselling case for any of the employees on the list over the life of the Employee Assistance Program. Using FSAMT staff eliminated the confidentiality problem. Even through we were in effect matching personnel files and case information, the company could not derive any further confidential data from the exercise. The close connection between the consultant and the FSA clerical person who was purposely kept naive to the purpose of the exchange by all parties was helpful to assure proper academic rigour.

The result, which impressed us all, was the program use by this "troubled" group proved to be about six times that of the total company population and, in the words of the consultant, "suggests effectiveness."

Outcome

This very extensive study moved us and our corporate client a tremendous distance in our knowledge as to the outcomes of these programs. The specific findings mentioned above were only one area in a long list of amazing tangible measurements, that demonstrated not only the effectiveness of the employee assistance concept to the firm, but also that we, as outside providers, were performing our assignment in an affective manner.

EXAMPLE III

A Client Feedback Study Developed by Family Service Association of Metropolitan Toronto for use with its Employee Assistance Clients, 1986.

Comments

This final example is one we are particularly pleased with not only because it has produced satisfying and consistent results, but also because of its simplicity. From a collegial point of view, we would very much like to provide the actual one page questionnaire as an Appendix item for all to see and copy but, alas, it is a competitive world we live in. We consider this tool very important in the maintenance of what the marketeers call "our edge."

A Description of the Client Feedback Summary

This one page feedback is headed to the casework client at the end of the final interview. There is no advance warning to the client that a study is in progress. The client is provided with a stamped self-addressed envelope and asked to return the questionnaire without signing, or in any other way indicating their position in the organization.

The questionnaire is comprised of 12 questions. The first 11 are answered on a continuum and a final question provides for general comments. Asking the question on an "extent to which" manner allows us to measure not only yes or no answers but also to determine a rough weighing.

For example: the extent to which your job performance was affected by your personal problem.

High				Low
[ ]	[x]	[ ]	[ ]	[ ]
1	2	3	4	5

The envelopes are opened and responses are tabulated only after a previously agreed to population size has been achieved. The results are expressed simply enough by showing the total responses on the actual questionnaire which allows the reader to readily see the frequency distribution of answers e.g. ($n = 30$).

The extent to which your job performance was affect by your problem.

High				Low
7	12	6	14	1
1	2	3	4	5

The comments are shown exactly as given in the order that the responses were opened.

The Results

This elegantly simple device has proven very useful to our joint committees, senior management teams, and in one case a Board of School Trustees, who were on the verge of cancelling their Employee Assistance Program.

Probably the most dramatic finding to date is the fact that on the two studies we have completed we have had a 100% response rate! As well, we have learned a lot about our subjects that we did not know, such as the dramatic extent to which they told us that their personal problem was affecting their job performance. Additionally, we have received very high marks from our casework clients in terms of both our work and their perception of the degree of positive change that they experience with reference to their problem.

SUMMARY COMMENTS

We have discussed in general terms three types of research methods used to evaluate the effectiveness of Employee Assistance Programs. Each one has been done for a somewhat different reason and used different techniques but each has in its own way taken us one step closer to excellence in the discharge of our responsibility in the employee assistance field.

The Development and Evaluation of a Case Management System in an Employee Assistance Program

Maria Roberts-DeGennaro

SUMMARY. This article suggests there is a lack of a conceptual framework for developing a system of intervention in an Employee Assistance Program (EAP). The author proposes that the development life cycle concept is a framework for planning a case management system of intervention in an EAP. Stages of the life cycle are used to describe the activities in planning and evaluating the activities of a case management system.

Googins and Godfrey (1987) suggest that except for personnel systems, Employee Assistance Programs (EAPs) constitute the largest program type among human service programs in the workplace. EAPs increased from about 500 programs in 1973 to more than 4,000 by 1980 (NIAAA, 1980). An employee assistance program is generally defined as the policies, procedures, and services which identify or respond to employees whose personal, emotional, or behavioral problems interfere directly or indirectly with work performance (see Schmitz, 1982, p. 15; Walsh, 1982, p. 495). Services range from providing information on how and where to get help to assessment, diagnosis, referral, and treatment. There is no precise definition for EAPs or universality of any program type among the EAPs. They vary in ideological assumptions and program orientations. In addition, there is a lack of a conceptual framework or a model for developing a system of intervention in these

Maria Roberts-DeGennaro, PhD, is affiliated with the School of Social Work, San Diego State University, San Diego, CA 92182.

programs (Wrich, 1974; Shain & Groeneveld, 1980; Walsh, 1982; Roman & Blum, 1985).

This article presents a conceptual framework for developing and evaluating a case management system in an EAP. This framework builds on an earlier article by the author (1986a, p. 65) which described eleven functions of a case management practice model applicable to EAP settings. These functions are as follows:

1. Developing a network of formal resources and services, including a network of contracted services that could assist the employees in problem solving and/or decision-making;
2. Accessing (casefinding) the employees to the goals and resources of the organization in which the case manager works;
3. Assessing the employee's strengths and needs, with an emphasis on the employee's strengths rather than on problems;
4. Developing the case plan by using the basic steps in goal planning for and with the employee;
5. Establishing an employee-organization contract and if appropriate, secondary/collateral contracts;
6. Designing an individualized service network and a natural helping network for and with the employee;
7. Implementing the case plan and mobilizing the employee's networks;
8. Monitoring the delivery of services under the case plan and modifying the plan, if needed;
9. Evaluating with the employee whether the agreed on activities were effective;
10. Closing the case by informing the employee of the reentry requirements into the system, discussing the employee's progress made and not made, and understanding what case closing means to the employee; and
11. Following up after termination to ensure that no new problems have emerged that require further intervention.

These case management functions are applicable to EAP settings where the case manager is restricted to coordinating and expediting care delivered by others. Depending on the nature of the services provided by the EAP, the intensity of care will be different. For example, in managing a health problem of an employee, the case manager would be closely working with the employee's family, in order to link them with the various medical services. In addition, the case manager would be closely monitoring these services.

Regardless of the intensity of care that is provided by the case manager, a model for developing a case management system is needed. Davis (1974, p. 413) used the development life cycle concept for providing a framework for planning the activities in the development of a management information system. This development life cycle consists of three stages: definition; physical design; and implementation of the system. He suggests the application of any system needs to go through essentially the same process when the application is conceived, developed, and implemented. The author has adapted the three stages of this development life cycle in an effort to plan the activities in the development of a case management system of intervention in an EAP. In addition, the author has added another stage, an evaluation stage. An administrative audit is presented as a process evaluation strategy in evaluating the case management system.

A planning committee should be responsible for the development of the system in the organization. Committee members might include EAP staff, if an EAP exists, representation from the management levels in the organization, the department proposing the system, and the union. In addition, employee participation is necessary and essential in the development of a case management system. Services cannot successfully be created for employees; they should be created with them. Spiegel (1974, p. 138) cites reasons for employee participation in the planning of an EAP:

1. Employees must be approached if their needs and desires are to be correctly described;
2. If employees are involved in the creation of a service, the credibility of such a service will likely be heightened;
3. The utilization of a service in which employees have played a planning role will be considerably heightened than if elitist planning created it; and
4. Employees's sensitivities about being used for ulterior motives

may be lessened if fellow employees have helped create, and continue to share in the control of, a service.

Each of the development life cycle stages will be discussed, in terms of the major activities that need to be completed in developing a case management system. Some of these activities may be given more attention than others depending on the nature of the EAP.

DEFINITION OF THE CASE MANAGEMENT SYSTEM

The first phase in this stage is to define the problem by preparing a report describing: (1) the need for developing a case management system of intervention in an EAP; (2) the expected benefits from such a system; and (3) the outline for conducting a feasibility study of the system. The need for a case management system should include a description of the problem(s) presented by the troubled employees in the organization. This report could be prepared by any member(s) of the EAP planning committee.

Weaver (1979, p. 66) suggests that 11.5% of the total employee population are troubled employees. The associated work performance problems of these troubled employees are costly to the organization in absenteeism and lateness, reduced productivity, disability and health care insurance, and employee turnover and premature deaths.

Besides documenting the work-related problems associated with troubled employees, the report should address the importance of providing case management services in the workplace. In other words, why are case managers needed in the EAP? What are the benefits from having case managers? Describe how the case manager is expected to coordinate the helping activities of the service providers and/or family members in the case, in order to monitor the employee's progress.

A cost containment or cost benefit analysis should be conducted in order to document the cost savings to the organization from a case management system. For example, health care costs could be contained if a case manager is involved with an employee's family in coordinating the complex array of medical services that may be needed for a family member. The expected benefits include the cost savings accrued to the employer as a result of service provision, such as improvements in work performance, decrease in absenteeism, lateness, grievances or disciplinary actions and on-the-job accidents, and savings resulting from reduced utilization of health and mental health care. In addition, there are benefits from increased morale and life-satisfaction, as well as a reduction in public expenditures for unemployment benefits, which result from retention of workers on the job (Donovan, 1984, p. 66).

The above report should be reviewed by the the upper level management in the organization and the EAP planning committee. If the report's definition of the system is approved, a feasibility study can be conducted. Three questions need to be addressed in this study:

1. Is it possible to develop the case management system with existing technology and staff? In other words, do existing staff in the organization have the competencies to perform the case management functions, such as networking, contracting, brokering, etc?
2. Are the expected benefits from the case management system greater than the cost of implementing the system? In other words, if additional staff need to be hired or contracts with community agencies need to be negotiated, will the costs from providing the case management services be greater than the benefits?
3. Will the case management system work when implemented? For example, are there any constraints or obstacles in the organization's behavior that will interfere with the operations of this system or in the integration of services within the organization?

The feasibility study should be reviewed by the upper level management in the organization and the EAP planning committee. If the system is approved, the next phase is a resource analysis. This analysis should provide a detailed description of the resources that are needed to implement the case management system. Specifications regarding the staff who are needed to perform the case management functions, and the network of contracts with community agencies that are needed to provide supplemental services must be identified. In addition, organizational resources, e.g., information, that are needed to assist the EAP in its marketing strategies should be specified. These specifications will complete the definition of what the case management system is to achieve.

PHYSICAL DESIGN OF THE CASE MANAGEMENT SYSTEM

There are three phases in this stage: (1) system design; (2) program development; and (3) procedure development. The physical design stage starts with the system design phase. This is the design of the systems that will direct the flow of work. Specifications need to be prepared on how the EAP staff will access the users, i.e., employees, regarding the nature of the EAP intervention. That is, how will employees learn about the EAP services. Both formal and informal methods should be used, since visibility is necessary and must be high in casefinding. Since casefinding is a function of case management, the case manager should use every available communication mechanism to furnish information about the program.

A good grapevine in the organization is particularly helpful in creating the conditions under which troubled workers can seek help. The case management system should specify how gatekeepers or significant employees in the organization are to be identified. Gatekeepers assist in interpreting the nature of the EAP intervention and in exploring how it can assist the employees in doing their job (Akabas, Kurzman & Kolben, 1979, p. 21).

A system flowchart needs to be developed to show communication and information flows within the EAP, and between the EAP and other departments within the organization. The EAP staff must interface with the union, personnel departments, equal employment opportunity offices, medical departments, groups of retirees, and training groups to establish working relations. Without such outreach efforts, the EAP would be an isolated appendage, contributing little to the dynamics of the organization. Linkages to relevant organizational units assure two-way communication as well as functional integration into the culture and operations of the organization (Googins & Godfrey, 1987, p. 125).

A control flowchart needs to reflect structural characteristics such as the EAP's sponsorship and organizational placement. Most EAPs come under the auspices of corporations. Some are sponsored by unions, labor organizations, professional associations, consortiums, or contractual arrangements with external agents, such as social service agencies. Because organizational placement of the EAP is both politically and symbolically powerful, the location in a particular department, e. g., a medical department versus a personnel department, can affect the perceptions of the program. In addition, the control flowchart should identify the controllers. For instance, what department would approve a contract with a community agency that is offering to provide alcoholism prevention services in the organization for the employees?

The physical design stage also needs to address the EAP record keeping system. The EAP records should be located in a protected area. Security provisions need to be established for insuring the confidentiality of these records.

The programming and procedure development phases can proceed concurrently. The programming phase involves the preparation of a program plan, which breaks the program into functions. The 11 case management functions were identified earlier in this article. These functions are applicable to an EAP setting where the case manager is restricted to coordinating and expediting care delivered by others. It is recognized that some case managers also perform therapeutic functions. This latter function can be provided either directly by the EAP staff or through a carefully developed information and referral service (Googins, 1975, p. 465).

Case examples of fictitious troubled employees should be prepared to illustrate the functions performed by the EAP staff in the case management system. Both successful and unsuccessful case outcomes should be identified. Through these case examples, potential problems can be identified before the system is implemented. This serves as a "trial run" of the system.

Procedure development involves the preparation of instructions. "In keeping with the suggested standards for employee assistance programs, each EAP should have a clear policy statement on which to base its operations" (Lewis & Lewis, 1986, p. 40). Extensive input from management, first-line supervisors, employee representatives, and service providers should be obtained in drafting the policy. Lewis and Lewis (p. 45) suggest an EAP policy should mention some of the following factors:

1. The organization's commitment to treatment and rehabilitation of troubled employees;
2. The importance of early identification of problems;
3. The voluntary nature of employee participation in the program;
4. The recognition that high standards of performance continue to be expected;
5. The need for supervisory referrals based solely on identifiable impairment in job performance; and
6. The assurance of confidentiality in services and counseling records.

In addition, the preparation of instructions for the following materials should be completed:

1. Information for the employees on accessing the case management system and participating in the case management intervention process;
2. Information for the EAP staff on the policy and procedures in performing the case management functions;
3. Information for any consultants and/or trainers regarding the preparation of training materials, etc.;
4. Information for supervisors on referring employees to the EAP, if supervisory referrals are policy mandated; and
5. Information for the controllers on contractual arrangements with community agencies.

Record keeping procedures need to be prepared. The EAP record keeping system should consist of scrupulously guarded confidential material that has been gathered through approved organizational channels and from outside treatment agencies, as well as from the employee (Googins & Godfrey, 1987, p. 127). Therefore, operating procedures need to be established for the EAP staff in accessing and closing files.

All of the above procedures should be written and tested for completeness, clarity, and ease of use. Written notification should be prepared and distributed to the employees on what the EAP is and how they can use it.

IMPLEMENTATION OF THE CASE MANAGEMENT SYSTEM

First-line supervisors play a key role in implementing a case management system, since they are often called upon to identify and refer troubled employees to the EAP. Successful implementation requires that supervisors develop the knowledge, attitudes, and skills needed to blend confrontation and encouragement. Training for both supervisors and union stewards should be provided on how to make use of the EAP as a supervisory support system (Lewis & Lewis, 1986, p. 43).

Recently, 85 companies in San Diego County completed a survey on the need for EAP related services (Roberts-DeGennaro, 1986b). Sixty-five percent (n = 55) of these companies were small, employing 500 or less employees. About one-half (n = 40) of the companies had an EAP. Over one-half (n = 47) of the companies judged the problem of alcohol and drug abuse to be somewhat serious in their work force. About 90% (n = 75) of the companies indicated supervisors were responsible for identifying troubled employees in their companies. Sixty percent (n = 51) of the companies believed training was primarily needed for their supervisors in assessing substance abuse problems, as well as family and mental health problems.

Clear communication with the organization's entire work force is also important in implementing a case management system. In order to know what the EAP is and how they can use it, orientation sessions should be conducted for the employees. The desired outcome from these sessions is that employees feel the EAP is a resource that can help them to enhance their personal well-being and to maintain their effectiveness as workers (Lewis & Lewis, 1986, p. 46).

About one-third of the EAP staff's time will probably be spent on maintaining the case management system. Staff will be involved in the day-to-day operation, modification, and maintenance of the system. Data need to be collected on the demographics and numbers of employees served and the type of services provided, as well as other relevant information.

PROCESS EVALUATION OF THE CASE MANAGEMENT SYSTEM

A process evaluation is an assessment of how much effort in the form of human and physical resources is invested in the system and whether the effort is expended as planned. Process evaluation is a way to monitor the degree to which a system is implemented as planned. It provides quantified information to summarize the type and amount of services provided and to whom these services are given. This information is needed to facilitate planning and decision-making, to anticipate problems, and to justify the existence of the program. An outcome evaluation can be done later and more easily after a process evaluation has been conducted (Posavac & Carey, 1980, pp. 103-105).

An administrative audit is an evaluation strategy that can be used to conduct a process evaluation of the case management system. The audit assists in monitoring the system and/or in improving the management of the system or the operations of the system, if it is not functioning properly. The audit describes what is done by the case management staff in relation to standards established by sources external and/or internal to the program (Tripodi, Fellin & Epstein, 1971 and 1978).

Tripodi, Fellin, and Epstein (1978, p. 64) suggest the audit as an evaluative strategy is a procedure to:

1. Evaluate the suitability of policies and practices directed toward compliance with those policies. For example, what case-finding efforts are being made to access employees? What are the profiles of the employees who are receiving services? Are the case managers adhering to nondiscriminatory practices in providing services in a confidential manner?
2. Evaluate the adherence of case management staff practices to designated divisions of responsibility and function. Are the case managers performing the 11 case management functions

as planned? What are the case managers' perceptions of their functions and responsibilities? What actual services are being provided?

3. Evaluate the organizational patterns of work in terms of preferred and efficient procedures within the program and/or between the program and other programs of a similar nature. What are the work loads of the case management staff? To what extent do existing staff practices correspond with the organizational patterns of work as reflected in the organizational chart?

Standards of service need to be articulated in order to conduct this process evaluation. In other words, what proportion of the employee population are expected to be served and what services are they to receive. These standards should be operationally defined as a percentage of the total employees who are to receive services and the types of services to be provided.

A client (employee) census can be used for monitoring the number and types of employees in contact with the program, the types of services requested, and the types of services received. Such a census provides a quantitative description of program contacts with employees and makes possible comparison of this information with previously planned standards of service delivery. As a result, this information will assist in making adjustments in casefinding and in the service delivery pattern. Since organizations are concerned with the cost per employee served, a client census can also document the cost of client contact (Epstein & Tripodi, 1977, pp. 59-64).

Standards of staff performance also need to be articulated. In other words, how do staff make use of their time? These standards should be operationally defined as the amount of time that case managers are expected to devote to the 11 case management functions. In addition, these functions should be rank ordered, from highest to lowest, in terms of the amount of time that should be allocated to each function depending on organizational priorities.

A time and activity study can be used in monitoring staff performance. This study describes the number and types of activities in which staff are engaged within specified units of time. The time frame should correspond to that used for recording employee contacts. Thus if statistics for client (employee) processing are recorded for a given month, the time and activity study should represent the same month. Programs are often required to demonstrate to the organization how staff are spending their work time. The information from this study can be used to estimate the costs in time and money of different aspects of staff performance. This information will also be helpful in making decisions about the structuring and restructuring of the case management functions (Epstein & Tripodi, 1977, pp. 70-75).

Tripodi, Fellin, and Epstein (1978, pp. 65) state, "The knowledge obtained from an administrative audit is usually in the form of facts pertaining to administrative and staff work patterns and the extent to which the program could improve its goals in relation to its management activities." They suggest the information gained from this administrative audit may be used to form judgments such as:

1. Whether discriminatory practices exist toward providing services to employees in the organization;
2. If there is a lack of compliance with specified regulations or functions in the case management system;
3. If there are personnel conflicts in the operation of the case management system; and
4. If there is a lack of compliance with accepted professional case management practices.

Based on this information, recommendations can be made concerning the efforts the case management system should make to be more effective and efficient in its practices. Information will be available on who receives what services from whom and when the service is given. This information can assist staff in developing rational plans for improving the case management system.

CONCLUSION

It is important that the case management system is designed and documented for maintainability. Davis (1974) emphasizes that neglecting any portion of the life cycle activities in developing a system may have serious consequences for the end result. The life cycle is important in the planning, management, control, and evaluation of the case management system. In order to manage and control the development effort, it is necessary to know what should have been done, what has been done, how well it has been done, and what has yet to be accomplished.

REFERENCES

Akabas, Sheila; Kurzman, Paul & Kolben, Nancy (eds.) (1979). *Labor and Industrial Settings: Sites for Social Work Practice*. New York: Columbia University School of Social Work.

Cohn, Anne & DeGraaf, Beverly (1982). "Assessing Case Management in the Child Abuse Field." *Journal of Social Service Research*, 5:29-43.

Davis, Gordon (1974). *Management Information Systems: Conceptual Foundations, Structure and Development*. New York: McGraw Hill.

Donovan, Rebecca (1984). "The Dollars and 'Sense' of Human Services at the Workplace – A Review of Cost-Effectiveness Research." *Social Work Papers*. Los Angeles: University of South California School of Social Work.

Epstein, Irwin & Tripodi, Tony (1977). *Research Techniques for Program Planning, Monitoring, and Evaluation*. New York: Columbia University Press.

Googins, Bradley & Godfrey, Joline (1987). *Occupational Social Work*. Englewood Cliffs, NJ: Prentice-Hall.

Lewis, Judith & Lewis, Michael (1986). *Counseling Programs for Employees in the Workplace*. Monterey, CA: Brooks/Cole.

NIAAA (1980). *Alcohol and Health, 4th Report to the Congress*. Washington, DC: U.S. Government Printing Office.

Posavac, Emil & Carey, Raymond (1980). *Program Evaluation: Methods and Case Studies*. Englewood Cliffs, NJ: Prentice-Hall.

Roberts-DeGennaro, Maria (1986a). "The Case Management Model in Employee Assistance Programs." *Employee Assistance Quarterly*. 1:63-74.

Roberts-DeGennaro, Maria (1986b). Survey of Need for Continuing Education in the Corporate Sector. San Diego State University: School of Social Work.

Roberts-DeGennaro, Maria (1988). "Developing Case Management as a Practice Model." *Social Casework*, forthcoming.

Roman, Paul & Blum, T. (1985). "Core Technology." The *ALMACAN*, 15, pp. 8, 9, 16, 18, 19.

Schmitz, Harold (1982). *The Handbook of Employee Counseling Programs*. New York: The New York Business Group on Health.

Shain, Martin & Groeneveld, J. (1980). *Employee-Assistance Programs: Philosophy, Theory, and Practice*. Lexington, MA: DC Heath.

Spiegel, Hans (1974). *Not for Work Alone. Services at the Workplace*. Springfield: National Technical Information Service. Contract #DL21-36-73-08.

Tripodi, Tony; Fellin, Phillip & Epstein, Irwin (1971). *Social Program Evalua-*

tion: Guidelines for Health, Education, and Welfare Administrators. Itasca, IL: F. E. Peacock.

______(1978). *Differential Social Program Evaluation*. Itasca, IL: F. W. Peacock.

Walsh, D.C. (1982). "Employee Assistance Programs." *Health and Society*, 60:492-517.

Weaver, C.A. (1979). "EAP's—How They Improve the Bottom Line." *Risk Management*, 27:22-26.

Wrich, James (1974). *The Employee Assistance Program*. Center City, MN: Hazelden.

One Organization's Experience in a Case Management/EAP Program: Implications for Monitoring and Evaluation

Charles E. Stanley
Marcia Murphy
Robert J. Peters

SUMMARY. Historically, Employee Assistance Programs (EAPs) have been viewed as an employee benefit even through there is documented evidence of their cost-effectiveness for the company. This article presents an integration of the Employee Assistance Program and Case Management as a way of providing a proactive method of containing health care costs. Such an integration will expand the focus of the Employee Assistance Program, strengthen our role as an employee advocate, and provide a method of demonstrating to corporations that EAPs do contribute to the "bottom line" profit margin of the company.

This article outlines the components of an effective, comprehensive Employee Assistance Program and discusses the process of integrating a Case Management system that emphasizes local demographic control within the EAP.

As we all are aware, Employee Assistance Programs (EAPs) are not new to the work force. EAPs have been effective to varying degrees in curbing costs associated with the "troubled employee"

Charles E. Stanley, MSW, LSW II, is President and CEO; Marcia Murphy, PhD, is Vice President; and Robert J. Peters, MSW, is Contract Manager and Clinician of Professional Employee Advisement Program (PEAP), P.O. Box 1591, Arvada, CO 80002.

at the workplace as well as reducing related benefit plan utilization costs. Studies have demonstrated that EAPs reduce insurance costs, save money through decreased absenteeism, tardiness turnover, and job related accidents; however, EAPs have been unable to statistically show the cost savings from increased production, quality, improvement, and quantity. We are able to speculate the cost of savings in these areas by pointing to research of the industrial psychologists which documents an increase in productivity as a result of changes in the workplace environment.

As EAPs evolved, they were viewed as a benefit to the employee. During the past five years contracting organizations have been increasingly concerned with the effect that health care costs have on the "bottom line" profitability of the organization. As a method of addressing these concerns, they have turned to Utilization Review Programs (URPs) to address the rising health care costs. To date, URPs have operated separately from the EAP. URPs characteristically utilize telephone consultations and second opinions as the primary methodology for generating cost savings. Typically, URPs have either excluded or have not effectively addressed psychiatric problems and/or substance abuse. This is primarily a result of the medical model philosophy underlying the URP's process and the lack of accepted standards for treatment modalities directly and expense similar to Diagnostic Related Groups (DRGs) for psychiatric and/or substance abuse treatment. Medical service providers and provider networks have marketed the medical model approach, by offering discounts for exclusive use of their facilities and networks. In the pressure for cost containment, traditional and sacred EAP tenets, i.e., provider care quality, appropriateness of treatment, and effectiveness, have been ignored or minimized.

To address the inherent conflict of interest which developed when the hospital-based or provider network URPs provided case management services, insurance companies, and self-insured medical plans developed contracts with third party administrators to provide case management for their health insurance claims. Limitations with this alternative include: no opportunity for constructive, preventive intervention based on accumulated data; no commitment to the unique needs and situations of particular organization contracting for the services; and an absence of reliable DRGs specifically for psychiatric problems and substance abuse. The utilization review is conducted far from the employee's residence.

The Professional Employee Advisement Program (PEAP) has developed an alternative to these two models – a program which integrates the EAP with a Case Management system (EAP/CM). This allows for case management services in the employee's residential area; the development of an ongoing process to continually evaluate treatment providers in the community; and the integration of the case management system with the preventive components of the EAP. An outline of PEAP's philosophy relative to the internal components of an effective EAP provider will serve as the foundation for discussion of the EAP/CM.

EAP's INTERNAL ADMINISTRATIVE COMPONENT

One of the most difficult tasks of an effective EAP is to develop a strong middle management structure which facilitates the implementation of the EAP in demographic areas outside the corporate headquarters. A high quality and effective EAP often becomes ineffective because the business has outgrown its management capabilities. One of the most critical times for an EAP is that period when the business is moving from a local or regional area of influence to a national marketing area. With more and more organizations having facilities in multiple locations, it is imperative that the EAP be able to offer services nationwide. This transition requires a foundation of strong, middle management, which can cultivate the philosophies of the EAP organization in geographic locations where the EAP develops its presence. Historically, EAPs have developed because of the leadership and charisma of a single leader; if the EAP is not able to make the transition from a posture of single leadership to a management team approach then national expansion will be difficult, if not impossible.

It is important that contracts be reviewed and monitored by a middle management person on a weekly basis. The intent of the monitoring is to both evaluate the effectiveness of the contract and challenge the contract manager with creative ideas, and discuss potential problems before they surface and weaken the effectiveness of the EAP.

ASSESSMENT AND REFERRAL COMPONENT

This component serves as the foundation for any effective EAP. It is important that the assessment component be comprised with the following elements.

All clinical and contract management staff are licensed or capable of licensure in a mental health subject area. The clinical group has an extensive knowledge-base in the disease concept of substance abuse. The clinicians are able to complete an extensive differential diagnosis which encompasses substance abuse as a primary disorder. Individual clinical supervision occurs on a weekly basis, group clinical supervision meetings are held monthly.

It is our belief that the effectiveness of an EAP clinician is determined by his or her clinical training (30%) and ability to develop a sensitive, empathetic, caring relationship with the client (70%). An EAP clinician would be extensively trained in the EAP philosophy, since through observation and experience we strongly belief that traditional therapists are fundamentally different from an EAP clinician.

Response time and location. A person's decision to reach out and ask for help can be a painful and difficult decision to make for an employee. That decision should not be treated lightly and responded with a call to a distant city. This initial request for service demands an immediate response by staff located in the employee's residential area. EAP staff located outside the employee's demographic area lose a very valuable element—they are unable to respond to the employee's request from an understanding of the local values and belief systems. As will be discussed shortly, one of the potential dangers for the future of the EAP field is if EAPs copy the PPO/URPs and providing services from a distance. One of the strengths of the EAP profession is an integration of the employee, employer, and the community components. This cannot be effectively accomplished without the EAP being diversified enough to allow for separate administrative offices and personnel in local and regionally accessible locations.

SUPERVISORY TRAINING

One of the most important areas of the EAP is the relationship between the EAP and the organization's supervisors. The importance of maintaining a high percentage of supervisor referrals is obvious. EAPs are designed to directly influence work related behaviors such as accidents, absenteeism, tardiness, productivity, employee turnover, and product quality. PEAP has developed an extensive supervisory training package that not only provides supervisors with training regarding issues of performance management and the methodology of using the EAP as a management resource, but also provides a constant, highly visible EAP within the supervisory ranks. The EAP needs to be accessible to the supervisor and be able to respond to the requests of the supervisor with a direct face-to-face intervention for the employee or a consultation with the supervisor.

An important service that the EAP can provide for the supervisor is to provide support to the supervisor before, during, and after the confrontation between the supervisor and employee. The supervisor often experiences many varying feelings during the employee confrontation; it is important that the supervisor have an arena to ventilate and debrief from the confrontation process. In order for the supervisor to trust the EAP and become an integral part of the EAP network the staff needs to provide on-site availability and consistent contact with supervisory personnel.

INTERNAL EMPLOYEE MARKETING AND EDUCATIONAL/PREVENTIVE SEMINARS

As external EAP providers, we are aware of the importance of marketing the EAP in the community to insure that we maintain a high visibility and continued expansion of our contract base. The same philosophy is true for the internal marketing of the EAP within the organization. We understand when an employee is having a personal crisis they will respond to those resources that are known and readily available. For this reason, it is important that the EAP maintain a high level of visibility within the organizational structure. This is achieved by offering a series of ongoing seminars to the employee population, so that an EAP representative is recognizable both by voice and face. Additionally, the rotation of different bulletin board posters, newsletters, and employee brochures maintain this high level of visibility.

EAPs present the organization with a number of hidden costs that increase the actual program cost. Historically, EAPs have presented cost savings data based solely on a reduction of health care costs, turnover, absenteeism, tardiness, and job accidents. These are all valid statistics; however, there are "hidden" costs that need to be factored into the equation: Management and support staff spend time tailoring the EAP to meet the organization's specific needs; the time that supervisors spend in learning how to use the EAP appropriately, the time employees spend in assessment sessions or preventive seminars during working hours; and the amount of time that management and liaison personnel spend evaluating and coordinating the EAP within the organizational structure. It is PEAP's position that the hidden costs cannot be recovered unless the EAP maintains a utilization rate of at least 8%. Considering the national average utilization rate accepted by many EAPs is between 7 and 8%, it could be assumed that many EAPs are not cost-effective for the organization.

In recent years, EAPs have enjoyed an increasing acceptance with the corporate culture as a benefit available to the employee/dependent. Many EAPs have not had to justify their existence and, as a result, utilization data and cost-effectiveness have been important, but not a priority. It is PEAP's belief that in the 1990s, we, as a field, will have to justify our contribution to the "bottom line" profit or we will not have the continued level of acceptance which we presently enjoy.

We believe that EAPs can affect the bottom line by an even further reduction in major medical claims than is presently evidenced by the EAPs or Utilization Review organizations. This is accomplished by integrating the EAP with case management of psychiatric conditions and substance abuse treatment.

THE EFFECTIVENESS OF THE CASE MANAGEMENT SYSTEM

If an EAP integrates a case management system into its program, a number of variables that must be considered to assure effectiveness of the merging:

1. The EAP needs to be autonomous from the contracting organization, health care companies, and preferred provider networks. Autonomy from the contracting organization limits the extent of management infringement on the EAP, maintains the confidentiality of the program, and permits the foundation for employee trust. Case management that is offered by health care corporations or preferred provider networks results in case management of their own internal networks, which provide many obstacles for cost accountability. The EAP must be able to choose from all the resources available in the community and select the highest quality, most cost-efficient treatment resource available to the employee without pressure from the corporation or treatment providers. EAPs that are connected with health care corporations or preferred provider networks are one of the most significant threats to the EAP field. The foundation of EAP services has always been based on autonomy. When the major treatment organizations use the EAP as a resource to promote their programs and services, then the EAP is no longer able to function within the basic guidelines of EAP definition. This becomes an even more critical issue as the EAP considers the option of integrating the case management program into its EAP.

2. The EAP must have qualified staff that are highly trained and able to relate to the ramifications of the differential diagnosis and the complexities of substance abuse treatment. Staff that are providing EAP/CM services should be licensed or licensable in their particular state. As we will discuss shortly, the case management services will be conducted in the offices located in the employee/dependents geographic area. Therefore, highly trained clinical personnel are necessary in all office-site locations. It is important that the organization provide ongoing clinical training in those areas of clinical staff weaknesses. It is PEAP's contention that the current ALMACA EAP certification does not adequately test the clinical skill level of the EAP staff to provide the case management ser-

vices. For this reason we use state's licensing as the baseline for selecting clinical staff.

3. The EAP that integrates the case management component into its program must be committed to providing EAP services at the corporate site locations and not via an 800 telephone number, except in specific instances. We believe that the EAP must understand the cultural and social variables impacting the employee population and their families. Additionally, as the EAP staff develops linkages within management systems there will be the opportunity for impacting the "bottom line" profit via preventive seminars and workshops, which specifically address the needs of that facility.

Another reason for providing the EAP/CM services on a local level is the opportunity for the local EAP staff to monitor the treatment resources for quality and fee rates. After the EAP/CM system develops baseline cost and quality data, the EAP then can become a powerful advocate for both the organization and the employee in the area of high quality, cost-efficient treatment.

4. The final variable for consideration is the necessity for the EAP providing case management services to maintain assessment and referral services as the core methodology for client service. When the EAP provides an 8 to 10 session model, the EAP is, in essence, providing short-term treatment. As mentioned earlier, it is difficult to conduct quality case management services, when you are also providing the treatment. The cost savings of the case management services are realized in those cases that require treatment extending beyond the short-term treatment model. In these situations, the EAP clinician must terminate the treatment, make an appropriate referral, and coordinate the exchange of treatment. This process lengthens treatment because of the termination process and the inherent difficulty associated with the rebuilding of the therapeutic relationship.

After the case management system is integrated into EAP, the EAP/CM system provides the following case management services within the structure of the EAP:

1. The case management process is to be conducted from the employee's residential area with an immediate backup to a centralized location which provides clinical consultation and program coordination. All offices are to be staffed by clinicians who have an

extensive treatment history in both psychological and substance abuse disorders. Cases enter the system either through the EAP or via request of the employee/dependent outside the EAP. Preauthorization for either inpatient or outpatient treatment via face-to-face evaluation would be necessary prior to referral initiation. As a result of the evaluation, the clinician completes a clinical assessment form which addresses such issues as DSM III diagnosis, problem priority rating scale, anticipated length of treatment, projected cost, and motivation of the employee/dependent. After the evaluation is completed the employee is referred to the appropriate resource located in the community. The referral is made immediately after the evaluation, and the provider schedules the initial session within 48 hours.

2. Insurance claims are monitored so that those employees who do not use the EAP as the entry point will be incorporated into the case management system prior to the initial claim being authorized for payment. An active promotional campaign at the onset of the case management system alerts the employee to the necessity of using the program. During the first year the employee is not penalized for not using the case management system, but is obligated to become involved after treatment is initiated by the employee. After the first year of implementation, the organization implements a graduated level of reimbursement for major medical claims; and the level of reimbursement is based on both case management involvement and the extent to which the employee follows the recommendations of the case manager.

3. Both inpatient and outpatient treatment requires preauthorization by the EAP/case manager. Historically, Utilization Review systems have focused their efforts on inpatient hospitalization, but considerable cost savings can be realized by monitoring outpatient treatment. As the system becomes more integrated, the EAP serves as an advocate for cost containment and negotiates a decreasing fee for treatment that parallels the length of treatment. Additionally, the treatment is reviewed on a scheduled basis to insure that the goals of therapy are in line with the DSM III diagnosis and priority rating scale. The EAP case manager assumes a proactive role whenever a discrepancy in the reporting materials exist.

4. As with outpatient treatment, inpatient treatment requires preauthorization prior to hospitalization. Emergency hospitalizations

are authorized for up to 72 hours, but a clinical assessment must occur within the 72 hours for treatment to be reimbursed beyond the preauthorization period. The hospital and attending physician provide the same baseline data required for outpatient treatment process. When discrepancies occur, the case manager discusses the situation with the treatment facility to reach an acceptable compromise according to the treatment plan.

5. Because the EAP/CM service is conducted in the employee's residential area, the manager is able to monitor the inpatient and outpatient treatment resources. This permits the EAP to regularly update its treatment network to reflect those facilities that are providing the best treatment at lowest cost. It also permits the case management system to provide "hands on" involvement with the clinical community. This is necessary because, to date, the treatment process for psychiatric and substance abuse disorders have not been challenged by the health care community. Accountability for this type of treatment has not begun to approach the level of sophistication attained by medical disorders.

6. As mentioned earlier, both the EAP/case manager and the treatment resource completes a DSM III diagnosis. The intent is to develop DRGs relative to the various diagnostic categories. We accept that the DRGs cannot be adhered to as rigorously as medical illnesses are categorized; however, the DRGs can serve as a baseline to determine effective treatment modalities, cost of treatment, and the anticipated length of treatment. With this baseline data the case manager then includes employee motivation, family support, and other relevant criteria to develop an effective case management plan.

7. The EAP/CM system monitors health insurance costs to establish baselines for "high risk" cases. When employees reach the baseline the EAP will initiate an "Intensive Onsite Case Review." The focus of the review is to evaluate the treatment plan to insure the employee is receiving the most intensive treatment, at the lowest cost, without sacrificing quality of care. Using this model, PEAP has been instrumental in working with treatment centers to develop an integrated model of inpatient and intensive outpatient treatment, as an alternative to traditional, long-term inpatient treatment of psychiatric and substance abuse disorders.

8. A final area of EAP/CM services is to develop baselines of

health care costs for individuals and families within the company's medical plan. When an employee and/or family reaches an 80% level of baseline data, the employee or family is invited to participate in a Health Risk Appraisal. The Health Risk Appraisal evaluates medical and emotional factors for the employee and/or dependent. If the employee participates the company increases their level of claim reimbursement; and when the employee agrees to participate in recommended programs the level of benefit claim reimbursement increases to an even higher level. This serves as an incentive for employee participation, which decreases the perception of the program as invasive.

One of the greatest assets of the EAP is its ability to work with supervisors in the identification and intervention process of the "troubled employee." This process permits the employee to become involved in an extensive rehabilitation process that involves early detection, intervention, and treatment of the identified problem. After the employee is identified and referred, the EAP manages the employee's treatment to insure the treatment is the highest quality and cost-efficient. When inpatient treatment is indicated, the EAP monitors the employee's progress, to ensure the treatment has resulted in the stabilization of the job dysfunctional behavior.

Chart I outlines the integration of the EAP/CM system within a contracting corporation.

The philosophy of the integrated EAP/CM consists of providing the highest quality, most cost-efficient treatment to any employee/dependent of the organization. At no time are the clinical needs of the employee compromised to save dollars. This model saves organizations significant dollars by monitoring treatment goals of resource clinicians and treatment centers, decreasing unnecessary inpatient hospitalizations, recommending intensive outpatient treatment, when appropriate, and developing a local base referral network which provides the highest quality, most cost-efficient treatment for the employees and their families.

Earlier in the presentation, we discussed the components of an EAP, and omitted the Usage/Reporting System. It is PEAP's belief that the combination of EAP and case management presents the most reliable method of monitoring effectiveness of the program. The contracting organization ideally has available information regarding the amount spent on health insurance claims for the year

Chart 1

EMPLOYEE ASSISTANCE PROGRAM CASE MANAGEMENT SYSTEM

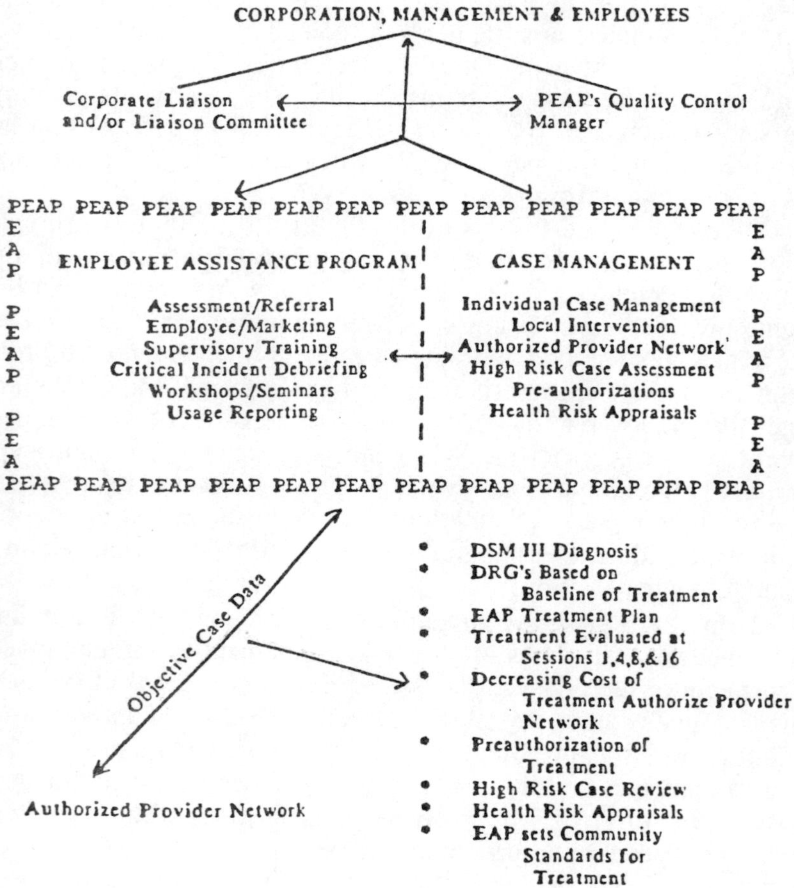

prior to the implementation of the program. The total expense for health insurance claims "paid out" during the year the EAP/CM is operational, minus, the previous year's expense which represents the gross cost savings. We subtract the cost of the EAP/CM service, and factor 10% of the total health insurance claims "paid out" in the given year to cover the "hidden costs"; and this gives us the "bottom line" net profit to the organization in the area of health insurance cost savings. Example: Organization A has 1,000 employees and in 1985 has a total expense for health insurance costs of $1,000,000.00. In 1986, Organization A implemented the EAP/CM service at a cost of $33,000.00. At the end of 1986, Organization A's expense for health insurance cost was $500,000.00. We subtract from the 1985 figure of $1,000,000.00 the 1986 expense of $500,000.00, plus 10% or $50,000.00 for hidden costs, and the $33,000.00 for the cost of the program and we are able to report a "bottom line" net savings of $417,000.00. This is profit to Organization A.

CONCLUSION

Employee Assistance Programs have proven their effectiveness in providing a cost-efficient, effective intervention resource for organizations and their employees/dependents who experience an emotional or substance abuse problem. In recent years, the EAP has been viewed as an employee benefit, which has a significant impact on the potential viability of the program. Traditional case management programs have relied on employee awareness and second opinions as a method of containing health care costs. PEAP believes that by integrating the Employee Assistance Program with case management the organization and its employees will realize a more sensitive, professional resource for managing employee health care and its related costs. Additionally, by providing a significant "bottom line" net profit the EAP will move from an employee benefit to an organizational necessity.

Establishing and Evaluating an Industrial Social Work Programme: The Seagram, Amherstburg Experience

R. G. Chandler
B. J. Kroeker
M. Fynn
D. A. MacDonald

SUMMARY. The process of establishing and evaluating an industrial social work programme in a small distillery using a third party university model is described. The programme is based on a participatory philosophy and the importance of joint management and union "ownership" of the programme is emphasized. The evaluation examined health and attitudes of employees, absenteeism and productivity, cost effectiveness and reduction in grievances. The overall finding was that both the employees and the corporation benefitted substantially from the project.

Employee Assistance Programmes (EAPs) that have a professional social work component can be categorized into three basic types according to the nature of their auspices (Chandler, 1983, p. 3). Some are entirely management sponsored with social workers employed directly, either in a separate department or as part of the medical, personnel, or other department of the industry. A few are entirely union sponsored, where a large union provides a social

---

R.G. Chandler, MSW, is Associate Professor, University of Windsor; B.J. Kroeker, MSW, is Professor, University of Windsor; M. Fynn, MSW, is affiliated with The Inn, Windsor, Ontario; and D.A. MacDonald, MSW, is affiliated with Syl. Apps. Correctional Center, Toronto. Address correspondence to R.G. Chandler, School of Social Work, University of Windsor, Windsor, Ontario, Canada N9P 3P4.

work service to its members. Still others are operated under third party contracts where an industry negotiates an agreement with a social agency, a university, or a private entrepreneur who employs the social workers and operates the service in the industry itself. In this paper, the development and initial evaluation of an industrial social work programme operated under a contract with a university is presented, with a focus on some of the issues pertinent to the stable establishment and effective evaluation of such a programme.

ESTABLISHMENT OF THE SEAGRAM, AMHERSTBURG INDUSTRIAL SOCIAL WORK PROJECT

The first industrial social work programme in Seagram's of Canada was begun in 1975 at the company's plant near Montréal, Québec, under an agreement with the School of Social Work at nearby McGill University. As a result of this experience, the company decided to expand the service to its plants in Waterloo and Amherstburg, Ontario and Gimli, Manitoba, using the same third party university model. While the company believed that the provision of an on-site social work service was an effective way of dealing with employee psychosocial problems affecting the workplace, it also believed that the service would be better accepted by employees if it were not administered by them. Consequently, in setting up its first service, it sought an outside organization with expertise in social work programmes, and a university school of social work appeared to be an appropriate locus for the administration of such a programme. After over two years of success in its relationship with the McGill school, it seemed logical to use the same model at its other Canadian plants, and the company, therefore, invited representatives of the university schools of social work proximal to each plant to explore the possibility of developing services similar to the ones in Montréal.

Following this exploratory meeting, the Director of Personnel at the plant in Amherstburg, Ontario, a plant employing some 300 employees, contacted the School of Social Work at the University of Windsor and a contract was developed outlining the responsibilities of the University, the company and the social worker, as well as the general objectives of the programme. The programme began in the fall of 1978 with an experienced social worker with an MSW degree employed by the University and administratively accountable to two social work faculty members. The social worker was present in the plant one day each week.

While the first social worker appeared to be accepted by the employees, use of the service was limited and, when disagreement between management and labour resulted in a strike in June 1979, it was mutually agreed that the programme should be temporarily discontinued.

Subsequent to this initial attempt to establish the programme, the University consultants reexamined the process and concluded that, while they had been assured that the union was supportive of the project, it appeared that union personnel had not been significantly involved, and that the programme was seen as "owned" by management. Consequently, the service was not actively endorsed by the union and its member were not encouraged to use it.

In an effort to ensure that union personnel would be effectively involved when the programme was reintroduced, visits were made to several other programmes. Two of the programmes visited operated under third party contracts with 15 different workplaces. From these visits and a review of the literature, it became clear that one way of ensuring meaningful involvement of union personnel was to establish a joint union-management committee to oversee the programme (Perlis, 1977, p. 31). Accordingly, when the company approached the University to start the service again in the fall of 1981, the first step was to establish such a committee, comprised of two members of the union, two members of management and the project social worker. This committee was active from the outset in determining the nature of the programme and even in interviewing and approving of the social worker prior to hiring. The committee has continued to meet regularly with the social worker and periodically with the University consultants.

> All policy concerns, involving the social work programme, are filtered through the Joint Committee. Statistical records related to the programmes are shared with the Joint Committee and policies and procedures are discussed and developed in

> this Committee and relayed to both union and management, to ensure joint support. (Fynn & McDonald, 1986, p. 20)

Since the reestablishment of the programme in 1981, there have been three different social workers, with the present one being employed since 1984. Use of the service has steadily increased, and even though the employee population has declined to approximately 250, the programme has been expanded to one and a half days of service per week. Suitable office space is provided on-site and in addition, the company has leased part-time office space in Amherstburg. Space is also made available in nearby Windsor at the University in order to accommodate employees and family members who may find it convenient or more comfortable to meet outside of the work day or away from the plant.

PROGRAMME FEATURES

Ozawa (1980) identifies four stages in the development of social services in industry. The first stage is that of service delivery to individual employees, focussing on specific problems such as alcoholism or drug abuse that are of primary concern to the company. Stage two is one in which the service expands to include a spectrum of psychosocial problems experienced by workers and their families and a wide range of preventive and educational activities in addition to direct intervention. The third stage shifts the focus from the individual employee to organizational intervention and the final stage is characterized by an emphasis on the common interests of management and employees, their loyalty to each other, and the incorporation of objectives other than profit-making. It should be noted that the final stage has seldom been reached (Ozawa, 1980, p. 469).

The initial design of the programme with the support of the Joint Committee included prevention and education as well as direct intervention components. The programme could be described as being at Ozawa's second stage with indications of movement towards stage three (MacDonald & Fynn, 1986, p. 21). While the programme has responded to a broad spectrum of psychosocial problems from the outset (although the company's initial concern and motivation for establishing the programme was the problem of alcoholism) and it has provided both on-site counselling and referral to appropriate community agencies, the social worker has provided leadership in the provision of "health promotion" programmes with films, speakers, and discussions on such topics as alcoholism and stress management, as well as weekly relaxation exercise programmes. All components of the programme have been offered to family members as well as the employees themselves.

As indication of movement to stage three, that of a shift in focus from individual to organizational intervention, the Joint Committee together with additional members of management and union participated in the development of a drug and alcohol policy for the plant as a whole. As a result, the policy has been accepted by consensus of both union and management and both are committed to its implementation.

Most recently, the company has provided a well-equipped gymnasium for the use of employees. Another joint committee with membership from union and management was set up to establish and maintain this facility. This development is perhaps an indication of some movement in the direction of stage four.

EVALUATING THE PROGRAMME

The concept of evaluation was built into the very foundation of the Seagram Social Work Project at Amherstburg. The *Statement of Understanding* between the University and Seagram's, prominently identifies the Joint committee as having overall responsibility for ensuring that an evaluative system is developed to test the success of the project. The scope of the evaluation is also outlined and it specifies the areas which the evaluation is to include. These are:

1. The health and attitudes of employees;
2. Absenteeism and productivity of employees;
3. Cost-effectiveness of the project; and
4. Reduction in grievances.

The concept of programme evaluation had been established but it was necessary to give the programme time to make an impact on the employees and the administration, which might be discernable. The evaluating, therefore, did not take place until a full three years had elapsed from the time of the present *Statement of Understanding*.

A number of factors had to be defined before the evaluation could be implemented, such as the philosophy of the programme, the roles of the Joint Committee and the University consultants, how the research project was to be staffed, and of course, the methodology to be employed.

The Philosophic Perspective

The Seagram project had been launched upon a participatory model that seemed to be working well. The evaluation, therefore, would need to be operationalized as a participatory endeavor if it was to be consistent with the operation of the project. Cunningham (1978) indicated that a high degree of participation "decreases the barriers to the utilization of the data . . . increases the probability that the results would be understood . . . and yields positive motivation to apply the results" (p. 34). All of these elements were of course highly desirable outcomes for a project which clearly was, in the first instance, intended to be developmental in nature and having an ecological perspective on competence enhancement. Such a perspective suggests that participants "should play active roles" and that they should "participate meaningfully in such areas as assessment, goal formulation, and selection of interventive strategies" (Maluccio, 1981, p. 15).

The evaluation of the Seagram project was intended to do more than merely produce a report on the "state-of-the-project." It was intended to become an integral part of the ongoing development of the enterprise. To achieve this intent it would, therefore, be necessary to involve both employees and management in all aspects of the evaluation, including the planning, data collection, and receipt of the final report.

The Joint Committee

The Joint Committee, comprised of representatives of both union and management and the project social worker, along with the plant manager, had all been party to the *Statement of Understanding* and, therefore, were cognizant of the reference to the evaluation of the project. It is probably true, however, that this part of the statement had not figured significantly in their concept of the project. However, when the University consultants presented the research proposal to them, the committee and the plant manager were in ready agreement—partly due perhaps to the fact that the proposal was consistent with the criteria in the *Statement of Understanding*, but also due to the rapport that had developed between the personnel at Seagram's and the University consultants. While the reason for support may have differed, what was important to the success of the research, was the fact that it was given unanimous support, along with an understanding on their parts to help to make the evaluation work.

Staffing the Research Project

While the concept of evaluation was built into the programme at Seagram's, Amherstburg, a matching budget-line had never been introduced. Since funds were not designated for this purpose, it would be necessary to find other means whereby the project might be staffed. Being associated with the University became a bonus, since graduate students in social work are required to undertake research projects to satisfy degree requirements, which are conducted under the direction of a three-faculty committee. The two faculty consultants to the programme, therefore, became the chairpersons and the internal reader on the committee and a third person was selected from the faculty of business to enhance the critical component of the business aspects of the evaluation. Two students in the graduate programme in social work were selected on the basis of their interest in undertaking such an evaluation as well as their competence to effect it satisfactorily, to become the researchers for this project.

Staffing for this evaluation was, therefore, effected without any actual budget, something not readily accomplished under usual circumstances.

Methodology

The evaluation covered two separate but related parts. One part dealt with the benefits of the social work project to the employees at this plant, while the other dealt with the benefits to the corporation itself. To determine whether the social work project was beneficial to the employees, it was deemed best to let them be the judges of this matter themselves and so a self-report questionnaire was designed, pretested by the Joint Committee and administered to all employees at the plant (Fynn & MacDonald, 1986, p. 27).

Special care was taken to assure the respondents of confidentiality of their respective returns by providing an envelope which they were asked to seal before returning it to the researchers. They were also informed that they might leave them in the security office, where a special box was left for such returns. Management cooperated fully with the project by agreeing to shut down sections of the plant, in rotation, to ensure that all employees would have an opportunity to hear about the evaluation from one of the researchers and the project social worker and to participate in the evaluation, if they wished to do so.

Data was collected related to six different areas: demographic information; employment history; involvement in the community and family; attitudes toward the project and the extent to which it was used; and help-seeking behaviour (Fynn & MacDonald, 1986, pp. 23-25). A total of 167 questionnaires were distributed and 86 were returned for analysis, giving a return rate of just over 50%.

To make an assessment of the benefits of the social work project to the corporation itself, an eight year period was selected for study: four years prior to the introduction of the social work project and four years following its inception, i.e., January 1977 to December 1984 inclusive (MacDonald & Fynn, 1986, p. 24).

To obtain data for this assessment the researchers used the criteria which Foote, Erfurt, Strauch, and Guzzardo (1978) specified as being the most essential, namely: rate of absenteeism; on-the-job accidents; visits to the medical unit; grievances; and, disciplinary actions. The personnel director of the plant provided the data related to these variables from the monthly statistical information compiled by the corporation (MacDonald & Fynn, 1986, p. 25).

Major Findings

While many findings resulted from this evaluation, the overall finding was that both the employees and the corporation benefitted substantially from the project.

Over 94% of the sample indicated that they had found the programme helpful. Some 65% indicated that they had encouraged others to use the service, while 78% indicated that they would use the service themselves if they had cause to do so. Ninety percent stated that they believed that such a programme would be beneficial to other companies.

From the corporation's perspective several findings stand out dramatically. Absentee rates have almost been halved, having dropped from a high of 11.9% in 1878 to a low of 5.5% in 1983. On-the-job accidents, too, have seen a considerable decrease from 562 in 1981 to 349 in 1984, and grievances have gone from 117 in 1980 to a mere 40 in 1984.

CONCLUSION

It is the aim of business to make a profit, and for most of our history the means of making a profit were deemed to require an exploitation of workers. It has become obvious though, to the students of business, that another means might be even more successful while at the same time being both more humane and more socially responsible. A Stanford University team made headlines recently by declaring that good business not only does not exploit its employees, but instead gives them significant say in the management and operation (Peters & Waterman, 1984). Dr. Megeed Rabag, of the University of Windsor, faculty of business, goes further to say that it makes good business sense to have employees participate not only in the operation of the business, but in the profits and ownership also (*The Windsor Star*, 1987-06-11, p. C11).

While the management at Seagram's has not gone as far as is

suggested by Dr. Ragab, it has made a very good start toward demonstrating an increased sense of social responsibility to employees by providing an in-house social work service to them, their spouses, and families. It is also obvious that the third party model has served them well, in that the employees do not see the service as being management controlled, and conversely management does not see the programme as being primarily a union matter. Hence, it does not become part of the bargaining process at negotiation time.

The Joint Committee, made up of management and union representatives, has given the service the objectivity necessary to garner the support and commitment of both groups. It is this committee that has given the employees the opportunity to participate fully in establishing the policies and to monitor the practices of the service and its evaluation. This structure in turn, has eradicated the barriers to utilizing the service, in that the work load of the service has continued to increase, and, because all parties understand the implications which it has for them, individually and jointly, it has brought with it a willingness to apply the findings which resulted form this evaluation.

While the motivation for the programme at Amherstburg began with a primary focus upon the problems of alcohol, it was in fact implemented as a "broad-brush" programme which recognized the fact that alcoholism does not travel alone. The programme has, therefore, from the beginning, provided service to spouses and immediate family members, along with provisions for an "off-site" location to meet in the town of Amherstburg and other facilities at the University of Windsor, if that proved to be more desirable to the clients.

This perspective on service, along with the recent establishment of another Joint Committee to oversee the operation of the gymnasium, suggests indeed that the programme at Amherstburg is moving to stage four of the Ozawa model (1980).

Finally, while a company audit was not part of the research, it is obvious from the findings that the programme has been extremely cost-effective, by way of reduced absenteeism and the improved morale which it has brought to the plant. To the extent that one can generalize from self-report satisfaction, other companies would indeed benefit from the establishment of similar programmes, ultimately resulting in increased morale, better relations between management and production employees, and greater productivity.

REFERENCES

Chandler, R. G. (1983). *Social services and the work setting: An overview and annotated bibliography*. Windsor, Ontario: Research and Development Unity, School of Social Work, University of Windsor.

Cunningham, J. B. (1978). *Community program evaluation: A suggested approach*. Ottawa: Ministry of Supply and Services.

Fynn, M. & MacDonald, D. A. (1986). *The Seagram, Amherstburg social work program: Is it beneficial to the employee*? Unpublished Master's thesis, School of Social Work, University of Windsor, Windsor, Ontario.

Foote, A., Erfurt, J. C., Strauch, P. A. & Guzzardo, T. L. (1978). *Occupational employee assistance programs for substance abuse and mental problems*. Ann Arbor, MI: Institute of Labor and Industrial Relations, University of Michigan.

MacDonald, D. A. & Fynn, M. (1986). *The Seagram, Amherstburg social work program: Is it beneficial to the plant*? Unpublished Master's thesis, School of Social Work, University of Windsor, Ontario.

Maluccio, A. N. (1981). *Promoting competence in clients*. New York: Free Press.

Ozawa, M. N. (1980). Development of social services in industry: Why and How? *Social Work*, *25*, 464-470.

Perlis, L. (1977). The human contract in the organized workplace. *Social Thought*, Winter, 29-35.

Peters, T. J. & Waterman, R. H. (1984). *In search of excellence*. New York: Warner.

Evaluating the Development of Employee Assistance Programs in Rural Communities

Barbara A. Dicks

SUMMARY. The development of Employee Assistance Programs (EAPs) has accelerated during the last decade. However, the impact of EAPs is slowly reaching small rural communities. A telephone survey of companies in North Central Louisiana was conducted to evaluate the development of programs there. Only 40% of the sample had EAPs and 13% were in the process of developing programs. Companies without EAPs generally assumed no responsibility in assisting with employee problems. This paper focuses on salient factors contributing to the limited development of rural EAPs.

The development of Employee Assistance Programs (EAPs) in the workplace has witnessed rapid growth during the last 20 years. Agencies and corporations have accepted a more humanistic approach to the resolution of problems confronting employees. Approximately 20% of the work force in the United States are reportedly experiencing work difficulties due to drug abuse, alcoholism, familial problems, emotional disorders, financial difficulties, marital conflict, mental disorders, compulsive gambling or a combination of these problems (Myers, 1984). These troubled employees

---

Barbara A. Dicks, PhD, MPH, is Assistant Professor, School of Social Work, Grambling State University, P.O. Box 907, Grambling, LA 71245.

The author wishes to thank Dr. Marvin Feit who served as mentor; to Sylenda Dixon for data collection; to Dr. Joanne V. Rhone for editorial assistance and to Shirley Lewis for secretarial help in preparing this manuscript.

frequently cause major losses to the company in terms of quality of work and economic costs that are reflected in work attendance, accidents, disability benefits, employee theft and insurance claims. In order to deal effectively with the diversity of employee problems, management and unions have strengthened efforts in developing Employee Assistance Programs to address such problems.

Although numerous volumes have been written on the development and evaluation of Employee Assistance Programs there appears to be a dearth of such information and data related to rural programs. Most of the focus tends to be related to urban based companies and corporations (Jerrell & Rightmeyer, 1982; McGuirk, 1980; Miller, 1986; Roman, 1981).

Given the migration of people and industry to the rural South over the past decade, a review of the literature pertaining to the development of EAPs in such areas is timely. Finding very limited data on Employee Assistance Programs in rural areas, the author decided to address the problem with local and regional rural companies and corporations. This study discusses results of a recent telephone survey of businesses and industries in rural North Central Louisiana, relative to the development and evaluation of Employee Assistance Programs. While preliminary results indicate a very low number of industrial Employee Assistance Programs in this area, it does not eliminate the need for such programs in rural communities. Rather, the converse is true due to the limited availability and accessability to social service programs in rural areas, rural values and ideology regarding treatment of sociobehavioral problems and general characteristics of the rural nationwide-based labor force and the increase in social problems.

In conclusion, an obvious necessity exists for the development of EAPs in rural communities. However, program development has been hampered by economic constraints of small companies; lack of unionization; adversarial relationships between labor and management; high unemployment; general rural attitudes regarding social services; and racial composition of labor and management. The major goal of the present research is to identify and discuss the major factors contributing to the slow and tedious development of EAPs in rural and small communities.

HISTORICAL OVERVIEW OF EAPs

The current trend in EAPs represents a deviation from the earlier focus of the Occupational Alcoholism Programs (OAPs) of the 1940s and 1950s that were geared solely towards the alcoholic in the workplace. However, the importance of OAPs should not be undermined since they served a vital role in development of EAPs. While the term Employee Assistance Programs is used most frequently to denote special services rendered to employees, many other titles are used: Employee Counseling, Personal Assistance Program, Employee Health Program and Employee Counseling and Assistance Service (Myers, 1984). Other programs designed for a specific problem may denote the problem in the title, i.e., Program For Alcoholic Recovery (Myers, 1984). With the myriad of social problems occurring during the 1960s and 1970s, the concept of EAP was readily adopted by unions and management. The EAP movement could be considered as one of the major revolutions in management due to several factors. The two most significant factors are union involvement and management's more humanistic approach in addressing employee performance. Much of the credit for management's response is attributed to the human relations movement that was promoted in the 1930s and 1940s, which stressed that performance was greatly influenced by employees' feelings about their work. The human relations movement paved the way for human services as a viable alternative to the traditional "work or be fired" ideology and provided for the security needs of workers through various fringe benefits (Googins & Godfrey, 1985).

EAPs also fit well into the open systems theory which emphasizes that organizations are not closed to their environment, self-sufficient or self-maintaining (Boone & Kurtz, 1987). A positive company image is promoted when it provides for emotional and psychological needs of employees. The rapid development of Employee Assistance Programs demonstrates management's acceptance of the interrelationship between personal problems, work performance and work productivity. Since the goal of most companies is to produce a product or service for economic benefit, EAPs are viewed as integral company assets.

The number of EAPs continues to expand, as over 5,000 were

recorded in 1984 (Myers, 1984). Today's programs vary in structure and services including in-house programs with social workers, psychologists, psychiatrists, alcoholism and drug abuse counselors, child care and health components, and programs that utilize external service providers for auxiliary services. The external programs might consist of referrals to individual therapists, clinics or hospital treatment programs. Although the scope of problems being addressed by EAPs has expanded over the years, the main focus continues to be an improvement of employee work performance and minimizing the costs of such efforts (Jerrell & Rightmeyer, 1982).

CHARACTERISTICS OF RURAL LIFE-STYLES

In order to develop a better understanding of the dynamics of EAPs in rural communities, some basic definitions, concepts and perceptions of rurality will be highlighted. The United States Census Bureau defines rural communities as those under 2,500 inhabitants. However, it may be worthwhile to view many large communities as basically rural. Since the U.S. Census Bureau uses 50,000 inhabitants as its measure of standard metropolitan areas, any town with less population should be nonurban or rural. A number of social scientists prefer to use towns with populations under 50,000 as the numerical designation for rural (Johnson, 1980). The latter figure will be used as the statistical definition of rural in this study.

Although there are numerous characteristics attributed to rural residents and communities, the majority of them can be classified as occupational, ecological or social/cultural in nature. The occupational perception usually focuses on rural areas as basically agrarian with plenty of open fields, and farm life, including streams for fishing. However, farm families are decreasing due to increased economic difficulties. Thus, many of the farm populations are confronted with problems of economic loss, depression, various familial problems associated with loss of the farms, and increased unemployment and underemployment. Problems related to health/mental health, education, leisure, the family, discrimination, crime, unemployment, and other stresses are as real for people in rural communities as they are for urban dwellers (Johnson, 1980). The ecological perception also focuses on density of population and closeness to a metropolitan area. Therefore, suburbs or "bedroom communities" with services available to them from a metropolitan area would not be classified as rural. The social/cultural perspective views rural in terms of life-style and relationships. The rural community is generally perceived as having traditional life-style, homogeneity of values, close personal relationships, fundamental religious heritage, strong family orientation, and resistance to outside influence. Other factors cited in the literature include: reliance upon informal systems; limited health, mental health, and social services; poor public transportation; skewed population of the very young and very old; and strong sense of independence, self-reliance, and privacy (Johnson, 1980).

Despite the three major categories utilized to highlight general perceptions of "rural," there are still different manifestations of rural due to regionalism. The diversity of regional differences must be considered as rural areas of the South, the Midwest, and New England are certainly very different. The differences can be viewed through social structure, economics, community culture, and regional problems. Even within a particular state, such differences may be apparent (Johnson, 1980).

Based on the foregoing discussion, it becomes very clear that rural communities might be somewhat reluctant to readily engage in pursuing EAPs due to traditionalism, provincialism, and general limited exposure to social service programs. The study that follows will highlight how rural residents in North Central Louisiana responded to EAP development.

STUDY SAMPLE AND PROCEDURES

An exploratory study was conducted utilizing a sample of 15 companies. In order to derive the sample population, consultation was made with several area professionals who had knowledge of companies with EAPs or identified those that might have EAPs. Based on the nominations of the consultants, a sample of 15 companies was selected. The companies selected included: retail discount stores, public utility companies, automotive manufacturer, and locally owned enterprises. This area of Louisiana is basically agrarian with forestry serving as one of the major industries. Small manufacturing companies and retail stores also contribute to the region's economy. This rural area is unique in having five major state universities and one private liberal arts college in its midst. The companies represented four parishes of North Central Louisiana, within a 100 mile radius of each other.

The Director of Personnel was contacted at each facility to ascertain if the company had an EAP. If the response was affirmative, then the manager of the program was identified in order to arrange for an interview. In the case of negative responses, the Director of Personnel was questioned as to whether the company perceived a need for a program to address employee problems.

A telephone survey was conducted with individuals in charge of the EAPs. The survey instrument consisted of a 10 item questionnaire focusing on:

1. Problems addressed by the program (alcohol abuse, drug abuse, marital problems, emotional disorders, financial problems, and familial problems);
2. Selection of participants;
3. Union involvement;
4. Provision of services (internal or external);
5. Program staffing;
6. Method of program evaluation;
7. Number of employees; and
8. Sexual utilization patterns.

The program managers were also asked to specify any desired improvements for their EAP.

FINDINGS AND DISCUSSION

The survey results demonstrated that of the 15 companies, only six (40%) had EAPs, five (33%) were developing programs, and seven (46.6%) did not have programs. The companies with EAPs consisted of one national food chain store, one public utility corporation, two subsidiaries of national automotive manufacturers, one local manufacturing company, and one subsidiary of a national glass manufacturing company.

The number of EAPs with union involvement, consisted of five (83.3%), while one (16.6%) was nonunion controlled. All programs had more than one service component. The majority of the programs (83.3%) provided at least three or more services, with alcohol and drug treatment common to all. Medical problems were identified as being served by half of the programs. Other problems addressed included emotional, marital, financial and familial problems.

In terms of the selection process for employee participation, 50% of the programs required initiation by the employee, 17% by supervisory referral, and 33% by joint action. The most common manner of service delivery was through external-based programs (50%), while combined services represented 33%, and internal services were minimal (17%). Nurses and physicians represented the only staffing for internal program while external staff consisted of social workers, psychologists and psychiatrists. One of the most noteworthy findings was related to sex related service patterns which clearly demonstrated that 50% of the companies did not have such records. Data from the remaining 50% of the programs revealed that males utilized the service more frequently than females. Another notable finding was that the programs with EAPs were all companies with from 300 to 3,000 employees with a mean for 1,150 employees, whereas the mean for companies without EAPs was 80. Several of the non-EAP companies stated that if an employee presents a problem it would represent grounds for termination. Those companies also specified that there was no need for EAPs. One of the companies indicated that if problems evolved interfering with job performance, the employee would be asked to sign a last chance agreement stating that if the problem reoccurred, the employee would be terminated.

In terms of improvements desired for their EAP, 66% stated none were needed, the remaining 34% cited removal of confidentiality and cost reduction as desired improvements. It is also interesting to note that none of the programs were pleased with their evaluation method, although the methods varied from internal to external methods. Some also felt that they collected too much extraneous data.

The results of the study supported the lack of EAPs in rural communities. Although the sample was geographically limited, it can be generalized to other Southern rural communities with similar characteristics. One of the limitations of this study was its small sample size. However, this might not prove too unusual given the general trend to EAPs in rural communities and the paucity of research related to this phenomenon.

The role of unions in the development of EAPs is consistent with the literature (Jerrell & Rightmeyer, 1982; Myers, 1984). The focus on treatment of alcohol abuse as a priority is consistent with the historical evolution of EAPs from occupational alcoholism programs (Googins & Godfrey, 1985). The programs are compatible with current trends as they generally offer additional services such as emotional, marital, medical, and financial counseling programs (Jerrell & Rightmeyer, 1982; Miller, 1986; Myers, 1984).

It is interesting to note that the national chain of retail discount stores and the regional chain of retail discount stores did not have EAPs. Major reasons attributed to this include: the use of cheap labor (basically college students and housewives as part-time employees), high employee turnover rate and abundant labor supply. Companies of this nature do not have to invest in employee services, since they can fire an employee and have a replacement available the next day. Companies with easily obtainable, abundant cheap labor sources are least likely to invest in EAPs. The automotive manufacturing companies have been pioneers in developing EAPs due to the large scale robotic-like quality of their assembly line style jobs which create stress for employees. It is typically the larger unionized companies that tend to have EAPs which is borne out in the literature (Jerrell & Rightmeyer, 1982; Steidinger, 1986). The smaller companies frequently do not invest in such programs due to concerns related to additional costs for providing such services.

CONCLUSIONS AND RECOMMENDATIONS

The development of EAPs in rural communities can work but there are some very essential factors specific to such populations that must be considered in the planning process. Development in rural areas, particularly in the Southern United States, is hindered by limited unionization, adversarial relationships between labor and management, cheap and abundant labor supply, a depressed economy, and general slowness to changes. The process is facilitated in companies that are advocates of the human relations school of thought and who are usually subsidiaries of national companies that have EAPs in the parent organization.

The challenge for the future lies in developing improved labor management relationships, social advocacy for workers in stress via professional organizations and schools of social work and improved marketing of EAPs. Research efforts should examine how companies in rural areas provide for the needs of their executives and the extent to which such variables as sexism, racism, and right to work laws affect development of Employee Assistance Programs.

Although the findings of this research do not have applicability to all rural populations due to the varying degrees of "rural" in relation to geographical dimensions, i.e., Appalachia, Ozarks, New England, and Western Mountains, due to each area's unique characteristics, it can serve as impetus for conducting similar studies in such areas. Continued studies of this nature including some of the variables specific to the designated rural area regarding local industries, management labor relations, and sex and racial distributions of the workplace can serve as valuable resources in this embryonic stage of EAP development in rural communities.

REFERENCES

Boone, Louis E. & Kurtz, David L. (1987). *Management* (3rd ed.) New York, NY: Random House.

Googins, Bradley & Godfrey, Joline (1985). "The Evolution of Occupational Social Work." *Social Work*, 30 (5) pp. 396-402.

Jerrell, Jeanette M. & Rightmeyer, Jonathan F. (1982). "Evaluating Employee Assistance Programs: A Review of Methods, Outcomes, and Future Directions." *Evaluation and Program Planning*, 5, pp. 255-267.

Johnson, H. Wayne (1980). *Rural Human Services: A Book of Readings*. Itasca, IL: F.E. Peacock Publishers.

McGuirk, Terry R. (1980). "Evaluation and Development of Employee Assistance Programs." *Alcohol Health and Research World*, 4 (3), 17-21.

Miller, Richard E. (1986). "E.A.P. Research, Then and Now." *Employee Assistance Quarterly*, 1 (4), 49-86.

Myers, Donald M. (1984). *Establishing and Building Employee Assistance Programs*, Westport, CT: Quorum Books.

Roman, Paul (1981). "From Employee Alcoholism to Employee Assistance." *Journal of Studies in Alcohol*, 42, 244-272.

Steidinger, John (1986). "The Current State of Evaluation Practices in Employee Assistance Programs," San Francisco. *Employee Assistance Quarterly*, 1 (4), 51-65.

Employee Drug and Alcohol Use Estimates: Assessment Styles and Issues

Angela Christine Browne

SUMMARY. Estimates of employee drug and alcohol abuse levels are increasingly used by employers to evaluate Employee Assistance Programs (EAPs). It is important to understand what goes into an estimate and the issues surrounding the utilization of such estimates. When estimates suggest that employee drug and alcohol abuse has not diminshed while Employee Assistance Program costs have been consistently high or increasing, these programs may be cut back or cancelled. Employees who are in need of these programs may lose them.

Increasing employee drug and alcohol use and abuse has become a central concern of employers in most, if not all, industries. Prior to developing or amending Employee Assistance Programs (EAPs) designed to counteract this trend, many employers want to establish a measurement of employee drug and alcohol use. This, they hope, will enable them to justify the costs of employee education, counseling, referral services and treatment, and the accompanying increases in employee benefits budgets.

Employee drug and alcohol use estimating is an evaluative mechanism that is gaining in popularity. Some employers have estimates of employee drug and alcohol use made regularly in order to evaluate the cost-effectiveness of their Employee Assistance Programs. The basic expectation is that employee drug and alcohol use will

---

Angela Christine Browne, LCSW, MPH, DSW, is at 2 Kenyon, Kensington, CA 94707.

decrease over time when employee assistance is effective. When drug and alcohol use remains steady or increases in the face of increasing employee assistance expenditures, employers are inclined to conclude that these expenditures are not cost-beneficial. Company budget and policy decisions reflect this thinking. Unfortunately, employees who may be deriving great benefit from the employee assistance services deemed to be cost-detrimental lose out when this is the conclusion. It is important, therefore, to understand how these drug and alcohol use estimates are constructed and the practical, professional, personal, and ethical attending issues. The estimate reports which follow provide examples of the styles and methods involved in reporting.

ESTIMATE METHODS

There are four commonly utilized methods of estimating drug and alcohol use in a workplace. One is to apply survey-generated or other national estimates of drug and alcohol use among the socioeconomic and occupational categories most similar to the particular work force being analyzed. Most employers express the sentiment that this tells them very little about what is actually occurring in their plants and offices.

A second method measures employee assistance service utilization. Employees in trouble with drugs and alcohol may seek confidential help from an employee assistance counselor. The number of such cases or the total number of visits per month can be recorded and this number will serve as an estimate of employees' needs for help in this area. However, many employees are reluctant to use workplace counseling and referral services even when anonymity is guaranteed. This form of estimate may therefore be a gross underestimate. Moreover, many small to medium size companies have no Employee Assistance Programs and cannot collect this form of data.

A third method is to establish indicators which reveal or infer a particular level of employee drug and alcohol problems. For example, data suggest that employees who have trouble with alcohol or drugs are tardy, absent, and utilize health benefits more frequently than other employees. Each of these employee behaviors can be measured and used as an indirect indicator of employee drug and alcohol use. Report #2 provides an example of this type of estimate.

A fourth method is employee reporting. This takes at least two general forms. A few employees may report or "reveal" to a manager that there is a certain level of drug and alcohol use in the workplace; or, a survey asking all employees questions about drug and alcohol use can be conducted. Report #2 provides an example of the former and #1 the latter type of employee reporting.

The third and fourth employee drug and alcohol use estimate methods described above are the focus in this discussion because they can be and are being utilized by companies in many different industries whose work forces vary in size and composition. The following are two sample reports, each consisting of different estimate methods. The companies' and employees' names have been omitted to protect the anonymity of all involved. Both Report #1 and Report #2 were commissioned by the owners of auto dealerships whose services include auto sales, auto maintenance and repair, and related clerical and finance work. Both reports include some initial recommendations to the employers. One estimate report, Report #1 is based on a survey distributed during an employee drug and alcohol education program.

A final comment about these reports. While they were delivered to the contracting employers in writing, they were also verbally presented. In both cases employers and their managers wanted lengthy discussion about the contents and implications of these reports.

ESTIMATE REPORTS

Report #1: Report to the "A" Corporation Regarding Employee Drug and Alcohol Abuse

Findings of Employee Survey

During a special and mandatory Drug Awareness Seminar Program, a questionnaire was distributed to all employees. Everyone was guaranteed complete confidentiality in answering the questionnaires (as well as in anything they might say during the seminars). Employees filled out questionnaires with pencils that were provided. They were instructed not to put their names on the forms. They then were asked to leave the completed questionnaires in a carton by the door.

The questionnaire asked employees about their use of alcohol, marijuana, cocaine, crack (a form of cocaine), heroin, methedrine and other drugs, both on and off the job. Because alcohol use is legal and socially approved of, this form of questionnaire can be expected to draw relatively accurate information about alcohol use. However, marijuana, cocaine, crack, heroin, and methedrine are illegal drugs and, consequently, questionnaires can be expected to draw underestimates of their use. Alcohol and drug use on the job are viewed as being inappropriate and, therefore, on the job use data may also be underestimated.

Approximately 90% of all who responded to the questionnaire replied that they had tried alcohol, approximately 60% reported having tried marijuana, 40% reported having tried cocaine or crack, 10% reported having tried heroin, methedrine, and other drugs.

Approximately 80% reported using alcohol at least once during the past month, approximately 40% reported using marijuana at least once during the past month, approximately 20% reported using cocaine or crack at least once during the past month, 2% reported using heroin, methedrine, and other drugs at least once during the past month.

Approximately 50% reported using alcohol at least once a week, approximately 30% reported using marijuana at least once a week, approximately 15% reported using cocaine or crack at least once a week, approximately 2% reported using methedrine at least once a week.

Approximately 5% reported that they were having trouble with alcohol, 2% reported having trouble with cocaine or crack.

Approximately 10% reported ever having used alcohol at work, with 2% regularly using it; approximately 5% reported ever having used marijuana at work, with none regularly using it; approximately 3% reported ever having used cocaine or crack at work, with 1% regularly using it.

Survey research is, of course, limited by the respondents' willingness to answer questions truthfully. The importance of this data is that it gives some indication, and probably an underestimation, of drug use in your work force.

NOTE: Employees were also asked if they would benefit from more educational programs concerning drug and alcohol at work. Approximately 50% responded "yes." Approximately 20% wrote in comments to the effect that they would benefit, but that they would not like the programs to be mandatory. About 5% wrote in comments to the effect that "the boss" should be more concerned with exposure to toxic chemicals in the workplace than employee drug use.

One group of 46 attendees was particularly agitated about the fact that attendance was mandatory. The majority of these persons were mechanics who work in the "shop." Many expressed anger about being made to do anything, about the amount of work they would be returning to, and about the fact that they would feel more pressured in their work now that they had missed time from it. A few suggested that this pressure would lead to drug use. When this presenter asked if they learned anything during the seminar, two-thirds of them answered "yes." When asked if they would have attended had it been voluntary, all of the answered "no."

The data show that there is marked drug and alcohol use among employees at Corporation A. Immediate and continuing action must be taken.

Recommendations

Open up lines of communication between management and first line employees, make counseling available, and let employees know that management and the boss care!

Workplace Changes

1. Provide a decaffeinated coffee and tea option where coffee and tea are already regularly provided. Employees are over-caffeinating themselves and undergoing the (pharmacological and psychological) effects of caffeine overuse.
2. Coca-cola and candy machines are presently in the workplace. Be certain that employees also have the option of buying sugar-free drinks, juices, and snacks other than candies and coca-cola.

3. Hang a bulletin board up in the workplace that posts current articles on health and information on drugs.
4. Make a no-smoking time-out room (without fluorescent lights and comfortably decorated) where employees can go on their breaks to take some time for relaxation and quiet.
5. Regularly investigate working conditions. Check to see if smoking during spray painting and other chemical work is profuse, and, if so, check to see whether or not it is dangerous.

Programmatic Changes

1. Institute an Employee Assistance Program.
2. Include an employee assistance counselor who can be seen off-site (because any visit to an office in your workplace is highly visible) and anonymously. Provide an employee assistance counselor or referral service or both for employees who want help with smoking problems. Provide a counselor or referral service or both for employees who want help with their drug and alcohol problems. Be certain that employees understand that the contents of their counseling sessions are confidential.
3. Institute regular ventilating (speaking up about tensions and pressures) sessions. Even a one hour group or lunch group once a month—voluntary—will help.
4. Provide annual seminars on drugs, mental health, and stress. Be prepared for some discontent if they are made mandatory.
5. Be prepared to send an average of 10 persons per year for two years through an addiction treatment program and its aftercare component, either via amending the existing employee benefits plan or setting up an equal access employer-subsidized benefit program.

Report 2: Report to the "B" Corporation Regarding Employee Drug and Alcohol Abuse

Findings of Employee Survey

Forty-two employees of B Corporation were interviewed following an initial meeting with Mr. K______, Mr. D______, and one employee who originally reported to Mr. K______ the existence of a drug and alcohol problem at B Corporation. Mechanics, parts department employees, office staff, and sales personnel in both the used and new sales departments were interviewed.

The goal of the interview process was to "Get an idea as to employee benefit utilization and employee comments regarding their employee benefits utilization." The interview process served as an indicator of the extent of the employee drug and alcohol problem at B Corporation in two ways. First, an employee's benefit utilization increased with his drug and alcohol intake and with his drug and alcohol problems and possible addictive behaviors. Secondly, the interviewers who were employed to do this estimate were highly experienced at reading beyond the words to signs of drug and alcohol use in the workplace.

Based upon the interviews and observations, it is clear that there is a marked drug and alcohol problem at B Corporation. This problem warrants extensive attention and the actions recommended later in this report.

Benefit Utilization Indicator of a Drug/Alcohol Problem

Note that 20.6% of those interviewed report frequent use of medical benefits – either by the employee or employee's family or both. *Addicted families use medical facilities more than nonaddicted families by a factor of 8.*

Absenteeism Indicator of a Drug/Alcohol Problem

Estimate mechanics' absenteeism reveals that 13.8% (4 in 29 people) are responsible for 58% of the absenteeism and 10.3% (3 in 29 people) are responsible for 50% of the absenteeism. Estimated salespersons' absenteeism reveals that 19% (3 in 21 people) are responsible for 68% of the absenteeism. *High absenteeism among a few individuals suggests a drug/alcohol problem among those individuals.*

Symptoms Indicator of a Drug/Alcohol Problem

Remember that these symptoms are perceived based upon the observations and intuitive judgment of the interviewers. Twenty and six-tenths percent of those interviewed presented symptoms of some kind of drug/alcohol use. (These are not necessarily the same individuals who use medical benefits frequently.)

Five and eight-tenths percent appear to be toxic or in some state of withdrawal at work. It appears that the drugs being used by this 5.8% of those interviewed were marijuana, cocaine/amphetamines and alcohol, not necessarily in order of amount or extent of use.

Note that it is highly probable that the 20.6% group presenting symptoms, (while not appearing to be using on the job) at the time of the Metatech interviews were probably working under the influence of some out-of-the- worksite drug/alcohol use or withdrawals from drug/alcohol use during nonworking hours. *This group and the 5.8% who appeared to be using on the job present serious morale, health, safety, and costly waste and liability threats to B Corporation. Judgment, coordination, attitude, and other capabilites are impaired in the drug/alcohol using employee*. Also, among the 20.6% not appearing to use on the job but presenting symptoms of use, there may be employees who will use on the job in other days.

Attitudinal Indicator of a Drug/Alcohol Problem

Some of the interviewing was met with poorly disguised hostility. For example, one service mechanic was very hostile and kept his head under the hood of the car he was working on and only answered in monosyllables. One young woman in the office was directly suspicious and hostile. *Rarely is a visiting researcher/interviewer met with this form of behavior unless there is some type of problem in the workplace*.

Interviewer's Outside Research as an Indicator of a Drug/Alcohol Problem in this Occupational Field

Auto dealerships range from 30% to 75% drug/alcohol use among employees. Most dealerships will benefit by implementing the following recommendations.

Recommendations

Based upon the findings of the on-site research and interviews and the general information we have collected about employee drug and alcohol abuse in auto dealerships, we recommend the following actions be taken at B Corporation:

1. The rewriting and subsequent posting of a new, more elaborate and stronger drug and alcohol policy.
2. The providing of a yearly drug and alcohol education program for all employees. Group size should be between 15 and 30 for employee nonmanagement seminars. Supervisor group size is to be discussed.
3. The development of a list of treatment options available to employees who have drug and alcohol problems. This should be posted and distributed by mail within two weeks after the new drug policy is posted.
4. The instituting of behavioral and performance documentation techniques in all departments at B Corporation.
5. The development and utilization of a computerized absenteeism and performance tracking system with cumulative totals and other special capabilities such as days-of-the-week absenteeism analyses.
6. Other measures including the instituting of progressive disciplinary measures suggested by B Corporation's attorney and the possible termination of certain employees should be determined only *after* the implementation and review of the above steps.

ELEMENTS OF AN ESTIMATE REPORT

Despite their differences in estimate methods, employee drug and alcohol use estimate reports usually contain the following elements:

1. An explanation of how the data were obtained.
2. The data.
3. Comments about the limitations of the estimates.
4. When requested by the employer, recommendations.
5. A verbal explanation and discussion about the contents of the report should accompany the written report.

Occasionally, employers who contract to have an employee drug and alcohol use estimate request that the reporter provide names of specific employees who may be or are using drugs or alcohol at work. The reporter must clarify with the employer whether or not these names will be provided *before* beginning this research for report. This author has consistently declined to provide names of employees stating that this is not the type of work she or her colleagues do. This is discussed again later in this article.

FACTORS IN EMPLOYEE DRUG AND ALCOHOL USE

Employee drug and alcohol use is influenced and even generated by several psychological, organizational, and sociological factors. Employers and managers need to be informed about these factors when they attempt to measure and then alleviate drug and alcohol use in their workplace.

Lack of Information. Most employees who end up in trouble with drugs suffer from a lack of information about how people become addicted and about how dangerous particular drugs are. Most employees who use drugs and alcohol even recreationally are generally unaware of the health risks involved. Most employees are also generally unaware of how to eat right "to keep fit" and to stay away from drugs. Every month, there is new information available on drug and health issues. It is difficult to keep up with this information growth. As a result, most employees settle for a lack of information. Unfortunately, this state of affairs can be dangerous and even fatal. For example, many persons can become addicted to cocaine because they do not know or do not believe that it was a dangerous and sometimes fatal drug. New designer or lab drugs are often used by people who share these same misconceptions.

Work-Life Stress. Work-life stressors include deadline pressure, pressure to be on time, dealing with authority and competition for promotion, and recognition or achievement of some goal. These stressors combine with the general stress of economic survival (the employee has to work to make a living) create ongoing tension. Drugs and alcohol have served as outlets and escapees for employees who have not learned other outlets for work-life stress.

Societal Pressures. We live in a society that advertises cigarettes and alcohol and glorifies legal and illegal drug use. It is difficult to be a member of this society and not feel the pressure to join the "Pepsi generation," "the happy hour," the drug using crowd, etc.

Peer Pressure. During a break at a seminar conducted by this author, an employee came up and, almost in tears, commented that he had no friends at work because he would not drink or drug with any of them. Many employees feel pressure from fellow employees to drink or drug socially. It is viewed as being part of fellowship. It can be lonely to say "no." This is a frequently verbalized complaint among employees between the ages of 18 and 35.

Fear and Denial. Once someone is in trouble with a drug, fear and denial sets in. Employees are afraid of losing the respect of their peers (by admitting that they are having trouble with a drug instead of "just using it") and they are even more fearful of losing their jobs or being arrested when they step forward and report that they need help. Also, most employees are extremely uncomfortable with the idea of reporting someone else's drug problem. Fear and denial are barriers that employees confront when they attempt to alleviate employee drug and alcohol abuse. Sometimes, employers, denying their own or their companies' drug problems, contribute to the building of this barrier.

Each of these factors influences workplace behavior and, consequently, drug and alcohol use estimating.

ISSUES IN EMPLOYEE DRUG AND ALCOHOL ABUSE ESTIMATE REPORTING

Recall that employee drug and alcohol abuse estimate reporting is becoming a common practice. Those who participate in this practice are confronted by a combination of practical, professional, personal, and ethical issues. While this makes such work professionally exciting, it also renders it professionally and personally demanding. Among these issues are the following:

Practical Issues

Selecting an estimate method. The selection of an estimate method involves the consideration of the amount of time to be allocated to the research, the skills of the researcher, and the ease with which surveys, interviews or other methods are applied in the work setting being studied. An understanding of what methods the employer and the employees will be most receptive to is important.

Determining the accuracy of the method selected. Once an estimate method is selected, its accuracy must be considered. Most methods will provide underestimates of the amount of use due to employees' understandable reluctance to report illicit or wrongful activities. Employers must be informed about the questions of accuracy typical in this form of research, prior to the beginning of this research.

Collecting the data. Data collection is often slow and tedious. A knowledge of the time involved in conducting interviews and tabulating the data from surveys or other research processes is essential. Contracting employers must be informed of the time involved in this process.

The costs of the research. Understanding the time and personnel practicalities of employee drug and alcohol use estimating will enable a researcher to estimate the cost of the project in advance.

Professional Issues

Responding to requests to do undercover work or pose as something one is not. Most researchers doing this type of work are psychotherapists, counselors, employee assistance or benefits personnel, or social scientists. These people are not professional actors or undercover agents and do best to deny this request.

Understanding one's professional background. The researcher must not commit to forms of investigatory activity that run counter to his or her profession. If the researcher is a licensed psychotherapist, confidentiality issues take the forefront. Employees may be confused about the role of the researcher. This confusion should be countered with a clear definition of the researcher's professional limitations and roles.

Understanding one's professional role during research. Whether or not one is a psychotherapist, as a researcher, there are also particular professional issues to be addressed. Research must be accurate or state its accuracy level. It must be objective. The anonymity of subjects, employees in this case, must be protected. Employers who ask for names of employees are asking the researcher to step beyond professional limits and should be so informed.

Personal Issues

Coping with scared, unhappy, angry or resistant employees. When conducting research aimed at generating an employee drug and alcohol use estimate, a researcher may have to interview or present questionnaires to employees who are uncomfortable with the research being conducted. Some of these employees will be coming from the perspective of chemical dependence, denying or angry about their drug problems. Others may be generally unhappy with their job descriptions, their pay, or their employers. In some workplaces, employees are intimidated by drug using or drug dealing employees and their fears will be acted out during the research work. A researcher must be prepared to deal with the difficult personal interactions that may arise during the research.

Remaining objective when the research brings out a subjective response. As a result of the personal experience of the researcher while generating an estimate, the researcher may find his objectivity difficult to maintain. A constant alertness to this possibility will help to control the interference of subjectivity in generating an estimate.

Ethical Issues

Reporting more than was requested. There will be times during the conducting of employee drug and alcohol use research when more information than the researcher would like becomes available. This should be reported if it falls within the original agreement with the employer and if it is professionally ethical.

Reporting employees' names or specific information leading to the detection of their names. Names of specific employees using or selling drugs at work may be mentioned to the researcher. Unless one has agreed in advance to provide such names, this information as well as the names of those who reveal it, must remain confidential. Also, any details which can lead to the identification of employees should be carefully considered before being written into a final report. These should not be included in the report when their inclusion is equivalent to providing actual names.

Conducting research that may be used as a justification for cutbacks in employee assistance. This is one of the most profound ethical questions in the fields of both employee assistance and social science research. Sometimes research produces information that leads employers to cut back programs and benefits that are helping employees. When a series of employee drug and alcohol use estimates show no improvement over time, workplace decision-makers may decide that their counseling or referral services are not working and terminate or cut back on them. Sometimes the funds are literally transferred to the security arm of the company, and an investigatory and enforcement emphasis may overtake the treatment and service emphasis which preceded it.

CONCLUDING REMARKS

This discussion has looked at current problems in the field of employee assistance: the measurement of employee drug and alcohol use and abuse. While the specific drugs used by employees are changing, we are a long way off from drug free workplaces. Keep in mind that even "OTC" (over-the-counter) and prescription drugs can effect employee performance, productivity, well-being and safety. Moreover, the quantification of employee behavior will continue as employers increase their emphases upon the measurement of indicators including employee performance as a predictor of productivity. As long as we want to generate statistics about employees, we risk losing real, humane, and treatment-oriented information about these employees. Their needs, their wants, and their problems with worklife become secondary to data about their behaviors. In our work, we must refrain from losing sight of the human element—the cry of the heart that employee drug use ultimately represents.

SECTION IV: EPILOGUE

Onward and Upward

M. J. Holosko
M. D. Feit

After completing this volume, which brings together for the first time the most current information and knowledge about Employee Assistance Program (EAP) evaluations, two questions seem appropriate to address—what have we learned from this "critical mass" of information and where are we going from here? By way of response, we have learned much about how EAPs have evolved and developed and also about how they are evaluated.

Depending on who you talk to, or what literature you read, EAPs have been in existence in North America for approximately 40 years. Over this time, the EAP field has gone through some marked changes and shifts. These changes have been influenced by the interaction of many factors including macro level societal, economic, and political trends as well as renewed research and knowledge about how individuals perform and function in a variety of organizational settings. More specifically, at this point in time, we are convinced that there is growing evidence to suggest that the personal well-being and health of individuals greatly shapes the productivity of any workplace setting. It is also apparent to us that the EAP field is dynamic and adaptable in its attempt to be responsive to workers in variety of settings. Further, it is probably this adaptability foremost that will shape the field's growth and ultimate survival.

As EAPs have evolved over time, three distinct generations of programs can be delineated with a fourth generation looming on the horizon. First generation programs were industry-based dealing basically with occupational alcoholism problems. These watershed programs were the front-runners of the EAP field and essentially focused their efforts on individuals with decidedly visible drinking problems which impaired their worker performance.

As these programs evolved, it became apparent that program participants had additional problems which needed to be addressed. Thus, was born the second generation of programs called "broad brush," in which the services offered were expanded to include the full range of addictions counselling, marital and family intervention, and mental health services. As EAPs expanded into a variety of more diverse organizational settings, e.g., educational institutions, health care, and human service organizations, there was an accompanying shift in organizational thinking that worker productivity, which was rather prominent and well-defined as the rationale for EAPs in the first two generations, was less well-defined yet critical to an organizations' well-being.

This shift set the stage for the third distinct generation of programs which have been referred to as "new wave" EAPs. These programs take on a more proactive and preventive focus, and address issues related to overall employee health, well-being and lifestyle. These programs have been recent developments requiring more specialized and costly multidisciplinary professionals for their implementation. Finally, the most recent development in the field is the emergence of a fourth generation EAP program. The "case management" approach encompasses all of the services of the previous programs, however, tailors services in a planned fashion to the unique needs of individuals. These programs concentrate on tracking and monitoring individuals as they are linked to specialized services within and external to the employment setting. We concur that EAPs will continue to change and evolve in these ways in response to their environments. Indeed, one vital sign of the field will be its malleability to influences which continue to shape its development.

As one can surmise, the issue of how one can evaluate such programs with disparate domains and growth patterns is more difficult than one would anticipate. The readings offered in this text suggest that meaningful evaluations can occur when they are setting-specific and take into account the organizational context and type of EAP offered by the organization. Further, evaluations should be guided by thoughtful planning, and all of the interested parties should be included in a cooperative fashion.

One of the most poignant themes we were reminded of in this text was that EAP evaluations should be guided by the phrase "the simpler, the better." This translates primarily in two key areas. First, the purpose of any EAP evaluation should be concise and meaningful to the overall objectives of the program. Similarly, the methods used to evaluate EAPs need not be complex, academic, or clouded in statistical "mish-mash." Further, if EAP evaluations are to have relevance at any level, their purpose, methods, findings, and ultimate dissemination should be understood by lay persons.

Bearing these issues in mind, EAP evaluators can make valuable contributions to their respective organizations and the field of evaluation research in general. Finally, we are convinced that any organization that doesn't evaluate their EAP is not able to render effective management decisions in the most appropriate ways possible.